Outward Evil, Inward Battle: Human Memory In Literature

Edited by
Benjamin Hart Fishkin
Adaku T. Ankumah
Festus Fru Ndeh
Bill F. Ndi

Langaa Research & Publishing CIG
Mankon, Bamenda

Publisher:
Langaa RPCIG

Langaa Research & Publishing Common Initiative Group
P.O. Box 902 Mankon
Bamenda
North West Region
Cameroon
Langaagrp@gmail.com
www.langaa-rpcig.net

Distributed in and outside N. America by African Books Collective
orders@africanbookscollective.com
www.africanbookcollective.com

ISBN: 9956-790-16-8

Selections and editorial matter copyright © Benjamin Fishkin, Bill F. Ndi, Adaku T Ankumah and Festus Fru Ndeh 2013

Individual chapters' copyright© individual contributors 2013

DISCLAIMER

All views expressed in this publication are those of the author and do not necessarily reflect the views of Langaa RPCIG.

The Editors:

Dr. Benjamin Hart Fishkin in his research has emphasized Nineteenth Century British Literature through each phase of his education. Prior to earning his Doctorate from the University of Alabama in May of 2009, he obtained a BA in English and Film from the University of Michigan, Ann Arbor and an MA from Miami University, Oxford, OH where he examined the interest of Charles Dickens in the theatre and how the stage influenced his novel writing. He has published *The Undependable Bonds of Blood: The Unanticipated Problems of Parenthood in The Novels of Henry James*. His recent research interest now include amongst other things the problems of marriage and the American family, and the relationship between the Blues and the single parent home in the works of William Faulkner, August Wilson, and F. Scot Fitzgerald. Professor Fishkin joined Tuskegee University in the Fall of 2009. Before taking up his position at Tuskegee University, Professor Fishkin was a Junior Fellow in The Blount Undergraduate Initiative at the University of Alabama. He has won several distinguished awards, amongst which, the Buford Boone Memorial Fellowship, the Oregon Shakespeare Festival Scholarship Award and the George Mills Harper Graduate Student Travel Award.

Dr. Adaku T. Ankumah received her PhD in Comparative Literature from the University of Wisconsin-Madison. With a minor in drama, her dissertation and initial research interests focused on revolutionary playwrights from the African Diaspora, writers like Kenyan Ngugi wa Thiong'o, Martiniquais writer Aimé Césaire, and African American Amiri Baraka, who use their creative efforts to work for the destruction of what they consider to be the colonial/capitalist foundation of post-colonial Africa. Ngugi's play *The Trial of Dedan Kimathi*, a play that examines the arrest and trial of one of the famous leaders of the Mau Mau revolt against the British in Kenya in the 1950's, has been the subject of her published research. She has also done research on the role of women in revolutionary theatre, voicelessness of African women, and gender and politics in the works of African women authors like Mariama Bâ, Ama Ata Aidoo and Tsitsi Dangarembga. Dr. Ankumah's recent research interest includes the writings of women in the African Diaspora. This includes the present research on memory in literature and its role in helping those dealing with painful, fragmented pasts forge a wholesome future in Edwidge Danticat's *The Dew Breaker*. She is also looking at memory and resistance in the poetry of South African performer and writer Gcina Mhlophe.

Dr. Festus Fru Ndeh is an Associate Professor of Theoretical and Multicultural literature at Troy University, Troy, AL. He holds a Ph.D. from the University of Duisburg-Essen, Essen, Germany. His research interest is in linguistic and Cultural theories, postcolonial literature, and transatlantic discourse and globalization studies.

Dr. Bill F. Ndi earned his Doctorate from the University of Cergy-Pontoise in 2001. He joined Tuskegee University in the fall of 2011. His areas of teaching and Research comprise among others English Languages and literatures, French, Professional, Technical and Creative Writing, World Literatures, Applied/Historical Linguistics, Literary History, Media and Communication Studies, Peace/Quaker Studies and Conflict Resolution, History of Internationalism, History of Ideas and Mentalities, Translation & Translatology, 17th Century and Contemporary Cultural Studies. He has published numerous articles and book chapters in these areas. Professor Bill F. Ndi has also published 9 volumes of poetry in English, 3 in French, a play and 3 works in translation. Amongst Professor Ndi's peer reviewed publications could be mentioned the following: Edward Coxere's *Adventures by Sea*, (2012), *Letters of Elizabeth Hooton, The First Woman Preacher*, (2011), Thomas Lurting's *The Fighting Sailor Turn'd Peaceable Christian*, (2009) (Annotated French Translations); "Names, an Envelope of Destiny in the Grassfields of Cameron" and "Extending educational boundaries" in Kumar, Pattanayak, Johnson – *Framing My Name*, (2010); Venuti, L. (ed.), *The Translation Studies Reader* (New

York: Routledge, 2004. pp. vii, 541) in *Australian Review of Applied Linguistics*, April 2008, Vol. 31, No. 1: Pages 11.1-11.4, « Discours de la vengeance dans les journaux confessionnels Quakers » in Marillaud, P & Gauthier R. *La Vengeance et ses discours*, «La première contestation de l'esclavage», *(A Translation)* Paris, Présence Africaine, « Quakerisme Originel et Milieu Maritime », in Augeron & Tranchant *La Violence et la Mer dans l'Espace Atlantique (XIIe- XIXe)*, « Littérature des Quakers et Clinique de l'Âme » in *Arts Littéraires, Arts Cliniques (Literary Arts, Clinical Arts)*, « Traduire le discours Quaker », in *Traduire 2*, «Globalization and Global Ethics: A Quaker Concern» in *Questioning Cosmopolitanism*.

Authors:

Dr. Loretta S. Burns is chair of the Department of English and Professor of English at Tuskegee University, where she received her bachelor's degree. She earned her M.A. at Ohio State University, where she was a Woodrow Wilson Fellow, and she received her Ph.D. from the University of Michigan. She has also studied at Columbia University and the Sorbonne, participated in a National Endowment for the Humanities Summer Seminar at Yale University, and conducted research at Harvard University as a fellow at the Bunting Institute (now called the Radcliffe Institute for Advanced Study). Her scholarly interests include American and African American literature, women's studies, southern literature, and interdisciplinary studies. Her ongoing research focuses on the influence of African American oral forms (blues, spirituals, ballads, and folktales) on written literature, and her articles and essays on black southern literature and culture have appeared in *Alabama English*, *More Than Dancing: Essays on Afro-American Music and Musicians*(Greenwood, 1985), and *The Companion to Southern Literature* (Louisiana State UP, 2002). She also writes poetry and fiction and has edited several literary journals. She recently published a book of poetry, *My Brother, My Sister* (Langaa, 2012), with Bill F. Ndi. Dr.

Burns has held faculty positions at Fisk University, the University of Florida, and Washington University in St. Louis.

Dr. Rhonda M. Collier, Associate Professor of English at Tuskegee University, holds a Ph.D. in Comparative Literature from Vanderbilt University. As a Fulbright scholar, she spent a year studying at the Universidade de São Paulo, Brazil's number one research institution. In São Paulo, she began her on-going Inter-American work on the contemporary poetry of Afro-Brazilian, Afro-Cuban and African-American women. She is concerned with the question of national history and how literature serves as a tool to give voice to black women in the African Diaspora. Her most recent publication "Hip Hop to Hip Hope: Art and Public Theology in South Africa" in *Walking Together: Christian Thinking and Public Life in South Africa*, is part of collection with diverse African and North American scholars and theologians (Abilene Christian UP, 2012). Her work "'Over the Rainbow': Finding Home in Cleage's West End Atlanta" is included in *Pearl Cleage and Free Womanhood: Essays on Her Prose Works*, the first-book length study on the works of African American author and activist by Pearl Cleage (McFarland, 2012). Dr. Collier is currently guest-editing a special topic volume of *Obsidian Journal: Literature of the African Diaspora*, on Afro-Brazilian Literature and Culture.

Eleanor J. Blount is Assistant Professor of English at Tuskegee University in Alabama. She specializes in the literature of African Americans, especially of the slave era, and also researches the history of antebellum America. The nineteenth century Transcendentalist writers of New England and fiction by and about diasporic Africans comprise some of her related scholarly interests. Dr. Blount studied history, journalism, professional writing, and creative writing at Paine College, Kennesaw State University, and at the University of Georgia where she composed neo-slave narratives as part of her Ph.D. work in English and creative writing. She was at one time a news reporter, and has taught English at Georgia Perimeter College and Gainesville State College among other places.

Dr. Adaku T. Ankumah is an Associate Professor of English at Tuskegee University. She holds a Ph.D. from the University of Wisconsin, Madison. Her areas of interest include women's literature (with a focus on African and Diaspora women) and the short story genre.

Dr. Festus Fru Ndeh is an Associate Professor of Theoretical and Multicultural literature at Troy University, Troy, AL. He holds a Ph.D. from the University of Duisburg-Essen, Essen, Germany. His research interest is in linguistic and Cultural theories, postcolonial literature, transatlantic discourse and globalization studies.

Dr. Bill F. Ndi, poet, playwright, storyteller, literary critic, translator, historian of ideas and mentalities as well as an academic has held teaching positions in several universities in Australia, France and elsewhere. He now teaches in the Department of English and Foreign Languages at Tuskegee University, Tuskegee Alabama, USA. He has published numerous scholarly works on Early Quakerism and translation of Early Quaker writings. He has also published poetry and plays extensively in both the French and the English languages.

Dr Benjamin Hart Fishkin is an Assistant Professor of English at Tuskegee University, where he specializes in teaching Nineteenth Century British Literature. He holds a Ph.D. from the University of Alabama where he served as a Junior Fellow in The Blount Undergraduate Initiative.

Table of Contents

Introduction: Towards a Paradigm of Memory in Literature..........v

Section 1: Power..........1

Chapter 1
Quakers, Memory & the Past in Literature. *Bill F. Ndi*..........3

Chapter 2
The Power of Memory: Crossroads in Works by Thomas Wolfe, F. Scott Fitzgerald, and August Wilson. *Benjamin Hart Fishkin*..........37

Section 2: Music..........53

Chapter 3
Memory, the Blues, and African American Slave Narratives. *Loretta S. Burns*..........55

Chapter 4
It Rains Inside: Parenting and Music in Works by William Faulkner, August Wilson, and Sherman Alexie. *Benjamin Hart Fishkin*..........73

Section 3: Resistance..........87

Chapter 5
Unwavering Insubordination: Rebellion & Memory in The Letters of Elizabeth Hooton. *Bill F. Ndi*..........89

Chapter 6
Memory and Resistance in the Poetry of Gcina Mhlophe. *Adaku T. Ankumah*..........*109*

Section 4: Trauma **131**

Chapter 7
Veiling the Past: Memory and Identity in Edwidge Danticat's The Dew Breaker. *Adaku T. Ankumah* 133

Chapter 8
Memorizing the Dark: Margaret Walker and Toni Morrison Compress African American Time and Space in Poetry and Fiction. *Eleanor J. Blount* 153

Section 5: Cultural Identity **169**

Chapter 9
There's No Place Like Home: Cultural Memory in Toni Morrison's Tar Baby and Edwidge Danticat's Breath, Eyes and Memory. *Rhonda Collier* 171

Chapter 10
"Go Back and Get It:" Spirit Possession as Rite of Passage and a Medium of Self-reinvention in Contemporary African Diasporic Literature. *Festus Fru Ndeh* 185

Index 209

Introduction

Towards a Paradigm of Memory in Literature

Memory is the act of remembering or recollecting events from the past. Past events come back to haunt us, or happy remembrances help to brighten our days. As the story line weaves in and out of time, memories play an important role in character development and the progression of the plot. Cultural memory also plays a role in literature. Read more about memory and literature. (Esther Lombardi)

In his seminal work *Time and Narrative*, the philosopher Paul Ricœur builds on an earlier analysis in *The Rule of Metaphor* to draw a correlation in what he calls a "healthy circle between time and narrative". As he argues, time is humanized to the extent that it portrays temporal experience; in fact, narrative is an experience of time. This is a theory that holds true to narratology, but even more so is its relevance to human memory.

The field of memory studies is such a catholic one, and an exhaustive treatment warrants perspectives ranging through psychology, neurology, philosophy, zoology, sociology, folklore and literature. However, due to the fact that most current research on memory tends to be more scientific and psychological, it seems very appropriate to address the subject from a humanities perspective i.e. a literary lens. It should be noted that the literature of memory can provide a rich array of data that is tantamount to field studies for capturing episodes of memory. In Greek mythology, Mnemosyne was not only memory deified but she was also the mother of the nine Muses (the goddesses of the various arts) by Zeus after sleeping with him for nine consecutive nights. Consequently, there is an inextricable yoke between memory and creativity, or better still, memory and literature as echoed in Lombardi's definition of memory which leads this introduction.

Using literature as a laboratory for the workings of the mind, and characters as the subjects of our experimentation and diagnostics, this book considers authors from all shades of society and from different time periods as subjects of study as it seeks to illuminate the functioning of human memory. In its conceptualization of memory, it does not seek to undermine the work of neuroscientists who seek to scientifically rationalize the workings of human memory, but it seeks to complement it with a humanistic touch. After all, literary theory and criticism has everything to gain from contemporary studies in neuro-criticism. As Jonathan Gottschall contends, in an era when everyone is talking about "the death of the humanities," a scientific approach can rescue literature departments from the malaise that has embraced them over the last decade and a half. He thus sees the use of neurological patterns to enhance literary hermeneutics as "a new moment of hope" (qtd. in Patricia Cohen). However, this leads to some obvious questions. Why is it so difficult to arrive at a generally accepted definition of memory? Also, why is this definition so hard to understand?

A possible answer is that memory is a term used in labeling a myriad of experiences and "Many very different things happen when we remember" (Wittgenstein 181). The heterogeneous nature of memory gives philosophers good reason to be wary of any attempt to explain it. The difficulty in finding a suitable explanation stems from the fact that,

> ...subtleties of subjective memory experience need not be neglected or obliterated by careful theorizing: an explanatory framework which omitted the phenomenological and interpersonal diversity of memory would fail on its own terms (Memory).

In an attempt to give some meaning to memory, it might be important to taxonomize and examine it from the works of various psychologists and philosophers dealing with declarative and nondeclarative memory.

John Sutton in his Memory entry in *The Stanford Encyclopedia of Philosophy* suggests three kinds of memory: habit memory, propositional memory and recollective memory. As he conjectures, "These varieties of remembering are marked by grammatical, phenomenological, and (on some views) psychological and neural differences." As he states, what philosophers call "habit memory" is referred to by psychologists as "procedural memory" and consists of:

> ... a range of phenomena, from simpler forms of associative learning through to kinesthetic, skill, and sequence memory. We naturally refer to procedural, habit, and skill memories with the grammatical construction 'remembering how'. I continue to remember how to type, play piano, or dance, even when I am not, now, occurrently engaged in the relevant activity. While some habit memories may have something in common with rigid, inflexible, automated conditioning mechanisms, others are flexible and open to the changing influences of context, mood, and personal memory.

What one gathers from the definition is that humans have an intrinsic propensity to retain things unconsciously. Such habitual retentions through repetition and trial-and-error learning survive human memory as they are retained in a different region of the brain - the basal ganglia. This can significantly influence human thinking and the conceptualization of ideas.

In defining 'propositional memory,' Sutton links it to 'semantic memory' or memory for facts which he sees as "the vast network of conceptual information underlying our general knowledge of the world." This is naturally expressed as 'remembering that.' So while 'remembering how' has to do with habitual memory, 'remembering how' falls within the gamut of 'propositional memory.' However, he defines 'recollective memory' also sometimes called 'personal memory', as 'episodic memory', 'experiential memory' or 'direct memory.' This kind of memory to him is "memory for experienced events and episodes, such as a conversation this morning or the death of a friend eight years ago." What is obvious about this category of long-term memory is that it involves the recollection of specific events, situations and experiences.

From his definition, because propositional memory deals with facts, and recollective memory is that which is informed by specific events, situations and experiences, both could be categorized under 'declarative memory' because they could be intentionally tapped from and expressed verbally and/or otherwise. This is conscious memory. It is the kind used by autobiographers and other nonfiction writers. Conversely, 'procedural or habitual memory' is implicit. This could be branded as 'nondeclarative memory' because it is memory about how things are done. It has to do with skills. Skills amount to activities performed automatically without conscious recollection of how they were learned. Nondeclarative memory involves multiple senses and systems. It utilizes multiple motor and cognitive pathways in its execution.

In the business of literary creation, writers pull from both declarative and nondeclarative memories. When they write, they tap from their conscious and unconscious memories. This has nothing to do with whether what they write is a true representation of memory or not, because in the field of memory studies, false memory is not memory at all. This is so because in developing a melody, painting or story the creative artist could think that he is remembering whereas he is imagining, confabulating or thinking that something new is being created while he is just tapping from his memory (Martin and Deutscher 167, 177). Patricia Hampl echoes this same idea when she says in *I Could Tell You Stories: Sojourns in the Land of Memory* that "we put what we want into the memories instead of what the memory itself wants." She argues that because we extract our feelings with images, we usually bring out what we wanted or wished in this memory. In our minds, we all have a created version of our past and when we want to express it, we usually do not have the full accurate "picture" in our minds. So, we reach down to the language of symbol. Here we embrace imagination to fill in our "holes." Now this process of remembering soon becomes reality. If we make memory like a story in a library, "we miss its beauty and also its function"(33).

In the end, memories bring out the relationship of our "older" self and our current self. It is in this regard that Hampl highlights:

> To write one's life is to live it twice, and the second living is both spiritual and historical, for a memoir reaches deep within the personality as it seeks its narrative form and it also grasp the life of the times as no political analysis can (37).

In her groundbreaking work that seeks to fill an interdisciplinary space in memory studies between science and literature, Suzanna Nalbantian studies the works of a variety of writers including Rousseau, Baudelaire, Rimbaud, Woolf, Joyce, Breton, Nin and Borges in *Memory in Literature: From Rousseau to Neuroscience*. The strength of Nalbantian's book lies in the fact that instead of just applying contemporary neuroscientific paradigms to current literature, she makes the texts themselves to, as Patricia Feito puts it in her review of the book,

> ...serve as laboratories for the workings of the mind," laboratories in which the authors are treated as "subjects" and their writings are explored as "a series of case histories of a variety of operations of human memory" (3).

While Nalbantian does introduce her study through an exposition of prominent nineteenth-century psychological theories regarding the function of memory, she allows each chapter and each writer to reveal a variety of memory processes, each unencumbered by external theoretical material. (Feito 30)

In fact, Nalbantian's book shows that neuroscience can help us break down memory into discernible elements and operations. These elements and operations - the initial creation of a memory in the brain, its storage there, and its later retrieval and experience by a subject - are a very different focus than the usual thematics of memory in literary criticism.

In another vein, in his seminal social scientific study, *How Societies Remember*, Paul Connerton identifies two major types of memory -

individual and social memories. On the one hand, individual memories consist of personal, cognitive and habit memories:

- Personal memory has to do with memory claims that take as their object one's life history such as, "I went to church at 10am today."

- Cognitive memory has to do with memory knowledge such as remembering a mathematical equation, a quotation, the road to work, the definition of a word etc. In this case, remembering is independent from the context in which it was first learned.

- Habit-memory deals with remembering how to do things such as reading and writing, driving a car, wearing a shirt etc. It is fully appreciated when one falls victim to amnesia, after an accident or in the case of an Alzheimer's disease's victim: one is unable to conduct a normal life in society. In that sense, habit-memory is a key element of social life; we can see here that cognitive memory can very quickly acquire the social value of habit-memory – the knowledge of how one's city is designed is crucial to knowing one's way home, for example. Understanding of the space in which one lives is at the heart of the feeling of belonging to a city; that is to say, to a community through which some of our sense of identity is negotiated and actually established.

It is noteworthy to state that these different definitions are not mutually exclusive.

Social Memory, on the other hand, is informed by the research of Maurice Halbwachs. He underscores the idea that the act of remembering itself is mediated through our belonging to a certain social group - be it a religion, a particular sort of kinship or class. Halbwachs argues that it is through these social groups that one is able to localize and recall one's memories. Furthermore, to lend credence to this, Connerton comments that "groups provide individuals with frameworks within which their memories are localized and memories are localized as a kind of mapping". (37).

He also adds that,

What binds together recent memories is not the fact that they are contiguous in time but rather that they form part of a whole ensemble of thoughts common to a group, to the groups with which we are in relationship at present or have been in some connection in the recent past (36).

Connerton further states that "Memory is retained through a community of interests and thoughts" (37). When one remembers, it very often depends on the context in which one finds oneself. This is to say that the act of remembering, although dealing with the past, remains almost entirely dependent on the present. That is why the study of memory would be incomplete if the process of transmission of the memories is not studied as well.

Based on the ideas explored above, it is obvious that any consideration of memory in this book will presuppose a perspective on forgetfulness as well. Diana S. Woodruff - Pak contends in *The Biology of Memory* that our knowledge of memory instructs and informs us on why we forget. Memory is the act of remembering and recalling past events. Although the act of remembering is often understood to be an individual act, here, memory is going to be approached in its various dimensions. The concept will be explored with the goal of seeking an understanding of how individual authors and societies remember.

This book draws on these various ideas on memory and is the result of a myriad endeavors rallied around a common fact that the tracking of memory in literature yields an astounding vista of orientations that are covered in separate chapters. The writers considered by the various chapter contributors are perceived as mediums for unleashing the memory process and its reconfiguration into artistic images. In ten separate chapters, different aspects of memory are variously reconnoitered in such memoric associations as power, music, resistance, trauma, and identity.

The first section on power is made up of two chapters. Chapter One investigates Quaker literature, memory and history as it argues that the Quakers use their memory to document their past to the extent that scholars of Quakerism tend to view them as modern and postmodern. In fact, by documenting their memories and their past (what they refer to as their "present sufferings") the author argues that these writers engage in a venture of preservation of the present for future generations. The chapter also explores the contribution of Quaker memory recordings to contemporary peace literature, given that the quest for "World Peace" is the bedrock upon which Quakers have built their philosophy. The documentation of the sufferings of Quakers turns out to be the foundation upon which their struggles against persecution and oppression would stand. Literature, created through memory, therefore becomes an instrument of power to the Quakers.

In the same vein, the second chapter builds on the notion of power drawing on the commentaries of a late nineteenth and early twentieth century religious scholar who said: "As memory may be a paradise from which we cannot be driven, it may also be a hell from which we cannot escape." The chapter examines how, in a perfect world, memory should be a source of comfort and support. It argues that, however, as the twentieth century progressed and gave way to the twenty-first, modern society has increasingly become out of touch with the needs of its inhabitants. Due to these changes, there is increase in the probability that memories are becoming psychological minefields that are difficult to move beyond. The chapter concludes that as memories persist and bleed into the present and the future, they become something that people, more often than not, struggle to be free of.

Section Two dwells on music and the construct of memory. Chapter Three borrows from Ralph Ellison's description of the Blues as "an impulse to keep the painful details and episodes of a brutal experience alive in one's aching consciousness, to finger its jagged grain, and to transcend it." It considers the influence of the blues on other African American art forms, including written literature and argues that long before the blues developed as a genre in the early 20th century, the blues impulse to confront adversity and to express and share one's anguish had been reflected in the foundation stones of the African American written tradition—the Slave Narratives. The chapter examines how *The Narrative of the Life of Frederick Douglass* and

Harriet Jacobs's *Incidents in the Life of a Slave Girl* exploit memory and language to transform and transcend the painful experiences of slavery. It conjectures that by revealing the horrors of slavery in their narratives, Douglass and Jacobs order the realities of their lives and construct their identities. In fact, through remembrance and discourse, they enact a cathartic ritual that in later years achieves its most sublime lyrical expression in the lament and affirmation of the blues.

Chapter Four, titled "It Rains Inside: Parenting, and Music in Works by William Faulkner, August Wilson, and Sherman Alexie" contends that contemporary American society across geography, ethnicity and economic status is either luxuriously ignorant or shrewdly terrified that it has forgotten the very support systems that was once its source of sustenance. Pulling from texts by Americans of various eras and ethnicities, the author argues that the idea of "a jolly home, a sympathetic reception, [and] a bright supper" table that people aspired to is now elusive (Dreiser 38). The home is no longer a place of comfort and a familiar source of support. In making this argument the author uses works written against the backdrop of various musical traditions. As he draws on a quotation by Faulkner who once stated that music is "the easiest means in which to express [oneself]."

In *An Introduction to the History of Sexuality*, Michel Foucault argues:

> Where there is power, there is resistance, and yet, or rather consequently, this resistance is never in a position of exteriority in relation to power... [but it is] a multiplicity of points of resistance: these play the role of adversary, target, support, or handle in power relations. These points of resistance are present everywhere in the power network. Hence there is no single locus of great Refusal, no soul of revolt, source of all rebellions, or pure law of the revolutionary. Instead there is a plurality of resistances, each of them a special case (95-6).

Foucault's ideas offer a critical approach to the practice of remembering and forgetting which are vital for resisting subjugation and overriding ideologies, especially his thoughts on the concepts of counter-history and counter-memory. In the quotation above, Foucault seems to frame the working of memory within the framework of power relations in terms of its concentration not only on what is remembered and forgotten, but by whom, how, and with what effects. Consequently, the practices of remembering and forgetting abet focus on issues of resistance and rebellion. This is the subject of the third section of this book. In this section the authors explore the use of memory in literature of subversion as instruments of power through which various writers respond to the forces that have held them captive.

In the chapter titled "Unwavering Insubordination: Rebellion & Memory in Letters of Elizabeth Hooton," the author investigates the conscious or unconscious silencing of the voices of women and their active participation in the events and ideas that have helped to revolutionize the world. It case studies Elizabeth Hooton, reputed not only as 'The First Female Preacher', but also as one of the first converts of George Fox's doctrine highlighted in the Quaker movement. Her works bring to the limelight the determination, enthusiasm and zeal with which she was ready to stand on the shoulders of the English society (both in the old and the New Worlds) to propagate the ideals for which she stood i.e. the Quaker ideals for an egalitarian society based upon the idea that all men are created equal and endowed with a divine *inner light* and *voice*. It is through her personal life story legated in form of letters that she wrote to Friends, dignitaries, opponents and priests that she unravels memories of her personal involvement, activism and rebellion in the Quaker resistance to the oppressive seventeenth Century societies and institutions. She did so in keeping with the Quaker tradition of documenting memories for posterity.

In another chapter on resistance titled "Memory and Resistance in the Poetry of Gcina Mhlophe," the author proposes that in dealing with different types of oppression and abuses of power, writers have responded in their creative works not by simply chronicling various atrocities, but also by resisting forms of oppression and, consequently, envisioning a future free of such brutalities. The chapter uses the South African example where apartheid left behind an inordinate amount of suffering. It posits that writers have at times gone back to their shared past to pull memories through which they voice their resistance. One such writer the chapter explores is Gcina Mhlophe, an actor with the Market Theatre in Johannesburg, activist, poet, playwright, storyteller, composer and director. Her poems rely on oral tradition and dig into the history of black South Africa. In them, she uses the past both to inform and to encourage resistance to the ugly past while envisaging a future which includes the voice of women.

Section Four explores the relationship between trauma and memory as probed in two different chapters that systematically examine individual and cultural memory from the Black Atlantic perspective. The chapters show how the remembering and forgetting of individual and collective traumatic experiences are crucial to the formation of an African diasporic identity. Ron Eyerman states that trauma as a cultural process "is mediated through various forms of representation and linked to the reformation of collective identity and the reworking of collective memory" (1). "Veiling the Past: Memory and Identity in Edwidge Danticat's *The Dew Breaker*" is a chapter that focuses on what happens to people who deliberately choose not to remember the past because of the pain associated with it. Using the *Dew Breaker* by Edwidge Danticat (an Haitian-American author) as case study, the chapter investigates the effect of remembering and forgetting on the construction of the self, and argues that 'voluntary amnesia' does not erase the past, but it leads to a present that is even more painful. This is the lesson learned by the dew breaker in the novel which could be taken for a collection of short stories.

"Memorizing the Dark: Margaret Walker and Toni Morrison Compress African American Time and Space in Poetry and Fiction" is another chapter that dwells on memory and trauma. The chapter postulates that Walker and Morrison use music, the paranormal and other stimuli to evoke sensory and subconscious memories of the institution of slavery experienced by African American ancestors, and the ways in which the legacies of slavery shaped African American life into the present. When their imaginative writings are studied in light of what scientists say about time and space, conclusions can be drawn to show how today's Black people are not disconnected to the dark experiences of their history and should not seek to forget them or compartmentalize them into meaningless categories of past, present, or future. Of the African American experience, the chapter therefore argues in support of what Derrida calls "metaphysics of presence", in which presence is privileged over absence. This position is further underscored by Hannah Arendt when she states:

> What has been lost is the continuity of the past as it seemed to be handed down from generation to generation, developing in the process its own consistency... What you then are left with is still the past, but a fragmented past, which has lost its certainty of evaluation (208).

Even though memory is an individual thing, contemporary research in social science studies reveals that personal accounts of memory have an effect on the formation of collective identity because the same kind of pain experienced by several individuals could result in cultural trauma. It is obvious that some of those past experiences are so traumatic that remembering and representing them in writing presents a painful dilemma to the writer. Nonetheless, a committed writer will obviously want to engage his readers by representing such traumatizing memories in such a way as to stimulate psychological and social consciousness.

Closely linked to the issue of trauma and memory is that of cultural memory and cultural identity which is the subject of the last section of this book. The ability of humans to recall and conjure specific events of their lives is what *The Stanford Encyclopedia* calls memory. The three main subcategories of memory: the working memory - stored in the prefrontal cortex, long-term memory - stored in the hippocampus and skill memory, stored in the cerebellum all contribute to identity formation. They are vital in the creation of new memories. Besides providing the individual with relevant information on how to act in response to situations, the act of remembering has a profound impact on identity-related abilities (4).

This section on memory and identity anchors on Richard Powell's statement that,

> The belief that black people, apart from physiognomic and genealogical ties with the inhabitants of Africa, had comparable experiences, identical struggles for full acceptance in society and shared destinies was widely held ... in the second half of the twentieth century" (24).

The first chapter in this section, "There's No Place Like Home: Cultural Memory in Toni Morrison's *Tar Baby* and Edwidge Danticat's *Breath, Eyes and Memory*" explores "cultural memory" from a post-colonial perspective in terms of it being a type of magic, agency if needed, that allows people the freedom to trace their individual histories with the aim of knowing the "truth" of their existences. The chapter reflects on the relationship between place and cultural memory and argues that for Toni Morrison's character, Jadine Childs and Edwidge Danticat's character, Sophie Caco, it appears that the use of words to contextualize important historical elements is the magic that empowers writers to return home. It is almost impossible to interpret historical events without being able to perceive the past, to appreciate the present and to anticipate the future. The chapter effectively shows how Toni Morrison and Edwidge Danticat use the idea of place to reflect a sense of identity that is rooted in history and memory.

The last chapter in this section and of the book is titled "Embodying spirit possession as rite of passage (and construction of the self) in contemporary African Diasporic Literature." It posits that African writers in the diaspora cannot escape the call of Africa upon them. Again, it is difficult for any one of them to truly pass for an African diasporic writer without having confronted Africa in some way. Such writers in a Janus-like manner use their African consciousness and Africa as repository and framework which foreground their interpretation of the present. This is usually the case in a postcolonial world, one in which writers are resolved to negotiating the bi-polarity of repulsion and attraction inherent to the past. This is both traumatic and triumphant. The chapter concentrates on an often ignored aspect of the literature of the African diaspora as it explores spirit possession as a technique used by African diasporic writers to create a memory of Africa. Writers, therefore engage in a reconfiguration of identity in a context within which, like their fictional creations, struggle from what Dubois calls "Double Consciousness." Spirit possession in this chapter is seen as a design by Derek Walcott in *Dream on Monkey Mountain* for his protagonist to reconnect with his African past as an attempt to reconstruct his identity and only after that can he move forward in life.

In the light of all that which precedes, it is evidently clear that the scope and field of memory studies is vast. Finally, it must be recalled that towards the end of a profound exploration of the concept of remembering in *The Analysis of Mind*, Bertrand Russell laments that his "analysis of memory is probably extremely faulty, but I do not know how to improve it" (187). Similarly, this book, though an important contribution in memory studies, does not holistically bridge the gap therein. It is a significant attempt to answer some questions that pertain to the relationship that literature has with memory. Literature as a subject at the core of the humanities cannot afford silence when the house of memory is "on fire". It is a direct consequence and offspring of memory. The title *Outward Evil and Inward Battle* is informed by the indictment literature has of society as the Voltairesque-deistic school of the Age of Reason holds: "the evil we battle is external, but we battle them inwardly." Consequently, our memories help us inwardly deal with those external past and present joys and tribulations remembered and/or forgotten.

In the final analysis, the respective authors of the individual chapters in this book, in their endeavor to rekindle the flames and passions of memory (so memory does not slip into oblivion) have had to bring to the fore their own experiences of and attitudes towards memory in an attempt to explicate their understanding of and critical reflections on the literary, historical, sociological, philosophical and psychological ramifications of memory and the curiosity it should stimulate. By leaving these authors to draw their respective conclusions as opposed to drawing a general conclusion, the editors believe that this book would provide a veritable menu for everything needed for an unforgettable memory banquet: appetizers, main dish, drinks and deserts.

Works Cited

- "The Memory Workbook", Mason, D.J; Kohn, M.; New Harbinger Publications
- Bhabha, Homi K. ed. *Nation and Narration*. New York: Routledge, 1990. Print.
- Bhabha, Homi K. *The Location of Culture*. London and New York: Routledge, 1994.172.
- Cohen, Patricia. "Next Big Thing in English: Knowing They Know That You Know." *New York Times* Apr. 2010: 1. *Academic Search Complete*. Web. 28 Nov. 2012.
- Connerton, Paul. *How Societies Remember*. Cambridge: Cambridge University Press. 1989.
- Dauenhauer, Bernard and Pellauer, David, "Paul Ricoeur", *The Stanford Encyclopedia of Philosophy* (Winter 2012 Edition), Edward N. Zalta (ed.)
- Dreiser, Theodore. *Sister Carrie: An Authoritative Text Backgrounds and Sources Criticism*. Second Edition. New York and London: W.W. Norton & Company, 1991. Print.
- Dubois, W. E. B. *The Souls of Black Folk*. New York, Avenel, NJ: Gramercy Books; 1994
- Eyerman, Ron, *Cultural Trauma* Cambridge University Press; 1 edition (January 14, 2002)
- Foucault, Michel. *An Introduction to the History of Sexuality*, London, Penguin. 1990
- Halbwachs, Maurice. *Mémoire Collective*, Paris, Albin-Michel, 1997
- Hampl, Patricia, *I Could Tell You Stories: Sojourns in the Land of Memory*, New York, Norton, 1999.

- Hannah Arendt, "Thinking," *The Life of the Mind* (New York: Harcourt, 1971)
- Martin, C.B. and Deutscher, Max (1966), 'Remembering', *Philosophical Review*, 75: 161–196.
- Nalbatian, Suzanna, *Memory in Literature: From Rousseau to Neuroscience*, New York, Palgrave-MacMillan Higher Education. 2004.
- Powell, Richard, *Black Art and Culture in the 20th century*, Thames and Houston, New York, N.Y. 1997.
- Russell, Bertrand. *The Analysis of mind*, London, G. Allen & Unwin; New York, Macmillan [1922]
- Sutton, John, "Memory", *The Stanford Encyclopedia of Philosophy (Winter 2012 Edition)*, Edward N. Zalta (ed.),
- Wittgenstein, Ludwig (1974), *Philosophical Grammar*, R. Rhees (ed), A. Kenny (trans.). Oxford: Blackwell.

The Editors:
BHF
ATA
FFN
BFN

Section I

Power

Chapter 1

Quakers, Memory & the Past in Literature.

Bill F. Ndi

Introduction

Seventeenth century English mindscape was notably characterized by millenaries' apocalyptic visions of the imminent end of the world. As a result of this, the period was marked by turmoil, changes and instability that affected every facet of social, economic, political, cultural, religious, ideological and literary life in both the Old and the New World. These changes and instabilities which have been carefully summed up by Christopher Hill in his historical *opus magna, The World Turned Upside-down,* pushed early English and American Quakers to launch a marginal literary creativity which turns out to be pivotal in the history of creativity in the English speaking world.

These Quakers so did by tilting their attention to documenting memory (happy as well as sad) and the past for future generations to remember who they were, what they went through and how they survived the odds they faced. The extent of this documenting of memory and the past have led scholars of Quakerism to a consensus on the postulation of Nigel Smith that these "early Quakers were at the same time modern and postmodern."

In the light of the aforesaid, early Quakers, belonged to a Christian sect and were persecuted for their libertarian ideas and ideals. They chose, in their tribulations, to document their "present sufferings" with the sole purpose being to catalogue for their offspring, what would constitute their own past. Consequently, Quaker memory in this venture would have to be preserved for future generations of Quakers and those who might take interest in their sufferings. Also these writings were all geared at validating

Quaker religious messages being conveyed as narratives to encourage those who might find themselves on the rough path of spiritual conversion and facing the same kind of difficulties that these Quakers of yore faced. In this guise, any exploration of memory and the past in contemporary literature should take into account the contribution by these precursors of this topical field[1].

This chapter envisages an exploration of the activism of early Quakers based on their works on, and documentation of, "Memory and the Past". An historical footnote here should evoke the total of 3750 spiritual autobiographies and conversion propaganda pamphlets and tracts that 17th century Quakers published within the first fifty years of the movement's existence. However, this chapter will also examine amongst other things, the legacy of their works in contemporary peace literature, given that "World Peace" was and still is the bedrock upon which Quakerism has built its religious philosophy and its philosophy of religion. Quaker collection and documentation of the *sufferings* of the times against this backdrop would turn out to be the foundation upon which their struggles for world peace and that against persecution and oppression would stand. Exploring these concerns will entail a critical examination of some Quaker writings including the works of Edward Coxere, Thomas Lurting and Elizabeth Stirregde.

However, before delving into examining how Quaker memory and the past and their recollection of that past exert an influence in literature it would be worthwhile to start by looking at the historical context in which Quakerism and its literature were born. 17th century English society was deeply characterized by chiliastic expectations, alongside with the Puritan Revolution that encouraged the birth of multiple religious groupings or sects. All these groups based, upon memory, their expectations and hopes that the end times and promise of a thousand years of bliss in a heavenly kingdom, made by Christ to His faithful followers was near. This was to occur after "His

---

[1] Lacan in discussing Freud in literary analysis highlights the unconscious as structured like a language. Cf. in Terry Eagleton. *Literary Theory: an Introduction.*

second coming". Early Quakers shared this characteristic of chiliastic and prophetic views alongside other religious groupings preaching to English Protestants the imminence of this universal revolution. Memory of the force and originality of this new Quaker messianic mission is contained in the spiritual autobiographies written by the adepts of the doctrine of *inner light* also called *publishing of truth*. These autobiographies, of which the most famous is *The Journal of George Fox*, (cf. Hugh Barbour & A Roberts, 1973.) assert various forms: novels, letters, doctrinal pamphlets and chronicles of persecutions which Quakers and other dissenters suffered. They all emphasize certain kinds of moments in the life of the adept, and most especially, those of moral redemption and/or relapses. Also, they track the journalists in their tribulation and sustain their narrative with constant reiteration of their memory of the events.

Historically speaking, it must be reemphasized, 17th century England was marked by turbulence in all facets of life: political, social, economic, cultural, ideological, religious, etc. Quakers were no exception of those who participated in actively bringing about these revolutionary changes. They contributed in a considerable manner in revolutionizing the ideas and mentalities of the times in such a way that some of the changes are still topical. The turmoil and turbulences in the 17th English society culminated in a revolution which was crowned with the Restoration of a constitutional monarchy. For the Puritans, this signaled the accomplishment of the religious Reforms that Luther had initiated in 1534. As such many radical Puritans asked for the adoption of the Lutheran and Calvinist doctrine of *Sola Scriptura* which would allow Christians to get closer to their brethren separated from them and whose faith was founded upon the *Bible* and the *Bible* alone[2].

---

[2] It must be noted that John Milton attached a great importance to this. Pointing out that Milton's ideas had its origin in part from Quaker ideas, Émile Saillens underlines what differentiated Milton from the Quakers. Milton venerated the bible while Quakers considered the bible to be a secondary source book of norms, subjected to the will of the Holy Spirit speaking directly to every man. Besides, Milton upheld that everything in the bible was to be believed. Cf. Émile Saillens, *L'homme, poète, et polémiste*. Paris : Gallimard. 1959.

It was in response to these demands by isolated groups of protestant radicals or separatists that the King, Charles I, imposed religious conformism onto all his subjects without exception. Knowing the task to be arduous, he appointed William Laud as the Archbishop of Canterbury in 1633. Once appointed at the head of the Church, William Laud took authoritarian measures to bring believers to conformity with the Church of England. He passed laws to make sure tithing was enforce and also ordered the dismissal of all puritan preachers. These measures only provoked anti-Catholic and anti-High-Church sentiments that were made evident many years later. As a result, Laud is noted in English religious History as one of the worst opponent of protestant radicalism. The immediate result of Laud's measures was that the various radical groups started breaking up to form organized religious movements which, besides flagging their religious aspirations, did not hide their socio-political agenda tinged with millenarist ideology.

Besides the Quakers, such movements as the Levelers, the Independents, Diggers, Men of the Fifth Monarchy, Ranters, Muggletonians and Seekers are worth mentioning here. However, after the 1st War, the idea of installing a theocracy split the puritans further. After this date, and under the Cromwellian Protectorate following the Revolt of the New Model Army, Quakers informed and advised the Army of their position. They stayed away from the infighting to control the New Model Army. This brought England as well as the New England colonies to the apogee of theocentrization and theocratization. These events led to many controversies. And Quakers contributed greatly to these controversies which gave birth to the process of democratization and modernization of the English speaking world. Who therefore were/are these Quakers? And what did/do they stand for and how did/do they translate their memory and past into literature? Or what ties Quakers to memory, literature and the past?

The Founding of the Quaker Movement & Fox

In the midst of the aforementioned struggle a few big sects or religious groups would go to war in the name of God and religion. The young George Fox, founder of Quakerism and a native of the northern part of England, aimed at drawing attention to biblical truths and started preaching the gospel at the age of 19 and according to what his memory could recollect from his childhood bible lessons. It must be recalled that Fox was not formally schooled to read and write nor were most of his followers. And historians of Quakerism such as, Edward Grubb (1925) in *Quaker Thought and History*, contend that

> His education, from the scholastic standpoint, was very imperfect; he read little except the Bible (which, however, he is said to have known almost by heart); and he had been unfortunate in his intercourse with theologians—not one of whom, during his early years of deep inward distress, had been able to "speak to his condition". (1)

Highlighting Fox's early years of distress establishes a foundational base upon which his doctrine was to be laid. It was all about an inward journey into the memory. Before *light* came to him, Fox records how, "[...] the Lord opened to me that being bred at Oxford or Cambridge was not enough to fit and qualify men to be ministers of Christ; and I wondered at it, because it was the common belief of the people."(10) He thus called his undertaking, the *Proclamation* or *Publishing of Truth* which has come to be synonymous to Quakerism (Brinton vii).

Fox prophesized a doctrine which highlighted a method of existence and thinking, in short a method of conduct for daily spiritual growth and dealings with fellow human beings. This movement essentially founded its belief upon the divine *inner light, inner guide & inner voice* shining the way of, leading, and speaking directly to all human beings irrespective of gender, race, class, profession, religion or other epithets that would project other human beings to act superior to the detriment of others. This assertion becomes the basis for Quaker daily rectitude and practice; thus leading to the adoption of a rigorous ethic. Moreover, these Quakers shocked their contemporaries by overtly affirming that *The Bible* was secondary and subordinate to the inspiration of the *divine inner light, guide* and *voice*. Worse still, Quakers relegated the historical Christ to the background and only paid attention to the Christ in each and every individual human being. For their contemporaries, this was heresy because they took it to mean that Quakers were simply saying they themselves were Christ. However, this, George Fox assures, unites each and every individual to God. This concept sums thus Quaker doctrine, philosophy and ethics. How did it all begin?

In 1647, George Fox began pulling crowds of people through his improvised preaching in public places. The main goal of this improvised prophet was far from the creation of a religious order or movement. It was purely for the purpose of contributing significantly to the religious fervor of his time; aimed at closing up on the initial goals set forth by Luther and Calvin. His exhortations consisted in the insistence upon the *inward* experience of seeking God as the sole source of authority here on earth. No laws were above God's laws and any authority not based upon God's laws was not worth obeying. This innovative message appealed to the famous *Seekers* of the Cromwellian Interregnum as well as many Baptists and Anabaptists.

For George Fox, the *inner light* and not vain outward rituals and fetishization of material things was the key to Christian faith and salvation. Besides he drove home the point that being educated at Oxford or Cambridge was not enough to prepare anyone for a true religious vocation. He treated the Clergy as a set of *hireling priests*. And went further to chastise and castigate the Church for imposing tithes. He treated churches as *Steeple Houses*. Another ethical *proclamation of Truth* by Fox was his insistence on the idea of a spiritual baptism and communion amongst all men. He thus denounced all forms of oppression, including slavery and war. As a result of all these, he invited the wrath of the High Church clergy who accused him of heresy. The result was that vexations and persecutions, torture and imprisonment followed from the very onset of the Quaker movement in their endeavor to *publish & proclaim the truth*. Thus, the Quaker religion and its doctrine find their genesis solely under the auspices of George Fox. And it was important for Quakers to keep records of their sufferings. This record keeping became a buttress of Quaker resolve and solidarity confirming God's support for their movement and its endeavor.

Memory of Fox's direct or indirect influence in the Quaker endeavor to *proclaim and publish the truth* as well as follow the *inner light*, is preponderant in the writings of Quaker converts. However, it would be hard to pinpoint a founding act of the Quaker movement. *The Society of Friends* (as it is also known) sprung from a spontaneous grouping of numerous *Seekers* in Preston-Patrick, North of England. They had voluntarily placed themselves under the leadership of George Fox who seemed to have better answers to their spiritual anguish and expectations. This was the beginning of a long period of persecution during which time (besides the reenactment of the Elizabethan Vagrancy Act) the 1662 & 1667 Quaker Acts, the 1664 & 1672 Conventicle Acts, the 1673 Test Act, the 1687 Declaration of Indulgence, the 1689 Toleration Act and the 1694 Triennial Act, were all promulgated laws targeting Quakers. These were just additions to many other laws directed against all *non-conformists* who refused to abide by the precepts and rules of the Established Church. But, one would ask: why the Quakers most specifically? And what grounds the appellation Quaker or its significance to memory and the past in literature?

From the very onset, Quakers had always considered themselves *proclaimers and publishers of truth*. They became thus called sarcastically for reasons that once when George Fox was summoned in front of Judge Bennett, Fox bade the judge to quake in the Name of the Lord. Judge Bennett made a mockery of him calling him a Quaker. Again, some members of the movement had been seized by feats of trance and trembling during their prayer meetings. These quaking trance and feat akin to spirit possession which have their grip on Quakers in their religious practice, spill over into their writing. The above mentioned episodes for many Quakers ground the origin of their appellation even if this appellation had existed on continental Europe designating a women's cult.

Fox and his disciples were therefore convinced they had found true and divine inspiration that would let them revive Christianity as practiced by Christ and His apostles. They aimed at establishing a parallel between their practices and those of primitive Christianity. As such, they mimicked the gestures of Christ and His apostles; all humble, persecuted, yet driven by unwavering faith. Prison sentences, humiliations of all sorts and beatings that followed were endured by Quakers and that did very little to quell their zeal. On the contrary, the ties between sympathizers and converts were strengthened and they both pulled their forces together against their persecutors. This paradox warranted the stabilization and growth of the Quaker movement and its documentation of memory. The consequences of the ethics of Quaker doctrine are evident in the adoption of the principle of plainness, humility and simplicity demonstrated in the language and speech pattern used by Quaker journalists/writers for whom keeping records of their sufferings had become crucial. As such, Quaker writing is void of linguistic and stylistic embellishments. This could also be explained by the fact that most of these early Quakers did not have any formal education or were simply autodidacts whose sole goal was to *publish* and *proclaim the truth*.

Understanding the doctrine propounded by George Fox goes hand in glove with the conception of his language and style. According to Hill, in spite of the strong manifestation of individualism by Quaker writers, « they use similar words and phrases » (128). In effect, Quaker literature comes across as a vehicle for Quaker ideology behind which seem to lurk a functional and operational tool and logic characteristic of the movement. What then would be the tool and logic thus mentioned?

Psychological Introspection

> O, rather like the sky-lark, soar and sing,
> And let our gushing songs befit the dawn
> And sunrise, and the yet unshaken dew
> Brimming the chalice of each full-blown hope,
> Whose blithe front turns to greet the growing day
> Never poets such high call before,
> Never can poets hope for higher one,
> And, if they be but faithful to their trust,
> Earth will remember them with love and joy ;
> And oh, far better, God will not forget.
> For he who settles Freedom's principles
> Writes the death-warrant of all tyranny ;
> Who speaks the truth stabs falsehood to the heart;
> And his mere word makes despots tremble more
> Than ever Brutus with his dagger could.
>
> Lowell, L'Envoi.

Introducing psychological introspection as a functional operating tool and logic for Quaker writers and quoting this poem by James Russell Lowell, a celebrated Quaker poet, is no critical accident because besides hammering home the principles for which Quakers stand, Lowell reiterates the desire for future memory by stating that "Earth will remember them with love and joy;". The poet pushes the recourse to memory to an all new and even divine height by tapping from his earliest memory of Christian learning and associating memory to God in the verse, "And oh, far better, God will not forget." This association of memory and its lapses with God becomes intriguing and spurs thoughts of the Christian concept of God's omniscience and omnipresence. Does God's memory have lapses at times with the exception of special cases like the deeds herein the poem described which "…God will never forget"?

In the same light Elizabeth Stirredge, one of the early Quakeress in her *Weakness in Strength*... starts her *journal* by highlighting her concerns and reasons for writing. She explains how she has found the beneficial effects of righteousness and will willingly tap from it to leave something for her children and grandchildren when she would be no more. She writes,

> ... I have found the blessed effect of keeping in the right way; therefore I have a great concern upon my spirit, for my children, that they may not be forgetful of keeping in the right way, whensoever the Lord shall be pleas'd to take me from them. (1-2)

This statement pre-empts such literary critics inclined to Freudian psychology to paying attention to the relationship between text and reader. Here, what Quaker *journalists*, Stirredge among others, are doing is laying a foreground for both the intrinsic and extrinsic concerns that they have for those who would read their works in the future. Griffith reiterates this approach and draws attention to the example of Norman Holland who argues for the textual content of the secret expression of the readers' desires and wants (129). Further illustrating that even though the reader may not be aware of the said desires and wants, the same underlie and explicate the reader's enjoyment of any textual content. Also, it could be argued that the much more recent development of hermeneutics in Germany which strives to highlight reception esthetics and/or theory hammers home the role of the reader in literature (Eagleton 64). Quakers in their writings who preoccupied themselves with concerns about the reader preempted this shift of literary concern from author or text to the reader for whom the texts exist.

In the above light, Quaker literature with its journaling approach strives to establish a relationship with its prospective readers, the writers' offspring for the most part and/or those who would take interest in the persecutions, trials, travails and tribulations endured by previous generations of Quakers. Thus, it offers a fertile ground for the elaboration and exploration of Freudian theoretical approach to literature. In addition, the fact that this literature is structured to talk of the stead, situation and plight of its writers to would-be generations of followers and adepts of Quakerism, it would be far from erroneous to assert that a considerable part of Quaker literature streams from the imaginary, the unconscious, the memory and the past. It thus takes a foot hold in literature even when the authors claim to be stating or basing their accounts upon historical facts expressed in the simplest form of language and explains why Nigel Smith considers any further analysis of early Quaker writings would prove them as "the zero degree of Puritan expression" (XIX-XX).

Quaker literature as a result becomes an introspective probe into the psyche of the adept and writers. He/she, through this process, digs out from the littlest remembrances of his/her tender years to those of the maturity years. These remembrances for the most part of their occurrences were taken for mishaps and now with their new found faith, they become blessings in disguise and only revealed many years later. These instances abound in the works of Quaker *journalists*. Lurting for example, remembering how at 14 he had been drafted in the army to go to war in Ireland where he had many "deliverances, too long here to mention", highlights the fact that "…at that time, wrought but little upon me." (16). From thence he moves on to inform the reader of the ship, the *Bristol Frigot*, on board of which he became a Quaker convert.

It is on board this ship that most of the narrative takes place. However, one cannot help the temptation of questioning Lurting's selective memory and the criteria upon which he chooses to dwell on specific events and not others. Is it because these memories are simply too long to relate here as he states or is it because they are too *painful* to be related? All in all, it is evident that this journey into the *journalist's* psyche prompts him to take a certain route while avoiding others all with the primary goal of leaving the reader with that which is from the depth of his mind and believed to help encourage and strengthen the reader in his/her spiritual journey through the inner thoughts and consciousness of the writer.

Quakers carefully worked towards what has gained currency and come to be known amongst critics as psychological realism. Quakers admittedly used their individual concerns to capture the psychological portrait of their society and its ills as they perceived it. The interest shown by Quakers in the individual as the focal point of autobiographical creativity helped to popularize the novel. This psychological exploration of private and personal lives, present in the works of Pepys and all 17th century Quaker *journalists* must have prompted Ifor Evans to assert in *English Literature: Values and Traditions*

> that [this]… helped the English novel to become in the 18th century, a means of exploring personality, motivations and above all the feelings of men and women who would have been considered ordinary had their psyche not been explored in depth. (72)

What precedes so far, begs a number of questions. How then do Quaker *journalists* decide on the information they include in their *journal*? What are the selection criteria for what is said or written and that which is unsaid or unwritten? What is fit for inclusion in or exclusion from Quaker literature? It is worth noting that Quaker *journalists* for the most part in their selective amnesia have recourse to such catchy statements as: "it is too long to narrate here.." and would only focus on what the writer sees as memorable, vital and potentially appealing and of some spiritual and religious importance to the would-be reader, oftentimes, the writer's own children and grandchildren. In this process is born a communication model which in modern communication theory parallels the interactional Sender <-> Receiver model. However, the Quaker communication model goes a step further because the writer takes into account the expectations of a feedback from the reader and the reader's possible reaction even though this feedback never really comes back to the writer/sender. This bi-directional communication model with the text as the medium could be mapped out thus

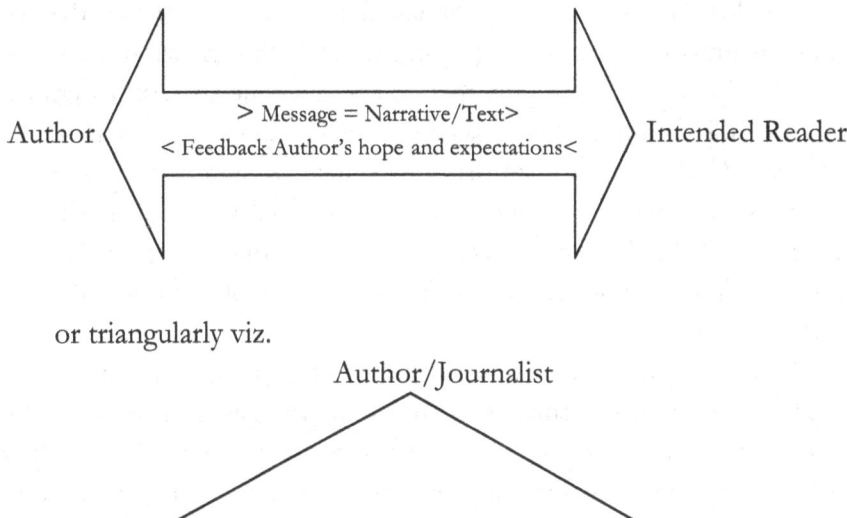

or triangularly viz.

These communication models call for the examination of the historical elements documented by Quaker writers/journalists as memory for posterity. Is the message or text informational, exploratory, persuasive and above all convincing? Would it serve the expected and highlighted purpose of the writer?

Documentation of History as Memory for Posterity

Exploring the introspective nature of Quaker literature, critical questions arose as to the deciding factor for elements included or excluded in this literature. Emphasis has also been placed on the fact that this literature has for primary purpose the spread of Quakerism through its own propaganda. Also brought to the limelight was the multiple persecutions (grounded by various Acts of parliament mentioned above) suffered by these Quakers. All of these foregrounded their specific interest in documenting issues of their own very existence, both spiritual and material, as memory for posterity. How did Quakers go about this? What was the *modus operandi* that instigated these writings which for Quakers became a *modus vivendi*?

Quaker Narratives share similar characteristics in style, themes and stream of consciousness techniques even though we had to wait for the 20th century for this to become a vogue in writing/critical circles. Hill summing Quaker writing in *The Experience of Defeat: Milton and some Contemporaries,* comforts this stance by stating that "Quaker writings thus become a kind of stream of consciousness that flows continuously and without forethought with one thing leading to another and most of the ideas directed against hireling priesthood" (128).

These narratives concerned with the exploration of internal as well as external problems of existence almost always start with the formative years which Quaker writers consider being the budding years of childish daydreaming, reveries and pursuit of carnal will. During these years everything that happens to the writer is at the time of its happening considered a mishap. However, at the time of writing, given the influence of the desire to heed the *inner voice*, the dominion over the writer of the consciousness of the *inner voice/light* engenders a supra individual will which overshadows the individual carnal will from the writers' mind. This individual carnal will is as such replaced by supra-individualism placed under the tutelage of divine will. The style and recurrent expression in Quaker texts demonstrate this principle generating concepts and ideas to which all adhere. By adhering to the Quaker principles of plainness and simplicity, these "journalist" make no attempts to be elegant in their writings. And besides, they are for the most part, autodidacts. This style of writing is highly likely what prompted Beckett to write in a language with which his familiarity was just basic, i.e. French. He said by so doing he wrote without style and it was not only easier but warranted an escape from everything with which he was familiar. Quaker narration of events of the past thus becomes divinely ordained occurrences. As such, the fears and insecurities engendered during their formative years find fervor in the authors' eyes as they would in the eyes of the reader. Here, memory is at play!

Edward Coxere, capturing the first meeting with his French foster mother during his travel on an exchange program in France, vividly remembers how subsequently he was mistreated by her and writes:

> My French mother, as I then called her, understanding that I was in exchange for her son, with that she kissed me and got me soon home to her house, which was a brewhouse. She being a widow, her father, who I then called grandfather, managed the affairs of the brewer, who was a fine ancient man, a Roman Catholic. They would be speaking to me in French, but I was like one dumb, and my mind not well satisfied for all my new kindred, for their loves did not balance the trouble of mind I had in being so far from home amongst such as I could neither speak to nor understand.[...]
> My mother proved not so kind to me as she appeared at first, which discouraged me very much, especially I not being able to speak for myself for about two months' time, but like a dumb boy making signs (as when I would go to sleep I would shut my eyes and lay my head on my hand) so long till I began to despair; it seemed so hard for me to learn. For my credit lay very much at stake, for most of my friends had so good opinion of me, which concerned me the more to have as much of it as I could. But by degrees I got one word after another till I did begin to tell a French story, and when I was entered I got courage in hopes to save my credit and satisfy my friends. (5-6)

Again, recounting his life at 15 and talking about his second job in the seafaring trade, he gives account of his acceptance to ship on board the *Oulld St. Georg*. He mentions his previous sea experience and expresses confidence in the St George. His previous voyage on board the *Malaga Factor* was unpleasant and his individual and carnal will made him to conclude sea life was not meant for him. In justifying his admiration for this second rate ship, *The Oulld St. Georg*, he adds memory of the fact that the ship's lieutenant of the Admiral had a son who was his playmate in addition to the fact that his own brother John was a seaman on board this ship. This account is followed by several other adventures at sea which all lead him towards his being "convinced" (i.e. Quaker parlance for converted into Quakerism or become a Quaker).

In documenting his adventures, Coxere stays close to his spiritual alertness and notes everything in the way of religious practice on board the ship in which he serves. He recounts serving as a mass boy. When writing about the accident on board *The Oulld St. Georg*, Coxere does not fail to attribute the fact that he and others survived as a doing/making of the Lord's. The seamen being trapped were left to die either by drowning or by fire caused by an explosion on board *The Oulld St. Georg*. This *journalist* brings to the forefront both the event and the overcoming of such a dangerous situation which could not have been anything else but the work of providence pure and simple. He writes: "… till at last it pleased the Lord that they overcame the fire before it got to the main powder room" (9-10). In short, Coxere's formative years are rich in accounts of many adventures at sea as well as memories of his encounter with people from other nations of Europe. He thus gives both historical and anthropological account of these peoples and their nations. He also gives account of some of the great wars that opposed these nations.

He skillfully documents his involvement in the wars that pitted European nations against one another. He fought for almost every nation (at one point) which was at war viz. the English, the Dutch, the Spaniards, the Turks, etc. Documenting his role in these wars, he remembers fighting for every nation possible at one point. He writes:

We being arrived at San Sebastian and delivered our goods, our ship then was taken up or hired to serve the King of Spain against the French, so that we were made Admiral of twelve sail of Spanish ships. At this time Bordeaux was the Spaniards', and we was to relieve it with soldiers and money. We had the general aboard and about two hundred Spaniards and Dutch. Though we were before the river of Bordeaux several times, our captain had no mind to put in; he still had an excuse to the general of non-convenience, so that we lay cruising in the Bay of Biscay about five months, taking of prizes, for every French ship we met with was our own. We took several prizes, by which our captain did enrich himself very considerably. The harbour where we kept our rendezvous was called Pasages[3], hard by San Sebastian, where we carried our prizes in. Our captain being a Roman Catholic, we had a friar aboard that said Mass. I kept all the trinkets aboard that covered the altar in a trunk, I being the chief cabin boy. The altar was the cupboard, which I covered, where on stood the picture of Christ, which since I wonder they would let me handle their Mass-tools, I being the captain's boy, I suppose it was not minded, for sometimes I was on my knees with them, as I remember. (11-12)

Even though his narrative does not reserve any important disclosure of his warring adventures, he mostly recounts his meetings with people who did not share his views and much less his ideas of peace militancy. He winds up with his stance against warring and fighting. He refuses to arm his ships before going to sea. Besides this demonstration of the Quaker peace principle, Coxere brings to light the arbitrary imprisonment suffered by his fellow Quakers and himself in English jails. His narrative ends with him waiting on the Lord (in a Quaker Assembly) and being taken and thrown to jail for his conviction. It is a spiritual voyage showing the stages of spiritual development through his voyages, his conversion to Quakerism, his experience of Quakerism and the travails and tribulations he and other Quakers had to endure.

Translated before a judge in Southwark, it is with well thought out effrontery that Coxere reminds the judge of his being a seaman who has been to places and has met with kindness that he expects the same from the judge. Here, he takes his coreligionists as his witnesses to what the judge promises for he knows he is not going to keep to his words. Coxere writes,

---

[3] From the sixteenth to the eighteenth century this was the starting-point of the Basque whalers, and Lafayette took ship here for America in 1776.

> When I came home in this vessel off the last voyage to London, I had not been above two or three weeks but I was taken out of Horslydown meeting by soldiers and carried away with more Friends to St. Margaret's Hill* before a judge in Southwark* on the account of banishment. We being before him, he took our names and where we dwelt. It being my turn to be called, he asked me what trade I was. I told him I was a seaman, and was newly come from sea, where I had been among several nations, and did wish I might find as much kindness here as I did among them. The judge told me I should. I bid the people standing by take notice of it. He passed sentence upon me, that was a fine of so much money and to be sent to prison. I was guarded to the White Lion prison in Southwark and there kept close prisoner during their pleasure. (113)

Furthermore, this spiritual journey through legal persecutions which constitutes Coxere's writing highlights what is hidden in the dark depths of the writer in spite of the Quaker principle of humility, simplicity and plainness in everything Quakers do. In one instance, he recounts a journey to Newfoundland and during which he was ready to defend himself in the eventuality of any war. He displays his willingness to put to use the 15 canons fitted on his ship. This clearly illustrates the toughness of sea life in the 17th century which G.N. Clark, a historian of this era underlines. He points out that,

> Armed aggression ... was the heart of commerce. To investigate the details of seafaring and colonial life is to find oneself in a world of hard men, exposing themselves to great risks, and putting up with great hardships, never slow to take the shortest way with other men whose presence might mean imminent danger *(59)*.

This is certainly the reason that must have prompted E.W.H Meyerstein, the first editor of Coxere's *Adventures by Sea,* to highlight that the visual and narrative qualities of Coxere's autobiography "transforms its reading into a personal and tragic experience".

Coxere's seems to show some objectivity when he relates facts and his emotional troubles caused by suffering in prison. He is not carried away by his conversion or by his new found faith to embellish his life story. Coxere's autobiography espouses, in this light, what sociological critical theorists would call social realism. His becomes to an extent a reporter's observation, a humorist's satire, the work of an historical linguist, a historian's documentation, the narration of a storyteller, findings of an anthropologist, etc. As a Quaker *Journalist*, Coxere makes memory a central "concern" of his writing. He constantly reminds the reader of the importance of this aspect of the human psyche (memory). Coxere, in his *Adventures by Sea,* points out how after many years of seafaring with the Dutch his linguistic memory begins failing him to the extent that he could not even remember words in his native English language. Also, he points out how after these many years when he happened to be on board an English ship he had to begin learning the names of riggings in English whereas he could remember them very well in Dutch. If upon returning home Coxere is taken for a Dutchman by his own aging mother, this is nothing but the result of a failing memory.

If literature in its etymological definition highlights the import of pleasure, learning, and emotion, viz. *"placere, doucere, movere"* Quaker literature tends not to emphasize the pleasing aspect even though occasionally in works such as Coxere's, humor is also a central ingredient that the author uses to alleviate the memory of imprisonments, torture, daily travails and tribulations with which he was compelled to be familiar. Coxere is not carried away as would post conversion Puritan writers in their representation of character marked by a dark picture of sin-bound pre-conversion self. These particularities exclude Coxere's work and those of other Quaker writers from the traditional puritan spiritual autobiography which as Jacques Tual states is "a subjective narrative in which the reader finds exaltation which describes on every page only subjective personal and emotional experience" (16).

In a nutshell, Quaker literature must be read bearing in mind the writers' first intention born of visionary and spiritual desires to portray personal resolve and serve as encouragement to the weak. As a result, the individual style of the Quaker *journalists* easily slips off and gives way to a group convention. Quaker writing style reveals what Crystal qualifies as "… a system of linguistic choices not used by only one writer but by a group of writers." (472). Quaker literature thereby becomes guided by what could easily be styled "Central intuition of the divine *inner light, guide* & *voice*." This is a peculiarity to Quakerism and its writing with the reader forced to confront a disturbing reality of a world in which the quest for freedom becomes the noose around the neck of freedom seekers whose tragic stance is overt defiance against established institutions. Nonetheless, as has been illustrated with *Adventures by Sea* of Edward Coxere's, the reader is left with a group think not void of the individual voice, tone and uniqueness. What then accounts for this?

Individuation/Collective Unconsciousness

Reading Quaker literature, memory and the past calls for the exploration and understanding of the process of self-actualization, realization and integration by which Quakers and Quaker writers tried to distinguish themselves from all other *journalists* belonging to other religious organizations of their time. This marked their writings and left imprints not only to the minds of the individual Quaker writers but their readers through their constant appeal to the individual conscience for a collective good. In a previous study of the Quaker *Journal*, the Quaker scholar Howard Brinton highlights this aspect. He further stresses that Jungian psychology has aptly described the period hitherto mentioned as one Quakers considered to be the budding years of childish daydreaming, exploration, reveries and pursuit of carnal desires; and has furnished an explanation to it and writes, "C. J. Jung in his writings, which are concerned with the integration or individuation of the self, has ably described the psychological characteristics and explanations of this condition" (23).

It should be noted that Quakers, memory and the past in literature have been facilitated by this psychological phenomenon. Quakers were adepts of a sect propounding internalization and individual conscience over externalization and outward appearances and/or issues of human existence. This phenomenon pushed Quakers to develop, in them and in their writings, the *supra-individual will* which overrides the *individual will* (in Foxian sense, *carnal will*). This *supra-individual will* operates under the divine will and accounts for the similarity in style and recurrent uses of the same expressions (words and phrases). Quaker writings therefore come across as those following conventions to which each and every writer adheres. The subtitle of Coxere's book follows this pattern. He spells out the things that occasioned his documenting of memory and the purpose of which is to give glory to God. He writes: "A Relation of the Several Adventures by Sea with the Dangers, Difficulties and Hardships I Met for Several Years as also the Deliverances and Escapes through them for which I have Cause to Give the Glory to God for ever."

Through this spiritual experience and documentation of memory, the psychological content of Quaker writing cannot only be circumscribed to the thinking, ideas and mentalities of the epoch. These Quaker fanatics, amateur writers, pamphleteers and roaming visionaries did not only preoccupy themselves with the dramatization of the soul and stories of religious conversions such as John Bunyan's (1666) *Grace Abounding to the King of Sinners,* (which had its 7th edition published in 1692), as was the vogue at that time. Quaker writings are marked by aspects of timeless universalisms that characterize the Quaker movement. They argued for intuitive response and spontaneity to the gospel and everyday events over careful study. Arguing that being schooled at Cambridge or Oxford never prepared anyone to be a true minister of God. And this was grounded by the ruthless and imponderable exactions perpetrated by these Oxford and Cambridge schooled priests who like those in Sir Walter Raleigh's (1608) political and religious satire "The Lie" constitute "… the Church, [that] shows/ What's good, and doth no good."

In Coxere's work he is also trapped in this dilemma and responding to his conscience, he vividly recalls and documents the burden of living a blatant lie as a seaman amongst other seamen who professed religiousness which did not follow the tenets of Christianity.

Our manner at sea of devotion is before night all the seamen with the master to read a prayer and sing a psalm; with whom I joined till it became my burden; for I had then more need to weep than to sing, as well as the rest of the seamen, who would be swearing, cursing, and lying, and with the same tongue come aft into the cabin and fall a-singing of David's words, as if they had been so many Davids and in his condition, instead of tears falling from their eyes, as David's did, laugh, scoff, and jeer, so soon as from their devotion, and, instead of singing with melody in the heart unto the Lord, vain, idle songs with ungodly words and actions. The Lord giving me a sight of this, my mouth was stopped, so that I sat by them and did not dare open my mouth to sing, neither at last to join with them in prayer, the prayers of the wicked being abomination to the Lord, but would walk on the deck by myself, which was no small cross, I having command over between thirty or forty men under the master, where the master and men's eyes were all at me to see me so much altered as not to come to prayer among them.

As also we had a feast aboard, with several English merchants, where many guns were fired off at healths. I walking at such a time like a stranger, where before I used to be active in firing off the guns, I had a check from the master, as if nothing were minded. This was not all, but the Lord tried me farther. I being among the complimenting Spaniards, so that I could not pull off my hat in answer to their complimentings, I found a daily cross as to outward behaviours, customs, and manners, beside the Enemy's workings within, that in this time the Lord let me see that fighting, killing, and destroying one another was of the Devil and not of Himself (91-92).

The above quote ends with the writer insisting, like most of his fellow Quakers in their writings, on a critic of externalization and the internal workings of the enemy to prevent self-integration. Though not systematically set down in any book of rules, inferences could be made by reading works by these early Quakers. It is in their process of self-realization, actualization and integration that Quakers believe and expound in writing universal truth and belief about the need for peace on earth as a divine duty not just a moral one. A duty Quakers believe should be executed with honesty, plainness, modesty and simplicity. The virtue of this execution which leads to the realization of self-integration is not only cathartic and psycho-curative for both the *journalist* and reader/future generation of Quakers but a foundation stone for world peace that the writers laid with the memory of persecutions, trials, travails and tribulations they suffered. These past sufferings imposed to Quakers from the external world become a *leitmotiv* for their strife to establish universal peace and testify to it in writing. Quakerism, unlike Marxism, does not call for popular uprising to overthrow the oppressors but calls for peaceful non-violence! So, Quakers in their obsession for freedom and integrity did not only defend the cause for themselves as individuals but did so for everyone in this world. Their memory, expected and projected hopes recorded in writing were for the fundamental stone for belief and practice of would-be adepts and readers to resolve and pursue a peaceful and spiritual journey through life with all its hurdles.

The Bedrock of Peace Literature

Should Quakers be admired for standing their grounds and undergoing all what they had to for the sake of equality, truth, peace, and justice even when they knew this was leading them to disaster? Besides, it has been established in literary criticism that such obstinate and passionate quest for freedom has been the pitfall of many a tragic hero. However, the Quaker appeal to non-resistance to violence solidifies the drift admiration rather than reproach. Tolstoy in his, *The Kingdom of God is Within You* opens the treatise with "The Doctrine of Non-Resistance to Evil by Force has been Professed by a Minority of Men from the Very Foundation of Christianity." He clearly highlights the import of Quaker writings on the ideas of peace. He postulates the irreconcilable difference between Christian theology and practice when it comes to the use of force stating how Quakers have maintained and proven fighting and killing more than anything else has contributed to obscuring Christian truth in the eyes of the heathen.

Further acquaintance with the labors of the Quakers and their works--with Fox, Penn, and especially the work of Dymond (published in 1827)--showed me not only that the impossibility of reconciling Christianity with force and war had been recognized long, long ago, but that this irreconcilability had been long ago proved so clearly and so indubitably that one could only wonder how this impossible reconciliation of Christian teaching with the use of force, which has been, and is still, preached in the churches, could have been maintained in spite of it.

Coxere, Lurting and Stirredge are part of these Quakers whose labors Tolstoy talks of in the above quote. Guided by the central intuition, mentioned above, Coxere comes to the realization "…that fighting, killing, and destroying one another was of the Devil and not of (the Lord) Himself" (92). Though Coxere's writing comes across as groans of pains and exclamations of joy through which he spews his anguish and frustrations in the face of religious and socio-political challenges as well as his hopes, joys and aspirations, Coxere like his fellow Quaker writers strives to transform the world into an arena of peaceful co-existence in which the need for wars would be uncalled for. The memory of Fox advising the New Model Army and insisting on the needlessness for war as stipulated in the book of Isaiah 2:4

> And he shall judge between the nations, and shall rebuke many people: and they shall beat their swords into plowshares, and their spears into pruning hooks: nation shall not lift up sword against nation, neither shall they learn war any more.

It must be emphasized here that Lurting uses this quote to justify his work which as he says was "First Written for Private Satisfaction, and Now Published for general Service." (9).

Quakers use this and many other biblical arguments to drum their stance against bearing arms and fighting and killing for whatever reason. They make it an issue of conscience. Coxere, in his narrative, tells us how he would rather suffer than fight or take away somebody's life even when this entails being out of job and source of sustenance. This, for him, becomes the only way to know true peace. He ponders on all of these and his previous life in which warring was the main source of his income. Now the label of Quaker makes everything impossible as he writes, "… out of employment, though I had good acquaintance with many masters of ships, but the name of a Quaker and not fighting shut me quite out of esteem with them." This documentation of his travails lay a foreground for his determination to see peace at sea. So he had to start looking to work for Quakers. He points out,

> … my desier was to be Imploid by frends up on which I went to Lundon whear I met with 2 or 3 frends who had a vesell which thay wear sending to sea & wanted a Mate. Thay hering of me came to me whear we agreed together for me to go mate for 50 shillings a month whear before I had 3 pound 10 shillings A month how Euer I was glad.

This desire to work for Friends who shared his views of not fighting led him to Edmund Tiddeman who, though not a Quaker, was willing to accept Coxere as mate. He unravels through this tale the multiple humiliations and smear campaign Quakers were subjected to then. The following passage is very telling of this.

This was in the year 1661. There was then but few Friends * masters of ships. I understanding that Edmond Tiddeman was bound to sea, I wrote to him to know if he would be willing to accept of me to go his mate. He answered me 'Very willing'. He then did not come among Friends. His wife's mother, which was old William Stradford's wife, soon heard of it, for it was noised abroad as a dangerous thing to carry a Quaker to sea, fearing he should also become * one too. They used their endeavours to, prevent it, but did not take effect. The old woman, being disturbed, sent for me to her house, where I found the old woman and old man together, where the old woman would a persuaded me not to go to sea with her son, telling me that she had said her prayers often in the night, desiring to be satisfied, but could not unless I would promise her not to go with her son, lest he should become a Quaker, and then what merchants would employ him? I told her I knew not how to comply with such a fearful spirit, but if he were not willing to have me go with him then I would not go. His wife and relations were wholly set against it, endeavouring to prevent it, so that I became as one not fit to be suffered in a ship, and how to maintain my family, which increased, I was in a strait, and knew not well how, unless I would deny the love of God unto my soul at that time, who shewed me to love enemies and not destroy them, so that my livelihood lay much on fighting, the more because I had been brought up to long voyages, where I was best acquainted to take charge as a mate: so that fighting was the great cross at that present with me to deny, and the more because I was more active at it, when occasion were, than many of my consorts, therefore was there the more notice taken of it that I should become a fool and what else they pleased to think of me.

In the face of these odds, Coxere as would any other Quaker remains peaceable and as he says, "… my desire was to be true to God and man and not deceive my soul" (92). This recollection actually urges him to give up a lucrative position of master on board *The Partners*. The argument for peace above all else and holding onto the tenets of his Quaker belief underscores this. He states:

> I, […], desired the owners, who were merchants, to send a man that understood more of merchandising than I did, though I was brought up a seaman, and was willing to officiate the place of a master, yet was to seek as a merchant. The concern being so

much as the whole cargo, to be at my disposing, I found it too heavy for me, though I was encouraged by wages. Also how to enter the vessel at the custom-house with an oath I could not, neither could I persuade another to do it for me. The wars with Holland breaking out with us, I saw little likelihood of scaping, the owners being designed to have me run alone, and also war with the Turks, so that I did desire to be discharged. The owners being very unwilling to do it, I at last persuaded them to it, and bought me a hoy, to use a home-trade. (111)

The mention of *The Partners*, Thomas Lurting and George Pattison is significant in underscoring Quakers, Memory and the Past as a bedrock for peace literature for it was on board this same Ketch that George Pattison and Thomas Lurting (whose autobiography, *A Fighting Sailor Turn'd Peaceable Christian...*[4] is a monument of contemporary peace literature) put to practice the Quaker peace principle of never returning violence with violence. To close this section of the discussion, it must not be forgotten that this literature has inspired many writings from Marvell *(Letters CCXXXVIII)* through Voltaire *(Philosophical letters* or *Letters on the English)* to Tolstoy *(The Kingdom is Within You)* and Gandhi, Joyce, Beckett, Walt Whitman and beyond. This begs the question as to what Quaker world view of life is in their literature or better still what perspective of life and its memory have Quakers legated to the reader and to our contemporary world in their endeavor to document memory and the past in literature.

Positive View of Life

Reading Quaker autobiographical journals does not give any impression of the authors lamenting over their sufferings, persecutions no matter how long and tedious their spiritual journey of self-examination had been. But, they always translate into a

---

[4] Cf. my French translation: *Le Marin Combattant Devenu Paisible...* Mankon-Bamenda, Cameroon, 2009 (1710)

wonderful working of the divine in favor of those faithful and trusting servants who can now *move forward* after self-reclamation and reformation. A positive note is always the outcome for Quaker appeal to the conscience and keen listening to the *inner voice* & *guide*. Given that the primary purpose of writing the *Journal* had always been to persuade future generations of converts that all the trials, travails, tribulations and persecutions undergone are for the Lord, anything done for Him is not in vain. It is in this process of validating their religious message that Quakers bear their testimonies to establish the crucial significance of an exemplary daily life led in the *light* radiating from within to without; inwardly to God and outwardly to man.

It is in this vein that Coxere, even after a year and a half as a slave to the Turks and a prisoner to the Spaniards, projects his happiness to be home in spite of the multiple challenges he has had to face. He talks of others pitying him and brushes off the journey in a way characteristic to Quaker *Journalists* escaping from painful and familiar memories; "Here ended this troublesome voyage." This Quaker characteristic style seems to confirm the Quaker belief that difficulties as well as anxieties were generated by external pressures or problems external to the self. He is unflinching at this point for he is in the constant presence and power of the *inner light*. Upon his return home, he writes:

> [...] and came home only my clothes to my back to my poor wife, but poor and penniless yet glad to see each other in health again after these troubles. My son Robert died whilst I was a slave, and Elizabeth was born. I was pitied by many, but counted unfortunate. At this time my wife did begin to keep shop, there being a necessity for something to be done for a livelihood.

Another instance of this literature documenting memory to legate a positive view of life is found in the narrative of Lurting, *The Fighting Sailor Turn'd Peaceable Christian,* briefly mentioned before. From the preface to the very end, Lurting's narrative refreshes the reader and unveils the Lord's working in favor of all who trust in Him. Lurting

(12) points out his is "First written for personal satisfaction and published for service." He then drums his message of peace, quoting from the Holy book, Isaiah 2:4. Besides, his narrative focuses on his being made captive by Turks and how he finally frees himself and his co-captives and in turn takes the Turks captive. Memory of his peace principle prohibits him from hurting a fellow human being and he heeds this and frees the said Turks unharmed off the coast of their country.

This application of the peace principle erects Lurting's treatise as a monument of peace literature and sheds a positive light on the triumph of the doctrine of the *inner light* over the external and internal workings and scheming of the enemy. This substantiates Quaker documentation of memory and the past in literature as a vital element in understanding the essence and quintessence of the Quaker endeavor of relating their travails, persecutions and tribulations to strengthen the resolve of future generations. This is clearly illustrated in Lurting's refusal to sell the Turks even when he has them at his mercy. He writes: *"That if they would give many Thousands, they should not have one, for we hoped to send them home again"* (68).

Again, he describes his return home and the reproaches he gets from the King for not acting like a conqueror and bringing the Turks to England. His answer to the King invites a smile from the latter. Through it, Lurting invites the reader to partake in his own contribution to the fight led by early Quakers to have their contemporaries and future generations accept the idea of peaceful coexistence (in spite of hostilities coming from without) in this world in general and at sea in particular. In the scene mentioned, he writes:

> And when we came for *England,* coming up the River of *Thames,* some Boats going before us; and King *Charles,* and the Duke of *York,* and many of his Lords, being at *Greenwich,* it was told them, *There was a Quaker's* Ketch, *coming up the River, that had been taken by the* Turks, *and had redeemed themselves, and had never a Gun.* And when we came near to *Greenwich,* the King came to our Ship's side, and one of his Lords came in, and discoursed the Master; and the King and the Duke of *York,* stood with the

Entering Ropes in their Hands, and asked me many Questions about his Men of War; I told him, *We had seen none of them*. Then he asked me many Questions, *How we cleared our selves,* and I answered him; he said, *I should have brought the* Turks *to him*. I answered, *That I thought it better for them to be in their own Country:* At which they all smiled, and went away (78).

This ending highlights what Lurting drives home in his Foreword where he writes:

For as Silence is the first Word of Command in Marshal Discipline, so it is in the Spiritual: For until that's come unto, the Will and Mind of God cannot be known, much less done. And as I know no way so Effectual to answer my End, than to Expose the following Treatise to public View, I commit it accordingly, hoping it may be serviceable to some in this and future Ages: Which is the only thing aimed at... (14)

And his conclusion: "*So I rest in that which can do Good for Evil, which ought to be the Practice of all true Men.*" says it all (80). And from every indication, it is evident that it required of these Quakers enormous strength and courage to tap from their memory and recount the horrors of their travails and tribulations. They have so did by choice to serve as a real life lesson that hedges the path towards peace, tolerance and oneness with the history and memory of their persecution being at odds with all Western values of liberty and freedom.

Conclusion

By carefully recording memory and the past, Quakers successfully expose what they had to endure as a people with conviction and ideas far too advanced for their time as well as the scheming of the enemy. They thus establish and confirm the victory of the ways of the Lord; a thing one of their contemporaries, John Milton, does in *Paradise Lost* in which he aims at "justify[ing] **the ways of God to Man.**"

Tilting attention to the individual's inner as well as outward problems of existence, Quakers through the documentation of memory and the past capture the psychological portrait of the society and its ills with the masks one puts on in everyday life while aware of the repressed emotions and feelings. As such Quakers validate their thinking that difficulties and anxieties relating to belief are generated from problems external to self. And further establish a wholesome world void of conflicts entails self-actualization and integrating the content of the psyche or that of the inner life consistent with the expected external life aspired after. Thus, collecting and documenting the *sufferings* of the times lay a foundation upon which any struggle for world peace and that against persecution and oppression would stand.

To Fox and his followers, the only possible way to experience total freedom void of any hindrances and entrapments of the enemy would require discovering the divine within and taking pity on those who cause harm. Their expostulation is based on the premise that to victimize someone, any civilized being in his/her right frame of mind, must have fallen victim to the entrapments of the enemy himself. This is how they substantiated the fact that Quakers living in *the light* and the power of the Lord would not hurt or cause harm to anyone by fighting. As a result such victims of the enemy's entrapment must be pitied and treated kindly. This explains all what the Quakers had to put up with; then posture in nonviolent resistance against the persecution in the hands of the Clergy of the Established Church, the government and law makers of their time. This principle in turn walked its way to us through their writings; to the works they inspired from such writers as Andrew Marvell, Voltaire, Tolstoy and Gandhi, amongst many others. Quaker writing and writers have inspired creative works: plays, novels, poems etc. In short, Quaker influence in writing in the English language is undeniably enormous. The Quaker narrative technique of introspection and having recourse to memory and documenting it is evident in the works of most writers in the English language from Defoe to Joyce and even Beckett.

Works Cited

- Barbour, Hugh & A Roberts eds. *Early Quaker Writings*. Grand Rapids, Michigan: William B. Eerdmans Publishing Company, 1973.
- Barbour, Hugh *The Quakers in Puritan England*. New Haven, London : Yale U. Press, 1964.
- Brinton, Howard H. *Quaker Journals : Varieties of Religious Experience Among Friends*. Wallingford, Pennsylvania : Pendle Hill Publications, 1983. (1972)
- Corns, Thomas N. (ed) et al. *The Emergence of Quaker Writing: Dissenting Literature in Seventeenth Century England*. Frank Cass & Co, 1996.
- Croese, Gerard. *The General History of the Quakers*. London: 1696.
- Crystal, David. *The Cambridge Encyclopaedia of Language*. London: Guild Publishing. 1988. (1969)
- Émile Saillens, *L'homme, poète, et polémiste*. Paris : Gallimard. 1959.
- Fox, George, *The Journal,* London Penguin, 1998
- G.N. Clark, *Seventeenth Century,* London, Clarendon Press, 1929
- Grubb, Edward, *Quaker Thought and History,* London, Macmillan, 1925
- Hill *The Experience of Defeat: Milton and some Contemporaries* London, Faber and Faber, 1984
- Ifor Evans *English Literature: Values and Traditions,* London : Unwin Books, 1966.
- John Bunyan's *Grace Abounding to the King of Sinners, (1666)*
- Kelly Griffiths, *Writing Essays about Literature: A Guide and Style Sheet,* San Diego, Harcourt Brace College Publishers, 1998
- Leo Tolstoy, *The Kingdom of God is Within You,* Lincoln, Bison Books, 1984.
- Raleigh, Sir Walter, "The Lie" a poem in *English Poetry I: From Chaucer to Gray*. The Harvard Classics. 1909–14.

- Russell Lowell, James. *L'Envoi* : To The Muse (poem Of The War)
- Stirredge, Elizabeth. *Strength in Weakness Manifest in the Life, Various Trials, and Christian Testimony of that Faithful Servant and Handmaid of the Lord, Elizabeth Stirredge*. Philadelphia: Benjamin and Thomas Kite, 1810.
- Terry Eagleton. *Literary Theory: an Introduction*. Minneapolis, MN University of Minnesota Press, 1983
- Thomas Lurting *Le Marin Combattant Devenu Paisible Chrétien…*, Mankon-Bamenda, Cameroon, 2009 (1710)
- Tual, Jacques. *Les Quakers en Angleterre, 1649-1700 : Illuminisme et Révolution*. Paris, Université Paris 3 Sorbonne Nouvelle. 1986
- Voltaire, *Philosophical letters* or *Letters on the English,* New York, Random House, 1992
- Wilcox, Catherine M. *Theology and Women's Ministry in Seventeenth Century Quakerism: Handmaids of the Lord*. (Studies in Women and Religion, Vol. 35), Lewistton, New York: Edwin Mellen Press, 1995.

Chapter 2

The Power of Memory: Crossroads in Works by Thomas Wolfe, F. Scott Fitzgerald, and August Wilson

Benjamin Hart Fishkin

In the early twentieth century, John Lancaster Spalding, a religious scholar commented, "As memory may be a paradise from which we cannot be driven, it may also be a hell from which we cannot escape" (282). In a perfect world memory would be a source of comfort and support. As the twentieth century progressed and gave way to the twenty-first century modern society has become increasingly out of touch with the needs of its inhabitants. This increases the probability that memories may be psychological minefields that are difficult to move beyond. They persist and bleed into the present and the future and become something that people, more often than not, struggle to be free of.

These psychological dilemmas cut across all of our racial, economic and social boundaries. Literary characters struggle to turn the page and move on from troubling components of their own personal history. It does not matter if the protagonist is an adult visiting his childhood home and reliving the events surrounding the death of a sibling, a successful businessman who reaches back into his teens only to realize that his life will never recapture the innocence he has lost, or a group of individuals in Pittsburgh's predominantly African-American Hill District who mourn the death of a local blues guitarist who falls short of the stardom that appears to be his destiny.

Sigmund Freud, in *Civilization and its Discontents*, analyzes the inherent tensions in modern society and states that in mental life "nothing that once has been formed can perish" (*Civilization* 16). In essence, everything is "somehow preserved" in amber and can reappear and be brought out into the open without warning (16). Literary works that do explore memory examine this lack of volition. Inherent within psychological trauma is a flooding of images - a persistent and debilitating tantalization from which no one is immune.

When Thomas Wolfe, in his novella *The Lost Boy*, takes the reader on a fun family outing to the Saint Louis World's Fair in 1904 and suddenly and silently pivots to turn this event into an unflinching look at how life irreparably wounds us all we see not only the power of memory, but also the poignancy of memory's involuntary persistence. Occurrences take place many years ago, even decades ago, have the power (instantaneously) to wound us again and again. Wolfe, early on, speaks of a "square that never changes, that will always be the same" where people and their attitudes are etched in stone (3). Such is the perception of an eleven-year-old boy whose use of "old brick" and "granite" to describe the streets of his North Carolina hometown symbolizes every child's need for grounded stability and reassuring routine (3). There is a particular sense of loss or reassessment that is universal and surrounds us all that no amount of parental preparation or support will prevent. Memory immerses Wolfe's Grover, and those around him, "with a moment's twinge of horror" for which there is no psychological armor (5).

More than a century ago Marcel Proust stated, "There is no man, however wise, who has not at some period of his youth said things, or lived in a way the consciousness of which is so unpleasant to him in later life that he would gladly, if he could, expunge it from his memory." This is the pain Wolfe refers to. The question is not why does this severe anguish exist, but why we are so vulnerable to its consequences? Proust's reference to an individual's youth is prescient and this emphasis lines up with and corroborates Wolfe's use of the month of April in his initial description of his older brother Grover. April is a reference to time and Wolfe quickly mentions, "the grass plots of the unbelievable intensity of green" to make it clear that he is thinking of spring, rebirth, and youth—all things that, once past, will not come again (3). The fact that it is three o'clock, a time when an elementary school would release a child to walk "home" to his father's shop, displays a boy's nascent steps towards an uncertain adolescence and adulthood.

Wolfe's use of bright optimism contrasts with F. Scott Fitzgerald's bleak and icy depiction of rural Minnesota. The latter looks to later life as a time when memory has no mercy. Fitzgerald's "Winter Dreams" shows us that "summer" is more than a meteorological condition; it is a reference to one's youth and (as yet) undiminished imagination. Young boys develop expectations that, when they are older men, remain unrealized. This is not a criticism, but individuals simply do not always get what they want nor do they always set their sights on attainable or even healthy goals. Hence we have the famous myth of Icarus who in an attempt to escape from his constraints soars too close to the sun. His failed ambition propels him in the opposite direction and exacts a very permanent price. This is what Fitzgerald means when he speaks of Dexter Green's "strong emotional shock" of pain and disillusionment (220). Dexter's love for Judy Jones not only does not develop as he wishes it to but remains a powerful memory from which he can never truly be free. The experience reveals that he, like Icarus, is not fully developed. When he first sees her with her nurse and "five small new golf-clubs" at the Sherry Island Golf Club she is described as a source of misery (219). Her exuberance as a life force is immediately noticeable. His nightmare has just begun.

This idea of women being a source of torment goes back to ancient myths and religious liturgy. The famous blues musician Muddy Waters famously states, "I been in the blues all my life. I'm still delivering 'cause I got a long memory" (Web. July 2, 2012). However, when August Wilson introduces Floyd Barton as an aspiring blues guitarist in *Seven Guitars*, a figure comparable to Waters in both age and potential if not temperament who worships the performer and upon seeing him play live in Chicago at the Hurricane Club says, "I am going to play like that one day.", it is his missteps and misappraisals that create irreparable problems (11). The reference to a violent, tropical storm is apt because Floyd's life is a series of self-inflicted chaotic episodes. As in the case of Herod, Lucifer, Pilate and others in *The Bible*, he himself is his own tormentor, and it is the community in Wilson's native Pittsburgh which must shake its heads and grapple with the memory of what might have been. Floyd's inability to establish a successful career and sustain it troubles the entire African-American community. *Seven Guitars* is an elegy to his unrealized dreams. Furthermore, the memory of his decision making—the steady and certain way in which he takes a winning hand and plays it into a poor one—becomes part of the collective consciousness of the theatrical players. The indiscretions in the Pennsylvania of 1948 will not dissipate in any discernible way; they will not fade back into the woodwork nor be put to rest with the funeral that commences the play.

As a child of poverty in Pittsburgh, Pennsylvania, you would think that Wilson would want nothing better than to forget the hurtful components of where he has come from. Kim Pereira in *August Wilson and the African-American Odyssey* talks of the concept of "lingering memory" as he refers not only to Wilson's understanding of the African-American working class, but also to the "sense of community in the traditional African setting" (2). His own youth may have been precarious, but it is the pre-diaspora history that offers answers about the past. The absolute impossibility is to know for certain whether or not it is better to retain a terrible memory about displacement or to forget it—and in the process—lose the insight and source of support that precedes it. Do we want the good with the bad, or both or neither? How is it possible to deal solely with either the good or the bad? A reunion with the past, a recurring theme in Wilson's play, can be as painful as the cure. Inherent within the theme of reunion is memory—what Pereira calls a "spiritual communion" (5). The solution for an unpleasant memory is the means to overcome it. To develop and advance in this resolution is essential.

An author who emphasizes childhood transforms the reader's mind into a museum that the owner does not necessarily wish to visit. Thomas Wolfe looks at his work in this fashion—as a window onto a troubled lonely past. More to the point he shows the reader the importance of his or her own perspective which, all too often, is less than idyllic. When these feelings of youth, with Wolfe's prodding, do resurface they are chaotic and instantaneous. The narrator's thoughts are sudden and disordered, while the reader is powerless to help.

At work here is a triangular relationship between the protagonist (or author), his or her past, and the reader. When Wolfe's readers look inward they see his trauma. They understand the eggshells that surround the minds of the young and know that no one reaches maturity without shattering more than a few of them. In *Of Time and the River,* Wolfe, almost exasperatedly, states that "All we know is that we lack a tongue that could reveal a language that could perfectly express the wild joy swelling to a music in our heart, [and] the wild cry mounting to a madness in our brain" (34). This gap between the intricacies of the human heart and the language formed by one's own cognition is the inarticulate speech this study hopes to provide.

Wolfe's past helps us fully comprehend the importance of our own experience. People are hungry, but somehow do not know what to ask for or even if it is on the menu. The pursuit of maturity and fulfillment is short-circuited by past-events that other participants have likely forgotten about shortly after their occurrence. Even more troubling is the notion that we remember painful events better than ordinary ones. There is a genetic reason for this. Matt Wilson, a professor of neurobiology at MIT's Picower Institute for Learning and Memory, states that a stimuli with a strong negative emotional component "seem[s] to be more easily retrieved than neutral stimuli or even those that are somewhat positive" (Blue in *Time Magazine* Web Edition, June 23, 2008). Part of what Dr. Wilson focuses on is how memories of places and events are encoded across networks of cells within the hippocampus—the portion of the brain that is involved in memory formation. More to the point, the way people sleep and dream may stimulate or influence the biology (*MIT*). This is the formation and reformation that Freud hinted at more than eighty years ago. It would be fascinating to hear what Sigmund Freud would say about a mind like that of Thomas Wolfe—a man whose artistry and energy was spent according to Rubin "trying to fix the illusory shiftings of memory before they should become lost" (32). The converse of this idea is that the suffering and distress people hope to be rid of is *not* lost with the passage of time. Herein lies the problem.

The romance between Dexter Green and Judy Jones can quickly be summed as a lovely rite of passage. However, when two people participate in such a relationship in their early twenties the circumstances may be far more challenging. For Dexter the inability of the love affair to continue is not an occurrence that he is able to put behind him. Judy represents the loss of a dream or an ideal and the pain is so persistent that Dexter never marries nor has any known emotional involvement with any other women. In looking back, Dexter comes to the harsh reality that "by his yielding he subjected himself to a deeper agony in the end" (233). He would like to remove her "stamp" or imprint (what blues singer Muddy Waters famously refers to as a "brand" or marking that one can never erase). That is impossible. It is not a consolation that everyone you know has been through it. The paradox is that he has no choice but to taste "the deep pain that is reserved for the strong, just as he had tasted for a little while the deep happiness" (233). The key word here is "little" because the two polar opposites are so unfairly out of proportion in terms of quantity.

In August Wilson's plays the misery of memory is never far from the surface. Wolfe and Fitzgerald battle the past, but they do so as solitary Caucasian figures. Wilson is just as severe, if not more so, but he is able to transcend with a broader cultural power. Embedded within his "Pittsburgh Cycle" is the history of African-American migration to the northern states which is dependent upon a separation from the past. Sterling Stuckey speaks of this when he says that,

> [t]he final gift of African 'tribalism' in the nineteenth century was its life as a lingering memory in the minds of American slaves. The memory enabled them to go back to the sense of community in the traditional African setting and to include all

Africans in their common experience of oppression in North America. (3)

The challenge is to hold on to the uplifting moments of the past—the shared support and the inherent connection to one another—while simultaneously processing and discarding the horrors of slavery which made this nostalgia for the past so necessary in the first place.

Seven Guitars is August Wilson's only play constructed on flashback. A sense of foreboding hangs over the neighborhood. This pain of loss, regardless of the lively dialogue, weighs heavy. The problem, as Louise accurately tells Vera in a heartfelt moment between the main female characters, is "You don't never get the full story" (30). Floyd Barton's wake, which follows his funeral, takes on the feel of a coroner conducting an autopsy or a forensic scientist reconstructing the circumstances of a great crime. We know something bad has happened, but we do not know why and when this occurrence has taken place. It appears that fate has played a cruel trick—that any other outcome would have been an impossibility. The surrounding characters, and not Floyd I would argue, are Wilson's main focus. They hear of his missteps involving women, business, and the law and see in him trouble spots that have plagued the African-American male for quite some time. His friends from the Hill District call him "Schoolboy" because he commits errors that a man of his age should not be making. Canewell, one of Floyd's backup musicians on harmonica and a member of Wilson's ensemble cast, says early on "I told Floyd if they put the record out it was gonna be a hit. They playing it all over. I told Floyd to get a cut of the money. They paid him a flat rate. I told him not to go for it. If he listened to me he would be a millionaire by now" (21). What is being discussed here is Floyd's willingness to take a flat rate for his new recording upfront rather than a percentage of each record sold. The revenue he would have earned by being patient, deliberate, and forward thinking would have set up his fiscal life for years to come. He is inherently flawed and squanders chance after chance to succeed in ways that most of Pittsburgh's African-American population can only dream of. Floyd even pawns his own guitar—his only means of earning a living—in an attempt to escape the financial peril he himself has wrought. These are the points of conflict that the other characters are unable to put behind them.

When a soldier suffers from post-traumatic stress disorder no one would doubt the veracity of his or her illness. There is something symptomatic about flashbacks and nightmares involving violence or abuse. The conflict can be corroborated, pointed to, and read about in the daily paper. It is another matter entirely to be immobilized or blocked by a day-to-day occurrence that is well hidden. The pain of isolation—suffering a torment that no one else can understand or even notice—is irrevocably associated with having one's own physical being in the present while his/her emotional cognition is in a time that once was and can never be any more. The pain authors of memory must reconcile is the back and forth between two disparate eras that seems as if it will last forever.

The conflict between past and present is very much like the pressure of a storm which gathers without warning. In *The Lost Boy* Wolfe presents his North Carolina hometown of Asheville as a "pleasant memory" and instantly changes the weather with a volatility that the protagonist and the reader are completely unprepared for (13). Suddenly, clouds collect "with a sulphurous and electric threat" that mirrors the psychological instability that has unbalanced the young boy who is learning, perhaps for the first time, that he is on his own (13). The crash of precipitation is of biblical proportions, with the author noting that this explosion is akin to the Mississippi River bursting in the sky. At the heart of the matter is an internal conflict— a battle that is staged in Grover's mind and in the minds of Wolfe's readers—about how to interpret time. There is an anger that cannot be altered and a shame that pain and negativity persist. Should it be forgotten as a past that is no longer pertinent or should it be remembered as nostalgia? This psychological bombardment of ideas, every bit as tumultuous as physical warfare, is the mainstay of literary modernism and a testament to Wolfe's ability to document and catalogue an individual's persistent inner conflict.

John Peale Bishop, a poet, critic, and friend of F. Scott Fitzgerald's, states that attention must be paid to Thomas Wolfe's uncommon memory. "He [Wolfe] could—and it is the source of what is most authentic in his talents—displace the present so completely by the past that its sights and sounds all but destroyed surrounding circumstance. He lost the sense of time" (130). I would argue that this is an affliction. Note Bishop's use of the word "destroyed" and that taking someone so completely out of the here and now has the inherent danger of being physiologically addictive. This is a conscience-altering narcotic in the worst and least therapeutic sense of the word. Wolfe taps into this negativity, an unhappiness and a bitterness that leaves us with a "furious hunger that haunts and hurts Americans so desperately felt—that being rich, we are all yet so poor, that having incalculable wealth we have no way of spending it, that feeling an illimitable power we yet have found no way of using it" (Wolfe, *Of Time and the River*, 34). Not only do the puzzles and mysteries of our pasts have no clues, but our own tailor-made troubles and tensions cannot be dismissed by the wealth, power, and prestige we spend every waking hour chasing.

When F. Scott Fitzgerald recounts a young, and not-so-young, man's experience he is not always so serious. There is a flirtation with lasting happiness—a tease that things may indeed come together in a lucky circumstance. The stakes are not quite so high and the words are so elegant that they seem to float off the page. There is something almost horribly cruel about this set-up which precedes a devastating disillusion. Not only does destruction appear to be an impossibility, but the golden summer makes everyone feel enchanted. To the innocent this is their birthright; to the experienced this is something to be enjoyed while it lasts because it never does.

The lack of attachment, or lack of an attachment that truly lasts, yields a loneliness for which there are no words. The protagonist's memory of Judy, which in the short term serves as some sort of rebirth, in the long term exposes a vast gulf between the way he would have liked his life to be and the way it actually is. When Dexter, seven years later, ponders this loss at a fragile age he looks backward, like a historian, in the hope of slowly understanding what happened in his twenties when there was a "fish jumping and a star shining" over the Black Bear Lake (223). Such a setting is more akin to the fantasy of a fairy tale than reality. Bryant Mangum refers to this activity in "Winter Dreams" as a "commitment to an idealized dream" (53). The dream is not only that of having a love that is (just slightly) beyond his reach, but also having the resources to share in the carefree life she seems to have.

Judy Jones is a heroine that, perhaps, only Fitzgerald could invent. On the surface everything appears easy and when she maneuvers her motorboat out towards Dexter's raft it is by no means clear whether she is there to rescue him or push him in. Her kisses, "like charity", will haunt him for years to come when Dexter will pay a psychological price that is impossible to calculate (226). His impression, which in the present is a sensation full of hope and happiness, in the future will be hurtful and chaotic. Dexter, like his rakishly tilted raft, is so off balance that he is unaware that she, and not he, has assumed the role of confident decision maker in the relationship (224). He yields without even knowing that he is giving ground. The experience is immediate and in the moment; analyzing and understanding this memory will take years and may never happen at all.

The shattering of illusions is very much like Proust's assertion that the individual needs not new events, but new eyes with which to see and interpret the old events. In theory this sounds good, but in reality it creates a terrible paradox. To truly embrace a brand new vantage point it is necessary to let go of the misreading that yielded the old. No one wants to give up the past in the hopes that pivotal elements can be carefully adjusted as to result in recreation, reformation, or omission. Of course, this is impossible, but it does not remove the longing or desire to bring about such a result. Like a phantom pain for a patient who has lost a limb yet still feels the sensation from a portion of the anatomy that has been amputated, the mind desires an orderly and satisfying result which can never be. This is the breach, gap, or loss which authors who scrutinize memory hope to bridge. The tease is that the break can be fulfilled and fortified. This is fantasy. The illusory past is so described because the evolution of our thinking right now no longer permits us to reason as we once did. We want to reclaim our innocence, but our thinking has become too sophisticated to let us do just that.

The idea of recreating happiness from an earlier time gets far more complicated when moving from an individual to an entire sum of people. This is the great difference between Wolfe and Fitzgerald, who examine the lasting hurt of Grover and Dexter respectively, and Wilson, who uses specific members of the Hill District to represent and authenticate the searing African experience in the United States. The personalities in Pittsburgh miss the memory they have been denied, but this is not a longing for love. It is a craving for a sense of community that proves to be unattainable. Human beings, and in this case specifically African-American human beings, do not have many reminders of their ancestry in the present-day United States. There are no physical memorials, there are few lessons in secondary schools on the subject, there are no photographs or paintings that are readily available. The human psyche has been damaged and immobilized by the more recent past. The terms that come to mind are "stuck" or "caught" in a whirlwind of pain that seems as if it is never going to end. Yet there is still an emotional connection with events that have happened *before* this disorder and confusion—occurrences that have happened so long ago that there can be no direct knowledge.

In *Seven Guitars* we see elements of what psychologists and cultural anthropologists call cultural transmission. This is a transfer of information, in actuality a non-monetary inheritance where information, not currency, is held in high regard. August Wilson uses music, and a plot centered on the musical form, to bring this about. "In Wilson's plays, the blues is the seam that threads the themes together. It also casts an emotional aura over the characters, uniting a group of seemingly diverse personalities with a bond forged in a common past" (Pereira 87–88). When Kim Pereira refers to "a common past", he is not looking back ten years, but rather centuries. He is not looking across town, but across the Atlantic Ocean. The characters (spiritually) want to leave the foreign and return to the familiar. Floyd Barton, like all of the other African-American men and women in these pages, has a "mythological lineage" (98). He wants freedom, and he can play the soundtrack to this very map, but that also means he has the freedom to fail. Much like *The Bible* passages which permeate Wilson's *Seven Guitars* Floyd must wrestle with a series of temptations as a thirty-five year old man with talent who hopes to make the most of his God-given ability. Liberation means the latitude to make bad relationship choices, poorly thought-out financial decisions, and careless evaluations about the law that will come back and haunt him. Unlike blues tunes, such as Floyd's "That's All Right" where a woman is the source of what seems like a permanent torment, Floyd is the source of his own dispossession. His identity leads him to rebel, and he has a talent that no one else in the African-American community has, but he is lost. An example of his flailing around for direction appears when he reminisces about his mother who is now deceased:

> If I could hear my mother pray again, I believe I'd pray with her. I'd be happy to just hear her voice…She out there in Greenwood [Cemetery]…Took me three hours to find the grave. They let the grass grow all over. I took and pulled up the grass and cleaned off her grave. Said I was gonna get her a marker. And that is what I'm gonna do. Because when I leave this time I ain't planning on coming back. I get her that marker and I won't owe nobody nothing (49–51).

This is more than a dutiful son looking after a family responsibility. This is an emotional response about memory and the past. The fact that "grass grow all over" the grave shows how difficult this is (Wilson 50). As you get older, understanding such circuitry gets harder, not easier, and you no longer "owe" those who precede you.

Floyd stumbles and falters, but this a problem that is larger than any one character. August Wilson creates such a figure because he is interested in this notion of being emotionally cut off from an environment of compassion and reassurance. The visit to the cemetery is simply one link to the past. The mother's rendition of "The Lord's Prayer" is only one generation removed from the subject—a heartfelt attempt to connect with the divine. What about the other many generations, perhaps more than ten, that must be meticulously traced back to Africa? In *Seven Guitars* Floyd is cut off from his own long-term past. When I use the term "his" it is in many ways a misnomer. This is a problem for the *entire* African-American population and Floyd is merely a recent representative of a very old and widespread problem. The fact that he is a blues guitarist--a figure who should have insight into the history of the African-American experience--makes this all very difficult to understand. He simply does not listen to the very music which Wilson refers to as "the bedrock of everything" (qtd. in Lewis 57). The blues has the potential to guide him and provide the stability he so desperately needs. His passion and imagination are discouraged because Floyd has forgotten the elements of memory that lie within and embraced the contemporary restraints of a world in which he is marginalized because he is not a white man.

When people reminisce they often get themselves into trouble. However, the authors explored in this study of literary memory present very different types of trouble. When it comes to music, August Wilson frequently introduces a character who is guilty of "hubris" (Pereira 18). Somehow, the plays present characters who have drifted away from the African-American mainstream and find themselves sidetracked even though they are unaware of this at the time. Now, this is not always their fault. Surely the characters in the plays are struggling for their very survival in precarious circumstances, but they also do not always act in their own best interest. Just moments after burying Floyd, one of Wilson's ensemble voices, Red Carter, states, "I believe every man knows something, but most times they don't pay attention to it" (5). This emphasis on "attention" has something to do with custom and inheritance. When Floyd inexplicably pawns his electric guitar he has, in essence, "fired" himself since he has no way to earn any money without it. He leaves the reader and the other cast members to wonder how this is possible. How does one get from isolation to self-isolation? Vera is right when she tells Louise, both of them arguably the smartest characters in Wilson's *Seven Guitars*, (and it is no accident that they are women) that "I believe Floyd means well. He just don't know how to do it. Everything keep slipping out his hands. Seem like he stumble over everything" (31). The "it" refers any goal of importance. It appears so easy for him to forget and overlook what is truly important. Whereas other Wilson characters "never lose sight of whence…[they]…came", Floyd seems content to forget about the past, or worse still, not even look towards it for inspiration (Pereira 20).

When Wolfe and Fitzgerald look back they face a very different set of problems. It is with anxiety and a considerable amount of perspiration that they seem powerless to cope with issues they thought had been long resolved. There is an element of gothic horror in both cases; a very humbling realization that what happened in our youth is not always pleasant. Even more to the point is the clamor and immediate pain that almost defies description. They do not run away from or ignore the pain, but they do not seem adept at handling it either. The difficulty is that, for a brief and bewildering moment, their individual conscious thoughts occupy two very distinct time frames and only one is subject to adjustment. The struggle against the shock of displacement is what connects these authors to other works of modern literature. Inevitably, and unfortunately, memory and surprise are violent collisions which disturb our security without promising to return it.

Works Cited

- Bishop, John Peale. *The Collected Essays of John Peale Bishop.* New York and London: Charles Scribner's Sons, 1948. Print.

- Blume, Laura. "Why Do We Remember Bad Things?" in *Time*.Time Mag., *23* June 2008. Web. 27 March 2012.
- "BrainyQuote" *Blues Quotes*. 2001 – 2012 Web 2 July 2012.
- Fitzgerald, F. Scott. *The Short Stories of F. Scott Fitzgerald*. New York, London, Toronto, and Sydney: Scribner, 1989. Print.
- Freud, Sigmund. *Civilization and Its Discontents*. New York and London: W.W. Norton & Company, 1961. Print.
- Lewis, Miles Marshall. "August Wilson." *The Believer* Nov. 2004: 56 – 66. Print.
- Magnum, Bryant. *A Fortune Yet: Money in the Art of F. Scott Fitzgerald's Short Stories*. New York and London: Garland Publishing, Incorporated, 1991. Print.
- McDonald, Christie. *The Proustian Fabric: Associations of Memory*. Lincoln and London: University of Nebraska Press, 1991. Print.
- MIT. *Department of Brain and Cognitive Sciences*. MIT, n.d. Web. 27 March 2012.
- Pereira, Kim. *August Wilson and the African-American Odyssey*. Urbana and Chicago: University of Illinois Press, 1995. Print.
- Rubin, Louis D. *Thomas Wolfe: A Collection of Critical Essays*. Englewood Cliffs: Prentice Hill, Incorporated, 1973. Print.
- Spalding, J. L. *Aphorisms and Reflections: Conduct, Culture, and Religion*. Fourth Edition. Chicago: A.C. McClurg & Company, 1907. Print.
- Stuckey, Sterling. *Slave Culture: Nationalist Theory and the Foundations of Black America*. New York and Oxford: 1987. Print.
- Wilson, August. *Seven Guitars*. New York: Plume, 1997. Print.
- Wolfe, Thomas. *Of Time and the River: A Legend of Man's Hunger in his Youth*. Garden City, New York: The Sun Dial Press, 1944. Print.
- Wolfe, Thomas. *The Lost Boy*. Chapel Hill and London: University of North Carolina Press, 1992. Print.

Section Two

Music

Chapter 3

Memory, the Blues, and African American Slave Narratives

Loretta S. Burns

Ralph Ellison famously described the blues as "an impulse to keep the painful details and episodes of a brutal existence alive in one's aching consciousness, to finger its jagged grain, and to transcend it. . . . As a form, the blues is an autobiographical chronicle of personal catastrophe expressed lyrically" (129). The influence of the blues on other African American art forms, including written literature, is widely acknowledged; however, long before the blues develops as an artistic and cultural form in the early twentieth century, the blues impulse to confront adversity and to express and share one's anguish is reflected not only in the oral tradition, to which the blues belongs, but in the foundation stones of the written tradition—the slave narratives.

Confronting a painful episode—of any duration—obviously involves reliving it in memory, which perforce modifies it, and giving voice to the experience transforms it even further. Hence the prisms of memory and language, together with the speaker's motives, both conscious and unconscious, create a verbal text that evokes the original event and simultaneously tells a somewhat different story. In effect, these elements coalesce not only to transform the past but to rise above it. To name adversity—to call it out—is to control it, to render it bearable, as the blues form so powerfully demonstrates.

Albert Murray compares the blues to classical tragedy by observing that "it would have the people for whom it is composed and performed confront, acknowledge, and proceed in spite of, and even in terms of, the ugliness and meanness inherent in the human condition." (36). In a typical blues lyric we are presented with the singer's situation, explicit or implicit, and his or her response to it, a response consisting of confrontation and endurance strategies. The essential situation and the sober emotions it produces are undercut by a variety of devices, including wry humor, irony, fatalism, and stubborn tenacity. The result, quite often, is an ironic tone, a certain detachment and restraint, and a controlled acceptance of life's absurdities and paradoxes. Moreover, the act of expression itself is cathartic and permits the protagonist to control and transcend the situation being described.

A blues statement is not strictly narrative but proceeds according to the emotional association between the structural units, and its ultimate attitude is not sadness but rather an unwillingness to abandon the struggle to survive, as the following selection, "Jailhouse Blues" illustrates:

(Lord, this house is gonna get raided—yes sir.)
Thirty days in jail with my back turned to the wall turned to the wall
Thirty days in jail with my back turned to the wall
Look here Mr. Jail Keeper put another gal in my stall

I don't mind being in jail but I got to stay there so long so long
I don't mind being in jail but I got to stay there so long so long
When every friend I had is done shook hands and gone

You better stop your man from tickling me under my chin under my chin
You better stop your man from tickling me under my chin
'Cause if he keeps on tickling I'm sure gonna take him on in

Good morning, blues [,] blues, how do you do how do you do
Good morning, blues [,] blues, how do you do
Well I just come here to have a few words with you

(Sackheim 52)

The audacity of the blues protagonist resides in her refusal to be undone by her circumstances. Instead of giving in to despair because she is in jail, the singer attempts to accommodate herself to the situation and tells the jailer to "put another gal in my stall." This line is followed, in the next stanza, by the sardonic detachment of "I don't mind being in jail but I got to stay there so long." In the third stanza she interrupts the story of her troubles to issue a wry warning to an unwary woman, and she concludes the lyric with an ironic dialogue with the blues. In a highly stylized line, the speaker addresses the blues as if it is a long-time acquaintance: "Good morning blues [,] blues, how do you do." By confronting her situation through memory and the act of creative expression, the singer brings her adversity under control, a control reflected and confirmed in the resolution of the final line, "I just come here to have a few words with you."

The singer, of course, is not only recalling her troubles, but she is sharing those troubles with an audience, presumably a sympathetic one. She is speaking to and for her listeners—those who have suffered the same or similar dilemmas. Hence the "chronicle of personal catastrophe," quickly becomes a collective history, and the individual memory evokes the memories of the group. Indeed the shared experience of speaker and audience is an important dimension of the blues catharsis.

This impulse to harness recollection and utterance to transcend and, in some measure, to alter experience is a primary dimension of the African American oral tradition from the spirituals to hip hop. However, it is also a key element in the written tradition, beginning with the slave narratives, in which former bondmen and women articulate and transform their past experiences. Robert Stepto correctly observes that "[t]he strident, moral voice of the former slave recounting, exposing, appealing, apostrophizing, and above all, *remembering* his ordeal in bondage is the single most impressive feature of a slave narrative" (26). However, the individual voice of the narrative also represents the voices of others, especially those who are unable to speak for themselves, and, by any measure, two of the most compelling and engaging narrative voices are those of Frederick Douglass and Harriet Jacobs in *Narrative of the Life of Frederick Douglass* and *Incidents in the Life of a Slave Girl.*

As the slave narratives and the blues ritual confirm, confronting the past through memory and language entails, paradoxically, bringing the past closer and detaching from it. Douglass's control of his narrative voice has been much noted and is a major dimension of the work's effectiveness. As a slave, Douglass experiences material deprivation, mental and emotional anguish, and physical abuse, but at no point in his account does he permit the details of his extraordinary journey from bondage to freedom to overwhelm him. On the contrary, he is the master narrator, creating order from chaos and translating his past experiences into a work of art. The "I" is the narrative's subject and its author, and it is the latter who rules.

One of the most oft-cited episodes in Douglass's *Narrative* is his discovery of the key to his freedom: literacy. When he is sent as a young boy from Colonel Lloyd's plantation to Baltimore, his new mistress, Sophia Auld, begins teaching him how to read but is abruptly halted by her husband, Hugh Auld, who warns her that teaching a slave to read is not only illegal but "unsafe." He insists that "if you teach that nigger . . . how to read, there would be no keeping him. It would forever unfit him to be a slave" (338). These words make an immediate and profound impression on Douglass, one that sets him on a new path:

These words sank deep into my heart, stirred up sentiments within that lay slumbering, and called into existence an entirely new train of thought. It was a new and special revelation, explaining dark and mysterious things, with which my youthful understanding had struggled, but struggled in vain. I now understood what had been to me a most perplexing difficulty—to wit the white man's power to enslave the black man. It was a grand achievement, and I prized it highly. From that moment, I understood the pathway from slavery to freedom. (338)

Although Douglass describes the effect of Auld's words as an epiphany, the full meaning of the event is not grasped until it is remembered and expressed. It can then be understood in the context of Douglass's entire life—at least up to the point of writing his story—and in relation to other episodes in that life. His determination to heed the valuable lesson that the incident imparts also acquires additional layers of meaning as it is recollected. He writes, "Whilst I was saddened by the thought of losing the aid of my mistress, I was gladdened by the invaluable instruction, which by the merest accident, I had gained from my mater. Though conscious of the difficulty of learning without a teacher, I set out with high hope, and a fixed purpose, at whatever the cost of trouble, to learn how to read" (338). Douglass the literate narrator recalls a time when Douglass the illiterate slave was struggling to learn to read. The significance of the event is fully apparent only after he has learned to read and write, escaped from physical and mental bondage, and recalled the experience in his *Narrative*. In remembrance and articulation, the experience is apprehended within the framework of his total journey from slavery to freedom and as a critical step in the formation of his identity.

The crucial discovery of the key to his freedom is succeeded some years later by an event Douglass refers to as "the turning-point in my career as a slave" (366): the fight with Mr. Covey. It is his description of this episode and the events surrounding it that illustrates most forcefully the cathartic effect of memory and language. Douglass's narration of this incident is compelling but unhurried; he does not cut to the chase but rather provides a detailed framework for the battle. He is returned to Thomas Auld, Hugh's brother, after years of living in Baltimore, and he describes the estrangement between him and Thomas Auld: "He was to me a new master, and I to him a new slave." He notes that Auld acquired his slaves by marriage and observes that "of all men, adopted slaveholders are the worst." He says Thomas Auld "was an object of contempt, and was held as such even by his slaves." He reports that Auld "experienced religion" but that he seemed "a much worse man after his conversion than before" and "found religious sanction for his cruelty" (351-53). These details concerning Auld's character help explain Douglass's difficulties in submitting to his rule. During his years in Baltimore, Douglass has succeeded in learning to read and write, and he has become the discontented, "unfit" slave of Hugh Auld's prediction. Thomas Auld now finds Douglass "unsuitable to his purpose," feels that living in the city has "ruined" him, and decides to send him over to Mr. Covey, a man with "a very high reputation for breaking young slaves" (354-55).

Douglass's framework for the decisive battle expands with his detailed description of Covey. As Vince Brewton notes, "Douglass devotes greater space in his first autobiography to the portrait of Covey than to any other character, black or white" (710). Covey is "the snake," the master deceiver who drives the slaves in his charge unmercifully and has an almost pathological fixation on catching them unawares. Like Thomas Auld, he is a religious hypocrite. He prays and participates in "family devotions" but purchases a female slave for breeding purposes, forcing her to live with a hired slave who is already married. The twins from this union Covey regards "as being quite an addition to his wealth" (359).

Douglass's memories of Thomas Auld and Edward Covey and the events leading up to his fight with Covey contextualize his memory of the fight itself. The battle and its meaning cannot be fully apprehended in isolation from the experiences and observations which precede it. Accordingly, Douglass recalls the beating he receives after only one week with Covey, devoting considerable space to the mishap with the team of oxen that precipitates it. He says that during his first six months with Covey "scarce a week passed without his whipping me" and that although he and the other slaves had enough to eat, they had "scarce time to eat it" (357). Thomas Auld's purpose in sending him out is fulfilled: Douglass is broken.

If at any one time of my life more than another, I was made to drink the bitterest dregs of slavery, that time was during the first six months of my stay with Mr. Covey... I was somewhat unmanageable when I first went there, but a few months of this discipline tamed me. Mr. Covey succeeded in breaking me. I was broken in body, soul, and spirit. My natural elasticity was crushed, my intellect languished, the disposition to read departed, the cheerful spark that lingered about my eye died; the dark night of slavery closed in upon me, and behold a man transformed into a brute! (359)

Douglass must set the stage for the battle—not only for rhetorical purposes but because he must unpack the memories surrounding the event as well as the memory of the battle itself in order to confront, control, and transcend his past. A primary purpose for writing the *Narrative* is to arouse the reading public to the horrors of slavery, but in so doing Douglass is also establishing and affirming his identity and human dignity, and to accomplish the latter, he must "drink the bitterest dregs of slavery" again though memory.

Before describing the fight with Covey, Douglass announces its significance: "You have seen how a man was made a slave; you shall see how a slave was made a man" (361). He then recalls being pushed past the point of endurance by overwork and physical abuse, at which time, bruised and bloody, he decides to walk the seven miles to his master's house, report on Covey's cruelty and abuse, and ask for protection. Finding Auld unsympathetic to his plight, Douglass is forced to return to Covey, but the narrative defers the account of the fight as Douglass continues to preface the encounter with details, telling of hiding in the woods to escape Covey's cowskin, encountering another slave, Sandy, who offers the doubting Douglass a root to be carried on the right side to prevent beatings, and running into Covey on his way to Sunday services and receiving a surprisingly civil greeting from him.

The rich details, beginning with Douglass's departure from Baltimore, are an elaborate overture for the recollection of the climactic battle with Covey. The battle and Douglass's memory of it assume added textures of meaning provided by the memories of the events that precede the fight and of those that follow it. When Covey surprises Douglass at work, attempts to tie him with a rope, and trips him as he tries to escape, Douglass lands on the stable floor, seemingly at Covey's mercy. It is then that he decides to fight.

Mr. Covey seemed now to think he had me, and could do what he pleased; But at this moment—from whence came the spirit I don't know—I resolved to fight; and, suiting my action to the resolution, I seized Covey hard by the throat; and as I did so, I rose. He held on to me, and I to him. My resistance was so entirely unexpected, that Covey seemed taken all aback. He trembled like a leaf. This gave me assurance, and I held him uneasy, causing the blood to run where I touched him with the ends of my fingers. (365)

The fight is fully engaged, lasting over two hours. And when, at one point, Covey asks Douglass whether he intends to "persist in [his] resistance," Douglass's answer is unequivocal.

I told him I did, come what might; that he had used me like a brute for six months, and that I was determined to be used so no longer. With that, he strove to drag me to a stick that was lying just out of the stable door. He meant to knock me down. But just as he was leaning over to get the stick, I seized him with both hands by his collar, and brought him by a sudden snatch to the ground. (365)

The fight ends only when Covey, "puffing and blowing at a great rate," releases Douglass, who judges that his adversary received "entirely the worst end of the bargain." The slave has taken a great risk and has triumphed. In daring to fight back, Douglass succeeds in ending Covey's physical abuse: "The whole six months afterwards, that I spent with Mr. Covey, he never laid the weight of his finger upon me in anger." But Douglass wins much more, as he explains:

> This battle with Mr. Covey was the turning point in my career as a slave. It rekindled the few expiring embers of freedom, and revived within me a sense of my own manhood. It recalled the departed self-confidence, and inspired me again with a determination to be free... I felt as I never felt before. It was a glorious resurrection, from the tomb of slavery to the heaven of freedom. My long-crushed spirit rose, cowardice departed, bold defiance took its place; and I now, resolved that, however long I might remain a slave in form, the day had passed forever when I could be a slave in fact. I did not hesitate to let it be known of me, that the white man who expected to succeed in whipping, must also succeed in killing me. (366)

Douglass reclaims himself not only by fighting Covey but by remembering and recounting this pivotal episode in his life; to find himself he must recover and confront his memories. In her work *Mastering Slavery*, Jennifer Fleischner contends that the slaves' declarations that their narratives are true reflect their total awareness "that the violent theft of *their* memories—of their own selves and of themselves by others—lay at the sick heart of slavery. When by way of their narratives they cross over the threshold of visibility into cultural memory, they effectively steal themselves back . . ." (3). Douglass assembles and confronts his memories not only to craft a powerful weapon in the anti-slavery arsenal but to transform "an authentic unwritten self . . . into a literary representation" (Baker, *Autobiographical Acts* 103).

Like Frederick Douglass, Harriet Jacobs movingly summons her recollections of slavery for both political and personal motives, testifying to the special horrors women suffered under slavery in *Incidents in the Life of a Slave Girl*: "Slavery is terrible for men; but it is far more terrible for women" (77). However, it is precisely because slave women are subjected to "mortifications peculiarly their own" that Jacobs's attempt to "finger [the] jagged grain" of her memories is especially fraught. She would rather not remember, insisting that "it would have been more pleasant to me to have been silent about my own history" (1). Nonetheless, she is compelled to break her silence to awaken the white women in the North to the suffering of her sisters in bondage and "to convince the people of the Free States what Slavery really is" (2). Additionally, her narrative provides a mechanism for coming to terms with the painful, almost unspeakable episodes of her own past.

Jacobs, like all autobiographers, must negotiate memory through a combination of confrontation and detachment, the latter facilitating the former. As the author of her own narrative, she is both subject and witness, and her function as witness is reinforced by her stratagem of concealing her identity as well as the identities of other people and places. She becomes Linda Brent, the "slave girl" of the title who relates the "incidents" of her life. As Hazel Carby points out, "The construction of the history of Linda Brent was the terrain through which Jacobs had to journey in order to reconstruct the meaning of her own life as woman and mother" (67).

These fictive elements help provide the psychological distance necessary for Jacobs to relive in memory and expression those aspects of her life she is reluctant to revisit. In Chapter V of *Incidents*, she begins her account of the merciless sexual harassment she suffered at the hands of Dr. Flint (Dr. James Norcom); however, as readers have noted, her description lacks specific details. She relates that when she turns fifteen, the master begins "to whisper foul words in my ear," but the reader never learns what he actually says. At other times Flint expresses his sexual designs through "signs," but these are not made clear. And the contents of the notes he slips into her hands and reads to her after she returns them are not revealed. As Jean Fagan Yellin explains, "Both determined and reluctant to address her sexual history, [Jacobs] consciously omitted 'what I thought – the world might believe that a Slave Woman was too willing to pour out – that she might gain their sympathies'" (xxi).

Despite her unwillingness to expose the precise details of her sexual history, however, what she does reveal and her mode of disclosure provide her readers with a sympathetic understanding of her vulnerability, isolation, and desperation as well as her courage and determination. She rises above the literary constraints within which she writes, and although the narrative "at times . . . appears trapped within traditional language and literary conventions inadequate to express her radically untraditional content, *Incidents*, like the great American romances, transforms the conventions of literature" (Yellin xxxiv). Furthermore, the interplay of memory and language transforms her story and permits her to confront its pain.

Jacobs's ordeal becomes her testimony, and her readers listen in rapt attention as she remembers the assault on her youth and innocence and unburdens herself:

> Sometimes he had stormy, terrific ways that made his victims tremble; sometimes he assumed a gentleness that he thought must surely subdue. Of the two, I preferred his stormy moods, although they left me trembling. He used his utmost to corrupt the pure principles my grandmother had instilled. He peopled my young mind with unclean images, such as only a vile monster could think of. I turned from him with disgust and hatred. But he was my master. I was compelled to live under the same roof with him—where I saw a man forty years my senior daily violating the most sacred commandments of nature. (27)

The fact that she fails to supply explicit details does not negate the powerful effect of finally being able to proclaim publicly her private torment. It may also be argued that her reticence and understatement are at times more effective than lurid details might have been. For example, she generalizes her experience with the presentation of a young girl learning "to tremble when she hears her master's footfall" (28). This image is chillingly concise, capturing the terror and helplessness millions of slave women experienced. Furthermore, what she is unable or unwilling to say about her personal experience is still *remembered*. In order to omit and select aspects of her life for her narrative, she must retain an expansive text of memory from which to draw. Although she is "pained by the retrospect" of what she suffered, she relives her misery for the sake of her "sisters who are still in bondage" (28-29), thereby releasing herself from the bondage of silence and seizing control of her own story.

Jacobs's predicament as a tormented young slave girl is made even more desolate by her inability to share her troubles, and her recollection of her isolation is a stirring cry of the heart.

> He told me I was his property; that I must be subject to his will in all things. My soul revolted against the mean tyranny. But where could I turn for protection? No matter whether the slave girl be as black as ebony or as fair as her mistress. In either case, there is no shadow of law to protect her from insult, from violence, or even

from death; all these are inflicted by fiends who bear the shape of men. The mistress, who ought to protect the helpless victim, has no other feelings towards her but those of jealousy and rage. (27-28)

Yet even as she expresses the misery of her loneliness, her longing to break out of her isolation is simultaneously being fulfilled. Her yearning for "some one to confide in," is fully realized when she summons her memories, finds her voice, and tells her own story.

Jacobs's story, like other slave narratives, functions both as personal narrative and as a representation of the suffering of others. Moreover, although her words seem directed primarily to white northern women, Andrea Powell Wolfe suggests that Jacobs "desires black northerners, especially those in power within abolitionist circles, to 'overhear' and understand" the importance of fighting for their rights (524). The shared experience of Jacobs and the slave women of the South and her political bond with northern blacks intensify the experience of remembrance and declaration.

As distressing and unpleasant as it is for Jacobs to recall and recount Flint's relentless sexual persecution, she finds it even more disturbing to call to mind and to reveal to readers her calculated decision to enter into a sexual relationship with Mr. Sands (Samuel Tredwell Sawyer) and the consequences of that decision. Recalling Flint's unremitting torment is distasteful and embarrassing for Jacobs, but he is the undisputed villain of the piece, and she is his unprotected target. Entering into a sexual liaison with Sands, however, entails a compromise of standards of virtue that she has attempted—up to that point—to uphold. Her decision involving Sands is a fateful one, as life-changing as Douglass's decision to fight Covey, the slave breaker. But whereas Douglass presents his battle with Covey as a means by which he unmistakably regains his manhood and humanity, Jacobs's decision and its aftermath are more problematic.

In *Blues, Ideology, and Afro-American Literature*, Houston Baker discusses what he refers to as "blues moments"—those times in black discourse when speakers "successfully negotiate an obdurate 'economics of slavery' and achieve a resonant, improvisational, expressive dignity" (13). In her recollection and retelling of her vexed decision to become Sands's mistress, Harriet Jacobs experiences such a moment.

The complexity of attitude and tone, characteristic of the blues, is nowhere more apparent in Jacobs's narrative than in her agonizing account of how she becomes Sands's mistress. Having evaded sexual contact with Flint by being among other people, she learns that he is building a house for her miles from town. But instead of bowing to her seemingly ineluctable fate, the teen-aged slave girl, with neither laws nor social conventions to shield her, swears to resist her nemesis in an astounding display of courage and resolve. She refuses to be a prisoner in Flint's house:

> I vowed before my Maker that I would never enter it. I had rather toil on the plantation from dawn till dark; I had rather live and die in jail, than drag on, from day to day, through such a living death. I was determined that the master, whom I so hated and loathed, who had blighted the prospects of my youth, and made my life a desert, should not, after my long struggle with him, succeed in trampling his victim under his feet. I would do any thing, every thing, for the sake of defeating him. What could I do? I thought and thought, till I became desperate, and made a plunge into the abyss. (53)

The defiant words with which she begins the preceding passage lead her to the perplexing question, "What could I do?" And her meditation on her predicament ends with a decision to undertake a desperate gamble. Caught between Scylla and Charybdis, she escapes "a living death" by a "plunge into the abyss."

Jacobs, as Linda Brent, seems to take a deep breath as she continues to relate this painful memory: "And now, reader, I come to a period in my unhappy life, which I would gladly forget if I could. The remembrance fills me with sorrow and shame. It pains me to tell you of it; but I have promised to tell you the truth, and I will do it honestly, let it cost me what it may." She refuses to excuse herself on the grounds of "ignorance or thoughtlessness" or "compulsion from a master." She insists, "I knew what I did, and I did it with deliberate calculation." Nonetheless, she indicts slavery itself for making her "prematurely knowing in the evil ways of the world." Slavery is "the demon," "the monster" that blasts her hopes, compelling her to tarnish her virtue and forcing upon her the task of "confessing what I am now about to relate" (53-54).

She recounts that Sands learns of her plight and expresses an interest in her and a desire to help her. He seeks her out and writes to her often. Jacobs is flattered by his attention and grateful for his offer of assistance, and in time "a more tender feeling" enters her heart. She understands the implications of his interest—"I saw whither all this was tending"—but explains why a sexual alliance with Sands is less distasteful than one with Flint:

I knew the impassable gulf between us; but to be an object of interest to a man who is not married, and who is not her master, is agreeable to the pride and feelings of a slave, if her miserable situation has left her any pride or sentiment. It seems less degrading to give one's self, than to submit to compulsion. There is something akin to freedom in having a lover who has no control over you, except that which he gains by kindness and attachment. A master may treat you as rudely as he pleases, and you dare not speak; moreover, the wrong does not seem so great with an unmarried man, as with one who has a wife to be made unhappy. (54-55)

The remembrance and retelling of this episode compel Jacobs to clarify her thinking—not only for the reader but for herself—and force her to confront head-on her complicated decision. She discloses that reasons of "revenge" and "calculation of interest" were added to those of vanity and gratitude. She hopes to "triumph over" Flint by favoring Sands. She hopes that Flint will react by selling her, and she is certain that Sands would buy her. She looks ahead to the prospect of obtaining her freedom and her children's freedom from Sands, recalling how Flint's slave mistresses and their children were sold off. These motivations, combined with the absence of any viable alternative, push her toward "a headlong plunge."

Jacobs's attitude toward her decision is as complicated as the decision itself. In the space of several sentences, she throws herself abjectly on the mercy of the reader; passionately underscores the contrast between her situation and that of her "virtuous reader"; forthrightly confesses her error and acknowledges her shame; and boldly declares that she should not be judged by conventions that do not comport with her circumstances.

Pity me, and pardon me, O virtuous reader! You never knew what it is to be a slave; to be entirely unprotected by law or custom; to have the laws reduce you to the condition of a chattel, entirely subject to the will of another. You never exhausted your ingenuity in avoiding the snares, and eluding the power of a hated tyrant; you never shuddered at the sound of his footsteps, and trembled within hearing of his voice. I know I did wrong. No one can feel it more sensibly than I do. Still, in looking back, calmly, on the events of my life, I feel that the slave woman ought not to be judged by the same standard as others. (55-56)

The last sentence of the passage is a powerful assertion of Jacobs's human dignity in the face of ferocious assaults against it, and it is memory, the process of "looking back" that makes possible this stirring assertion. After asking for pity, Jacobs rejects the consolation of both forgiveness and judgment in favor of an integrity undergirded by a sense of her own worth.

As Fleischner emphasizes, "Southern slavery, a system of labor that utilized abuse and deprivation, was an assault on each slave's memory, a crucial basis of each person's sense of self and reality" (27). Douglass, Jacobs, and other slave narrators constructed their identities through memory and discourse, facing and transforming their struggles, which also represent the struggles of others. The inclination to confront and transcend life's wounds and injuries through memory and language is reflected in both the oral and written traditions of African Americans from their beginnings to the present and serves as an important link between these traditions. The slave narratives enact a powerfully cathartic ritual that would achieve its most sublime lyrical expression in the lament and affirmation of the blues, which embraces—rather than resists—the impulse to recall and give voice to a painful experience. The life-affirming tenor of the blues is achieved only after the pain and absurdity of life have been confronted and expressed. But what if words fail? What of those experiences beyond words? Both Douglass and Jacobs, articulate and persuasive writers, sometimes find themselves groping for language that cannot be grasped. As a child Douglass witnesses a brutal beating administered to his Aunt Hester, but he lacks the words to adequately describe his emotions, saying, "I wish I could commit to paper the feelings with which I beheld it" (319). Although Jacobs is committed to relating truthfully the sorrowful and bitter events of her life, she feels at times that her pen is insufficient to the task: "The degradation, the wrongs, the vices, that grow out of slavery, are more than I can describe" (28). Even the blues singer, at certain interstices between emotion and utterance, must hum, moan, scream, whoop, or wail. What cannot be expressed in words, however, can still be felt; it can still be kept "alive in one's aching consciousness." Even when words fail, the text of memory remains.

Works Cited

- Baker, Houston A. "Autobiographical Acts and the Voice of the Southern Slave." *Critical Essays on Frederick Douglass*. Ed. William L. Andrews. Boston: G. K. Hall, 1991, 94-107. Print.
- ---. *Blues, Ideology, and Afro-American Literature: A Vernacular Theory*. Chicago: U of Chicago P, 1984. Print.
- Brewton, Vince. "'Bold Defiance Took Its Place'—'Respect' and Self-Making in *Narrative of the Life of Frederick Douglass, an American Slave.*" *Mississippi Quarterly* 58.3-4 (2005): 703-717. Print.
- Carby, Hazel. "'Hear My Voice, Ye Careless Daughters': Slave and Free Women before Emancipation." *African American Autobiography: A Collection of Critical Essays*. Ed. William L. Andrews. Upper Saddle River: Prentice-Hall, 1993. 59-76. Print.

- Douglass, Frederick. *Narrative of the Life of Frederick Douglass, an American Slave. The Classic Slave Narratives.* Ed. Henry Louis Gates, Jr. New York: Signet Classics, 2002. 299-403. Print.
- Ellison, Ralph. "Richard Wright's Blues." *The Collected Essays of Ralph Ellison.* Ed. John F. Callahan. New York: The Modern Library, 2003. 128-144. Print.
- Fleischner, Jennifer. *Mastering Slavery: Memory, Family, and Identity in Women's Slave Narratives.* New York: New York UP, 1996. Print.
- Jacobs, Harriet. *Incidents in the Life of a Slave Girl: Written by Herself.* Ed. Jean Fagan Yellin. Cambridge: Harvard UP, 1987. Print.
- Murray, Albert. *The Hero and the Blues.* Columbia: U of Missouri P, 1973. Print.
- Sackheim, Eric, comp. *The Blues Line.* New York: Grossman, 1969. Print.
- Stepto, Robert. "Narration, Authentication, and Authorial Control in Frederick Douglass' *Narrative* of 1845." *African American Autobiography: A Collection of Critical Essays.* Ed. William L. Andrews. Upper Saddle River: Prentice-Hall, 1993. 26-35. Print.
- Wolfe, Andrea Powell. "Double-Voicedness in *Incidents in the Life of a Slave Girl*: 'Loud Talking' to a Northern Black Readership." *ATQ* 22.3 (2008): 517-525. Print.
- Yellin, Jean Fagan, ed. Introduction. *Incidents in the Life of a Slave Girl.* By Harriet Jacobs. Cambridge: Harvard UP, 1987. xiii-xxxiv. Print.

Chapter 4

It Rains Inside: Parenting and Music in Works by William Faulkner, August Wilson, and Sherman Alexie

Benjamin Hart Fishkin

At the turn of the last century, it was "a jolly home, a sympathetic reception, [and] a bright supper" table that people aspired to (Dreiser 38). The home was a comfort and a familiar source of support. This idea proved elusive, and as the twentieth century progressed, modern society swerved erringly to become a mechanism that is out of touch with the needs of its children. This is a dilemma that cuts across all of our racial, economic and social boundaries. It does not matter if the protagonist is a Spokane Reservation Indian boy from eastern Washington, an African-American child from Pittsburgh's Hill District, a descendant of either race, or of a spiritually complex family in northwestern Mississippi. Our nation is either luxuriously ignorant or shrewdly terrified that we have forgotten the very support systems that once sustained us.

Much of modern life speaks of reclaiming American values. Such an emphasis brings to the fore the issue of memory and whether or not earlier eras did indeed possess the attributes we give them credit for. Lewis H. Lapham recently contemplated the evils "likely to befall a nation that is deprived of its memory," but he is talking about a cultural amnesia in terms of history and politics which is too broad to be the source of any one study (26). Lapham is looking at collective memory—in some ways taking the national pulse and examining the vital signs--whereas I am looking at individual memory and even more specifically at the memories of the young who must endure some sort of psychological trauma involving the marginalization or absence of a home and supportive family. If there were once support systems for our children where have they disappeared to and have adults forgotten the most important part of the bargain? On a personal level, the suffering is so palpable that a self-deprivation of memory may be preferable. We may be willing, if not eager, to "pull the wool" over our own eyes. The norm of modern parenting seems to be a set of loose and intermittent constructions that our grandparents would never have dreamed of, let alone implemented.

Sherman Alexie, early on in the introduction to *The Lone Ranger and Tonto Fistfight in Heaven*, refers to his father as a "randomly employed blue-color alcoholic" (xii). And he is the lucky one. Out of the trio of children to be explored here at least this male parent is on the scene and sporadically available. The joy of having an alcoholic and diabetic father, even one who has lost a foot due to the latter illness, is superior to the bad fog of loneliness that now victimizes our youth. The children in William Faulkner's *Go Down Moses* and August Wilson's *Fences* do not even have this comparative luxury. Their conversations are in monologue. As America grows more and more complicated, and it becomes more and more acceptable for parents to live apart from their children, issues that pertain to race, gender and music converge to construct an unimaginable to dysfunctional identity that threatens our order and stability.

There is a storm-like quality to these relationships involving parents who are themselves broken. Alexie wonders "if memories of his personal hurricanes would be better if he could change them. Or if he just forgot about all of it" (4). Unfortunately, he can do neither. There is no button to push to eliminate the horror he sees within his tribe. Instead he takes a meteorological cyclone of accelerated speed and precipitation and alters it so that it becomes an inward psychological condition—just as Shakespeare did in *King Lear*. The losses do not disappear; but they become an almost personal characteristic of the thought process. It rains inside. The memories are involuntary and all too comprehensive: "Each dangerous and random" (Alexie 5). The American Indian would give anything to let go of the specifics of this stream of consciousness narration repeatedly overwhelmed by pain.

Like a skilled improvisational musician Sherman Alexie takes a series of intertwined stories and speaks to the disunity of a people who know no other way of living. If life on a reservation does anything it displays for all how hard it is to be cut off from one's own past. The ironically named Victor, a nine year old, literally lies down between "his alcoholic and dreamless parents" when they are passed out after a night of boozing (10). All he wants is for the family to make progress together. These are the goals articulated by Alexie's characters—cultural lines and markers that always seem distant no matter how much ground has been traveled. The participants are tired when they begin their journey as the mere effort to get to the start of the race is exhausting. Their quest seems to be what to do with the gnawing dread that things have gone so horribly wrong. For as long as anyone can remember, things have not worked out and there is no guarantee that they ever will. As a poet, Alexie self-identifies with his lonely and angry subjects surrounded with unemployment, addiction, and hunger. His fiction reads like a diary. One always gets the feeling that these anecdotes are thinly veiled biographies with a modern soundtrack for the majority of his audience that neither knows anything about being a Native American nor lives in the Pacific Northwest. Music reverberates and provides a foundation that attempts to make sense out of all this family turbulence. It means something and people look towards it, or listen to it, to help them combat an absence of control. It is, quite possibly, Alexie states, "the most important thing there is" (29). In a third world where sons both love and hate their fathers, music may be the only "medicine" that can bring them closer together (29).

William Faulkner once stated that music is "the easiest means in which to express [oneself]," but it is not an elixir (Web. July 2, 2012). The tension between father and son, or descendent and antecedent, is in such a state of putrefaction that the relationship(s) are beyond repair or rapprochement. A sense of despair and desperation hangs over Faulkner's characters. They endure so much and get precious little help from those around them. He states in a section of *Go Down Moses* entitled "The Old People" that "we have to live together in herds to protect ourselves from our own sources" (167). This is a complex remark. We need psychological protection from and battle tested fortification against the very same people. There is, perhaps, no way to tease out these two qualities and herein lies the conflict at the heart of all literature that deals with the issues of family and parenting.

There is a betrayal when the young do not get the help they need and this not only brings with it a loss of innocence, but a sense that the world will never again be ordered as it should be. The British use the term "muddle" to mean something that cannot be easily untangled – a complex mess that cannot be easily solved or understood with a change in behavior. Unlike a "'mystery" which has an actual solution a muddle is beyond complete comprehension and so are family relationships where diction, cadence, and hesitation indicate volumes to the trained eye of a meticulous composer. We want our parents to offer insulation against circumstances contrary to commonly accepted opinion, but they are flawed figures in their own right. Their own behavior is neither always common nor acceptable. Faulkner sees the self-contradiction and, if possible, creates a setting that is even more complicated than the condition of the Native American. *Go Down Moses* involves children created across racial lines – where the very identity of their parents becomes an issue of conflict. In the case of Sam Fathers, we are told that "the blood of the warriors and chiefs had been betrayed" (168). He is the son of an Indian chief and is part Choctaw, part African-American, and part Caucasian. As if all of this is not enough, Sam and his mother are sold into slavery by his father. This violation of trust creates problems for people comprised of each of these three bloodlines. Their memory is indelibly associated with trauma and the consequence of this parental failure is they have no idea how to proceed or even where they belong. Not only do the ancestors in *Go Down, Moses* not help their children but also their behavior appears to be a hindrance. The human men who are trying to "write down the heart's truth out of the heat's driving complexity, for all the complex and troubled hearts which would beat after them" present a narrative that is too difficult for words (260). It is more fitting as an elegy of lament or despondency for a situation that is irreparable. The novel, like the Negro spiritual for which it is named, is best experienced as a mournful musical composition complete with the bitter anger and sorrow that transcends all races. The psychological inheritance of a memory that is spiritually lacking or isolating is so overwhelming that it cannot be told forthrightly, and Faulkner conceals it for much of the novel just as the human mind obscures facts that are too painful to address directly.

It is hard to be optimistic. These interrelated short stories take the questions of bloodlines and heredity and mix and rearrange them so that issues of parent and child become nearly impossible to untangle. Individuals must come to terms with the fact that they are not brought up by their biological parents, Isaac McCaslin is raised by his cousin, but that is by no means the end of their suffering. They also must reconcile the fact that their patrimony is immoral and filled with displacement. Faulkner, who often uses biblical imagery, knows full well that "He[God] will by no means leave the guilty unpunished, visiting the iniquity of fathers on the children and on the grandchildren to the third and fourth generations"(Exodus 34: 6-7). "Uncle Ike" is also aware of this and once he fully understands what his people have done - enslaved the innocent, impregnated women who did not have the ability to deny these improper advances, and then enslaved the resultant offspring so that those in captivity are literally imprisoned by their own fathers - he is left alone to wrestle with and define what is moral in the Deep South. Inherited characteristics in the author's fictional Mississippi that are truly loving and giving without the hope of recompense almost never come from biological fathers. Isaac's spiritual teacher is Sam Fathers and as a caring surrogate the paternal reference in his name comes from the fact that he himself has had "two" fathers - the one who sold him and the one who raised him. The qualities that count do not come from those with similar chromosomes. They are borne out of a narrative that appreciates characters who are comfortable in the woods away from the bondage of modern civilization. For the South to truly become moral there must be a confrontation with plantation life and that voice of incongruence must come from without rather than within.

When August Wilson presents *Fences*, his own treatise of father-son conflict, he states, "My greatest influence has been the blues. And that's a literary influence, because I think the blues is the best literature that we as black Americans have" (qtd. in Lewis 57). Inherent within this particularly African-American art form is the ability to improvise and attempt to handle things "as they happen." This is a wonderful philosophy for six talented musicians when they are actually onstage and before the public, but does this translate when the players step off the stage at an afterhours club and into a household setting? It is the decidedly unglamorous decisions which require careful forethought that threaten to undo Wilson's male characters in the second half of the twentieth century. Their families, who do not share in these problems, suffer for misdeeds that are not their own.

For all its history involving the gradual progression of the African-American community in the years following World War II, *Fences* is also a modern Shakespearean tragedy. Kim Pereira accurately sees how Troy Maxson is a tragic hero in that he is the source of his own destruction. His memory of how he had been ill treated by America is something that he cannot get over even though he would be healthier and happier if he could let this go (or at least let it fade away and be replaced by more recent occurrences). Memory stands in his way and he rigidly holds on to it when it does him a terrible disservice. In his attempt to do what he thinks is best for his family-Troy refuses to acknowledge that things are indeed changing for the African American in the fifties-"he finds himself estranged from the very family he is striving to protect" (Pereira 38). Like Othello, Oedipus, and Icarus the best of intentions only lead them to the worst possible outcome. In keeping with our emphasis on music, the circular and cyclical hurdles Troy introduces into his domestic life are "that same concerto of grief" that has captivated theatergoers for centuries (Pereira 42). He cannot relinquish the fact that more than twenty years earlier he was not allowed to play major league baseball, and while this is an undeniable problem, he lets it bleed and coalesce into an even greater source of bodily pain. By forbidding his son Cory the chance to play college football Troy has inflexibly possessed "too good" a memory. Whereas Bono, Troy's loyal friend, speaks constantly about absent fathers, Troy creates a rift with his son where there is none and guarantees that another African-American son will be deprived the devotion of his father. The fact that Troy had an equally explosive break with his own father implies that it will not be the last.

August Wilson, who himself as a young man was not interested in Jazz music because it did not have any words, changed his mind completely in October of 1966 when he saw two hundred people gathered outside the Crawford Grill in Pittsburgh to hear John Coltrane because they did not have the ninety cents per drink to sit inside. In 1966, "that's a lot of money" and this crowd was in the street wrapped up in a religious fervor (qtd. in Lewis 57). As he stated

> ...the brothers outside, they prayin. This is their music. This is what has enabled them to survive these outrageous insults that American society has forced on them... [the people were] stunned into silence by the power of art in the music of John Coltrane and his exploration of man's relation to the divinity... (58)

Jazz has the ability to captivate. It must be part of the narrative. This is why Lyons, Troy's son by his previous marriage, wants to be a musician and spend his time in clubs. "The only thing that matters to me is the music" (Wilson 18). Part of the reason that Lyons needs music is that other components of his life are so difficult. He states, "I need something that gonna help me out of the bed in the morning. Make me feel like I belong in the world" (Wilson 18). The question is why does a thirty-four year old man need to step outside his home to belong to something? Why is music the source of spiritual escape? And what, precisely, is there a need to escape from? Lyons is in a double quandary. Not only must he seek out his identity as an African American male in Pittsburgh in 1957, but he must also struggle with the self-definition that comes from growing up without his father who has been in prison for much of his childhood. He must grab onto music because there is little else. When he does see Troy, his father is angry, but it is Lyons who has the legitimate complaint.

In each of these literary texts the dominant theme is that children must reconcile and find a way to make sense of their parents' decisions. Our overarching societal views of marriage, family, and relationships have changed and it is the children of these formations, more so than their biological parents, who suffer the most. James C. Coleman in his *Intimate Relationships, Marriage, and Family* states that "investigators have concluded that contemporary marriage and family are deteriorating if not downright disintegrating" (25). In Faulkner, Wilson and Alexie, we see the "coming attractions" of these problems at (roughly) the beginning, middle and end of the twentieth century. All deal with what Coleman calls the "reorganization" stage and this is a challenge that harms children indiscriminately (407).

Fences focuses on the family, but it is a family in turmoil that is not dissimilar from the Native American family in "Because My Father Said He Was The Only Indian Who Saw Jimi Hendrix Play 'The Star-Spangled Banner' At Woodstock." In an eight-year stretch of time, "Wilson traces the fortunes of the Maxson family for three generations. In their thwarted hopes and ambitions, their battered pride, their fears, their stubborn faith, [and] their infidelities" (Pereira 37). The difference is that Troy's family is more likely to be surrounded by the blues of Bessie Smith than the sad refrain of Hank Williams. Sherman Alexie's parents met at a cowboy bar where they shuffled along to "I'm So Lonesome I Could Cry." When the progeny of this ill-fated romance tells his father that "Hank Williams and Jimi Hendrix don't have much in common," the father replies, "Hell, yes, they do. They knew all about broken hearts" (30).

Inherent within this caustic debate is that, left unaware, we all grow up to be our parents. This is what makes the sharp and painful shift of Isaac McCaslin and Jim Bono so essential to their ultimate well-being. There must be a clean break to prevent these problems from repeating themselves. Anything less would be inconsequential. Each of these texts, including Sherman Alexie's *The Lone Ranger and Tonto Fistfight in Heaven*, needs the blues to confront heartbreak. The blues is a theoretical approach to American Literature. It is an African-American art form that is embraced irrespective of the race of the author with the potential to make these problems bearable. "The Walking Blues" Bono notices his father's absence is just as devastating in its Southern as well as Northwestern ramifications. The blues serves as an acknowledgement that not only are our pasts not perfect, but that these imperfections must be wrestled with if individuals hope to turn the page and move on. Literary theorist Houston A. Baker states that it is the blues critic who must "decipher" the often unobserved skirmish that we all find ourselves in the midst of (115). In a sense the reader of these works is this critic who must both evaluate and comment upon this form of expression. The blues is an art form which arises because people are left lonely and cold, but even more to the point it is an answer for the rudderless and nomadic condition whose roots reach all the way back to the improvisational music that predates slavery in the United States. This is the jazz of Coltrane, whose parent is the blues, which mirrors the uncertainty of the African American adrift in the west before being appropriated by the population at large (Jones 17). The origin of this sophisticated form of music reaches back centuries and this is apparent to a careful reader who realizes that this is a timeless component of what we read, listen to, and talk about (Baker 117). The issue of race is such a problem that Baker terms it a "sharp dilemma...a critical orientation that looks, not to real history, but to the limitless freedom of myth" (122). To find some sort of solution one must abandon the normal rules and constraints to form a music that will make it possible to survive.

When August Wilson discovered Bessie Smith, in a 1965 rooming house, it "gave him a way to define himself in relation to the world" (Meson-Furr 6). What's more without her, the music of Williams and Hendrix would not have been possible. Without the blues music would not have had a "tear" embedded within it. With the blues that "tear" transcends. It links everyone who has the courage, or the naivety, to have relationships together. It aids our convalescence when these relationships, all too frequently, do not work.

Again, it happens that we are in the parenting business or at least nearly everyone is in the parenting business unless he or she purposely makes a conscious choice not to be in such a circumstance. When Wilson expands on the issue of parenting, I would argue that it is the character of Jim Bono, Troy's friend for several decades, who makes the most telling observations. Bono states that his father had "The Walking Blues," and this has more to do with it than merely a geographical issue involving travel. The need to "roam" implies that Bono's father has been involved with several women and that these women were in more than one place. The result is a controversial set of facts that create yet another dilemma or "muddle" that cannot be reconciled. The problem is that men, like Bono's father, who may have children in more than one city, cannot be reliable parents to each of them simultaneously. Even if they wished to be conscientious in regard to childrearing they simply cannot be in more than one place at a time. This very problematic circumstance has, somehow, been recycled so that the blues musician who is popular with women and has several love affairs sees his popularity enhanced by this so-called "bad" behavior. From a business or economic standpoint this is devastating as there are several households to be maintained—often from one income. The issue of responsibility becomes even more important when one realizes, as Wilson does, that a man who has "The Walking Blues" has the potential to create disunity at a *faster* pace than a reliable parent can create stability. Troy Maxson creates three households and then is often away from each of them as a professional baseball player, a prisoner, and an adulterer. This creates a sociological problem that has the potential to travel. People suffer from behavior that they had no part in.

Not only is Isaac McCaslin innocent he is unaware. He is simultaneously an "Uncle to half a county" and a nephew and son whose name, if corroborated, is besmirched (Faulkner 3). In *Go Down Moses*, whose title refers to a biblical figure whose parentage is famously unknown, the "reliable parents" do not have "The Walking Blues." That is because they can wreak havoc on their own families without leaving home. The behavior of Isaac's ancestors leaves him with a tangled mess to organize and order. His persistence and perseverance lead him to uncover the fact that the men in his family, just as the men in Wilson's *Fences*, have more than one family. The fact that this is financially profitable creates an unspeakable horror. The result of all of this is that these truths are opaque. In a world where subtext—what is below the surface—threatens to overwhelm the text we have a setting whose reality is purposely obscured. The source of Isaac's dilemma is a hidden past whose problems are exacerbated by the fact that there is no one to guide him.

Sherman Alexie has a guide, but, for the most part, he is alone as well. "On an Indian Reservation, Indian men who abandon their children are treated worse than white fathers who do the same thing. It's because white men have been doing that forever and Indian men have just learned how" (34). When Alexie misses his father he listens to blues music. "The first time I heard Robert Johnson sing I knew he understood what it meant to be an Indian on the edge of the twenty-first century, even if he was black at the beginning of the twentieth" (35). Children miss kinds of stability that today, even though fleeting and intermittent, hurts when it is not there. All three men are connected by their struggle to adapt and improvise to a world that is no longer concerned, or even aware, of how things should be. The responsibility of parenthood is so difficult, and the transgressions so common, that Isaac McCaslin and Jim Bono state that they never will have children of their own. The reason for this admittedly severe remedy is that this is the only guarantee that they will not repeat the sins of their fathers. This act of self-denial is a preemptive strike to ease their own consciences. It makes their lives less complicated, but it exacts a price that cannot be measured or calculated.

On Independence Day of last year, Mitch Pearlstein, in *The Weekly Standard*, commented that "family fragmentation" is not only something corrosive that can damage a child's (psychological) wellbeing, but it has a direct relation to how well educated that child will become (34). While education is not at the heart of this study, the class ramifications of being without it are front and center in each of these three works. Troy Maxson, while forbidding his son Cory from playing football, prevents him from obtaining the economic and social mobility he himself desires. The college scholarship that is within Cory's grasp could be a passport to the middle class. Troy stands in the doorway to prevent an occurrence he yearns for. Cory must not only deal with the formidable challenge of being an adolescent African-American in the late fifties, but he must also stiff arm his own father to make something of himself. What has happened to the notion of a parent wanting more for those who follow? The parent here, while well intentioned, is a problem. He makes the playing field harder for his own son and as a black man then, it was hard enough to begin with. Cory's survival is made more difficult, his progress short-circuited from within.

If there is resistance to success in the Native American community, it does not come in the form of a parent. The parents in *The Lone Ranger and Tonto Fistfight in Heaven* don't have Troy's anger, but they do not seem very interested in the future. There is an apathy that comes from being hurt too many times and knowing that this is unavoidable for both themselves and their children. Instead of planning poorly there does not seem to be any planning at all. It took Alexie's own initiative to attend a high school off the Spokane Reservation. He states "I knew how to live in poverty, having grown up on an American third-world reservation" and it is nothing short of astonishing that he got beyond such an environment to be discovered by an editor at the *New York Times Book Review* (Alexie xiii).

In terms of memory how does an author forget "being a poor Indian growing up in an alcoholic family on an alcoholic reservation" or is it better not to forget and take such severe pain and then create a series of stories that are funny, entertaining, and plumb elegant (Alexie xviii)? The author's talent is his ability to take desolate reality and be transformative, but this is a uniquely personal and individual experience. As one of the few people from this environment to even go to college Alexie has crafted a career not with his family's help, but by eluding the problems that would have trapped or ensnared anyone with less persistence.

The notion of a family disintegrating, collapsing, or breaking down has always brought with it a degree of turmoil. However, as time has progressed these situations have become more frequent and the hardships more complex. Not only are questions unanswered but they are also unstated. The consequences of the narrative are unspeakable and difficult to bring to light. The psychological limitations - how people approach their own pasts and the pasts of those who precede them - have no easy solutions. People are deceived and cheated and then they misplace confidence in those who are also deceived and cheated. That said, it is essential to note that these occurrences tend to be repetitive. William Faulkner, in arguably his finest novel *Absalom, Absalom*, states that "we see dimly people, the people in whose living blood and seed we ourselves lay dormant and waiting" (*Absalom, Absalom* 101). Unless compelled, as Faulkner's characters are, we scarcely look at the playbook that is before us. Without such scrutiny it is impossible to know what to retain, what to discard, or when to let go once and for all.

Works Cited

- Baker, Jr., Houston A. *Blues, Ideology, and Afro-American Literature: A Vernacular Theory*. Chicago and London: The University of Chicago Press, 1984. Print.
- Coleman, James C. *Intimate Relationships, Marriage, and Family*.

Second Edition. New York: Macmillan Publishing Company, 1988. Print.

- Dreiser, Theodore. *Sister Carrie: An Authoritative Text Backgrounds and Sources Criticism.* Second Edition. New York and London: W.W. Norton & Company, 1991. Print.

- Lapham, Lewis H. "Ignorance of Things Past." *Harpers*, May 2012: 26

- Lewis, Miles Marshall. "August Wilson." *The Believer* Nov. 2004: 56 – 66. Print.

- "iCelebZ.com." *Famous Quotes.* 2006 - 2009 Web. 2 July 2006.

- Faulkner, William. *Absalom, Absalom.* New York: The Modern Library, 1964. Print.

- _____. *Go Down Moses.* New York: The Modern Library, 1940. Print.

- Jones, Leroi. *Blues People: The Negro Experience in White America and the Music That Developed From It.* New York: William Morrow And Company, 1963. Print.

- Meson-Furr, Ladrica. *August Wilson's Fences.* New York: Continuum International Publishing Group, 2008. Print.

- Pearlstein, Mitch "Broken Families, Broken Economy: The Real Obstacle To Growth." *The Weekly Standard* 4 Jul. 2011: 34 – 36. Print.

- Pereira, Kim. *August Wilson and the African-American Odyssey.* Urbana and Chicago: University Of Illinois Press, 1995. Print.

- Wilson, August. *Fences.* New York and London: Plume, 1986. Print.

Section III

Resistance

Chapter 5

Unwavering Insubordination: Rebellion & Memory in *The Letters* of Elizabeth Hooton

Bill F. Ndi

The love that I bear to the souls of all men makes me willing to undergo all that can be inflicted on me.

Elizabeth Hooton

Introduction

Over the centuries, the voices of women and their active participation in the events and ideas that have helped to revolutionize the world have been silenced consciously or unconsciously. The above quote by a well-known early Quakeress, Elizabeth Hooton, reputed not only as the first Female Preacher (Manners, E. 1915) but also as one of the first converts of George Fox's doctrine, the founding doctrine of the Quaker movement, brings to the limelight the determination, enthusiasm and zeal with which she was ready to stand on the shoulders of the English society (both in the old and the New Worlds) to propagate the ideals for which she stood i.e. the Quaker ideals for an egalitarian society based upon the idea that all men are created equal and endowed with a divine *inner light* and *voice*, shining the way of and talking to each and every one of them without exception nor consideration for race, gender, religion, class, profession, etc.

Again, these early Quakers took a serious stance against oppression in all its forms as a sign of their rebellion against state and High Church orchestrated persecution. Elizabeth Hooton was no exception. Her declaration cited here above is not just a vain statement by an angry young man or woman, but a significant affirmation of the sacrifices Quakers were willing to make in order to guarantee the establishment of the ideals for which they stood. Quakers were ready for everything even if this entailed opposing and disavowing every established order against the backdrop of changing the status quo.

In this Quaker struggle, women played a very significant role. This important role has not escaped the attention of critics, analysts and historians of this period in general and those of Quakerism in particular. Pointing out women's role and active participation in this strain of 17th century radicalism, Antonia Fraser draws attention to the fact that,

> ... Quaker women were able to exercise responsibilities within their own religious organization denied to any other Englishwomen of their time [...] These women as a result were able to practice a certain kind of admirable nonconformist philanthropy from which much reforming richness has flowed in the English social life. [...] the *Inner Light* drew Quaker women into a more challenging and adventurous way of life, not only did they themselves suffer hideously, but they also pulled down upon their whole sex still viler imprecations concerning the nature of womankind (358).

In the light of the foregone, this chapter proposes to bring to light, through Hooton's *Letters* the specificity and constituting elements of rebellion and memory as a veritable source of historical affirmation and information for the hows and whys of Quaker feminine rebellions and documentation of memory. Besides the fact that Quaker literature comes across as a piece of literature whose primary goal is to serve as propaganda aimed at converting or encouraging and strengthening the resolve of new converts, Quaker *journalists* exploited the expressiveness of their rebellion and memory at times in form of letters as is the case with Hooton's. The body of this primary literature left by this early generation of Quakers not only as legacy but as memory that should never be forgotten does not only speak of the physical persecution endured in the hands of religious and political tyrants over the years but also of the moral and psychological scars left by these persecutions as well as the inward battles led by these Quakers. They documented all of these to fertilize the resolve of generations to come.

Hooton's letters as would be demonstrated hereunder establish a relationship between her memory of the historical events of her time and her personal as well as Quaker defiance and refusal to submit to established order in spite of the cruel persecution directed against Quakers who resorted to an inward spiritual to ward off such external impositions. Thus Hooton's letters become a permanent place for rebellion and one where remembrances of the past could be tapped. For it is in this rich primary literature that all Quaker writers inscribed not only their group participation but their individual participation in the Quaker bid to hasten the second coming. These writings thus constitute a socio-political statement motivated by the happenings of that age.

Hooton in Context

Amongst the chiliastic movements of 17th century England, the Quakers are well reputed for everything and above all their rebellious tendency; and the memory of which they inscribed in their writings which in the first instance was to serve as propaganda for their libertarian ideas and ideals. Amongst the numerous definitions or attempts to explain Quakerism, the aforementioned rebelliousness has come to be used as a hallmark of this movement. Christopher Hill, explaining the emergence of religious dissent and contestation in England during the 17th Century, emphasizes the spirit of rebellion as the driving force against the established order as a key element to understanding the Puritan Revolution and especially radical religious groups and sects such as the Quaker movement. He goes on to highlight that it would be worthwhile considering "the Quaker movement as a rebellion of young men against their parents (this was not apparently the case with young girls/women)" (118).

Beyond these considerations, historians of Quakerism also view this movement as one that has continuously exerted a non-negligible influence at the height of its glory and still continues to do so today, even if somewhat neglected (Tual 447). It is in this light that the question of the influence(s) exerted in the area of memory and rebellion by Quakers in general and most especially by Elizabeth Hooton (being an old woman and one who became a convert almost in her fiftieth year and was the first to embrace the doctrine) become(s) crucial.

Rebellion and Memory of Rebellion

Mention having been briefly made of Hooton as the first female preacher and convert to the Foxian doctrine of the *inner light*, nothing has been said as far as her memory of the Quaker rebellion or the Quaker rebellion and her documentation of memory for posterity are concerned. As one of the First converts, Hooton transformed her home into a meeting house and participated actively in the rebelliousness of this movement which consisted amongst other things in interrupting priests during sermons and drawing their attention to the ills that plagued the society and to which ills the Established Church and its *hireling priests* turned a blind eye. It was mostly as a result of this rebellion that many Quakers were thrown into jail and persecuted oftentimes for asserting freedom of expression which, at the time, was the reserve of divine right monarchs and their lackeys. So Quaker rebellion and its memory take center stage in Quaker activism and literature such as Hooton's.

Paradoxically, Hooton's/Quaker rebellion is one incrusted in silence and followed by a sudden outburst of logorrhea directed against both their persecutors and the Established Church priests whom Quakers considered and labeled as *hireling priests*. It is in the spirit of silence and rebellion that Elizabeth Hooton is thrown into jail for the first time in 1656 after being charged with interrupting a local priest. Hooton's participation in this rebellion and her documenting of its memory for posterity as Quakers so desired puts a feminine voice to the rebellion and the participation of women hitherto silenced and/or ignored by the male dominated society. This documentation of memory gives Hooton the opportunity to address concerns informed by her plight as a woman, and one speaking for all the other voices silenced by centuries of humiliation and non-recognition for their worth. By taking to preaching as a woman, Hooton put up a much more daring fight in an era when women were not defined by who they were but by whom they were married to or whose daughters they were; in short they were nothing more than chattels and/or belongings only to be seen and not heard. Such privation left women with the craving for the humanity as Barthes would centuries later state in *A Lover's Discourse* in these terms: "when you crave truth as you crave air, then you will know what truth is.... It is by this asphyxia that I reconstitute my "truth"..." (17).

Hooton in the course of her ministry lived and experienced a dramatic life of a rebel and wrote letters documenting memories of her labors, ministry, persecutions and tribulations for posterity. The hideousness of her sufferings, amongst many other things according to Fraser, "also pulled down upon [her] whole sex still viler imprecations concerning the nature of womankind" (358). These letters were written to her friends, detractors and adversaries: priests, magistrates and judges, mayors, the King, and political leaders of her day. In them are underscored, the most captivating elements of the memory of her participation in the quest for truth, peace, freedom, justice and equality for all irrespective of gender, race, religion, class, age, etc. as well as her memories of political and religious persecutions that dissenters in general and most especially Quakers suffered in both the Old and the New World during the Cromwellian Interregnum and after the Restoration and beyond. Therefore, through Hooton's writing, the memory of the yoke under which women had been held hostage psychologically and otherwise is shattered and the same memory thus finds life in these letters she wrote. What then accounted for this?

Sources of Memory and Rebellion

The fact that Quaker *Journalists* like Elizabeth Hooton canalized their energies with equal, and if not surpassing, vigor of the violence directed at them, leave their writings as a primordial ground from which recently converted adepts to Quakerism or historians of the movement specifically and Historians in general would gain knowledge of and familiarize themselves with the bitter and/or sweet memories of both violence and persecution suffered by these early Quakers as well as their responses to such ferocity against a belief system using religion to transgress all socially established norms at the origin of oppression. These letters also show both Hooton's and Quaker astute defiance and refusal to bow to what they believed was far from the truth in their endeavor to *publish* or *proclaim the Truth*. It is therefore in this light that Hooton's *Letters* transcend their original goal of propaganda pieces to become a source of memory and rebellion for the purification of established institutions. Hence, this rebellion proceeds from that which is borne in the mind and manifested outwardly; the inner depth of which mind was at odds with a societal paradigm depriving women of the basic rights.

Hooton's *Letters* provide graphic details of her daily sufferings as a Quaker. They also give accounts of her own imprisonments and those of other Quakers, the arbitrariness of the imprisonments she and others suffered, her experience in jail houses for her convictions, the beatings and torture she received, what she witnessed done to other victims in her unfortunate circumstances and her proposals to the jailers, rulers, leaders and politicians on what needed to be done to reform the penitentiary system. These letters are therefore decorated with her personal life experiences and autobiographical tidbits as well as those of all who experienced and witnessed firsthand the acts of violence and persecution ordered and perpetrated by the authorities in their attempt to silence voices of dissent and rebellious activism.

It is noteworthy to highlight that Hooton's *Letters* besides being addressed to specific dignitaries or politicians and rulers including magistrates and judges contain in them historical testimonies tied to both her religious beliefs and convictions about the ills of the society in which she lived. Moreover, do Quakers not categorize their writings or accounts as witnessing and/or acts of testifying on the events they lived and experienced in their quest for truth and its proclamation and publication? Hooton's accounts become an attempt to flood the world with memory of the material world to the benefit of that which is deeply rooted inside.

Hooton's writings like those of her fellow Quakers and other contemporaries do not steer clear of the detail of accounting and chronicling persecutions and sufferings in both the Old and the New Worlds. Hooton's most especially, reveal her tenacity, determination, patience, intrepidity and courage in the Quaker rebellion to *proclaim* & *publish the truth*. Hers is complementary information which provides memories that should have been lost otherwise were they not carefully recorded. Isn't it true that the 17th century was characterized by censorship? Isn't it true that religious radicalism suffered more from this than others? History has it documented that many acts of parliament were promulgated targeting religious dissenters and most specifically Quakers. Amongst the many laws cited the following: The Quaker Acts 1664 and 1667 and also the 1650s laws in New England mentioned by Hooton, levying a £100 fine to any ship masters who brought in Quakers and their books or pamphlets. Is it not for this reason that the historian and scholar of this era, Christopher Hill, draws attention to the fact that collecting information about this period is very problematic because of censorship? Isn't it in the same light that he writes in *The Experience of Defeat: Milton and some Contemporaries*, that,

> One problem to be faced in dealing with the seventeenth century England, and particularly with radicals, is censorship. It was there all the time before 1640, its strictness increasing in the 1630s. In the 1640s it was intermittent and rarely effective: it was

gradually restored in the 1650s, though there was still greater freedom for radical voices to be heard than after 1660 (21).

The above quote thus paints a disturbing picture of the atmosphere in which Quakers struggled to document their memory of events and their daily travails viz. imprisonment, beatings and other forms of dehumanizing violations of human rights that they endured. These however, did not quell their zeal and enthusiasm but led to a paradox whereby sympathizers and converts pulled their forces together against the persecutors. This paradox (whereby, instead of persecution having the expected effect of tampering the resolve and zeal of converts encouraged many more people to side with those early Quakers or become Quakers themselves) however warranted not only the internal growth of the Quaker movement but also highlighted Quaker rebellion and documentation of memory of the sufferings incurred as a result of their resolve to thrust their belief in the *inner light* and *the proclamation* and *publishing of truth* for, as Lurting writes in the preface to his autobiography, "First Written for Private Satisfaction, and Now Published for general Service." It is therefore not surprising to recognize memory in this writing as being far removed from merely verbal recollection of happy and/or sad remembrances but a desperate effort to complement absolutely essential views of historical truths and reality even in the face of censorship.

Individual<->Society, Binary Opposition

The themes of rebellion and memory are practically inescapable in literature in general but it is most especially marked in Quaker literature. It is clear and incontestable that from a certain perspective, any literary work comes across as a commitment undertaken by a writer with the goal of establishing a conversation between the individual's recordings of remembrances of events and societal handling of events and/or its people or class of people during a given time and space. Rebellion and memory can thus be streamed down to the writer's souvenirs of carefully recorded resistance to oppression and wanton abuse of power by those in authority so nothing is lost of the struggle to overcome evil and its pervasiveness to crush the voices of dissent and contestation in a battle for freedom. Quaker rebellion is one expressed in many forms passing through linguistic rebellion and outright interjection and interruption of priests during religious services and outright violation of what is considered acceptable or not in society e.g. "thouing" and "theeing" all without exception[5]; rejection of/opposition to tithing or societal imposed codes of respectability viz. doffing hats, curtsying to greet, revering, appearing in public in sackcloth or even parading naked, etc. In short, non-conformism to the High Church and societal conventions esteemed not to be guided by the *divine inner light*. This binary opposition of individual rights and societal imposition also becomes the playing field for feminine rebellion in women's attempts to develop personal selves in spite of societal attempts to mystify and falsify history. This rebellion according to Manners, E. (1915) was from every indication heralded by Hooton, *The First Woman Preacher*.

From reading Elizabeth Hooton's *Letters*, one of the first things that comes through her life long struggle as a mark of rebellion against the male dominated society from which she hailed is her willingness to sacrifice everything for her religious convictions and to address her views as well as those of her kind on the wrongful stance of society vis-à-vis womankind. She so does without the least timorousness. It has been noted that upon embracing Quakerism, the priest vehemently opposed to it and exhorted her husband to divorce her. Though Elizabeth Hooton's husband was not in favor of her becoming a Quakeress, he later on threw in the towel after realizing that the strain in their matrimony brought about by this new found faith of hers could only be resolved by him becoming a Quaker himself (which he did and so remained all his life). In spite of the exhortation of the priest and opposition from the husband and other

---

[5] This Quaker contribution explains the linguistic absence of this singular form of you in the English language hitherto used to denote inferiority as opposed to the plural you for an individual to denote superiority.

family members, Elizabeth Hooton stood her grounds as an independent minded woman operating within her new found religion whose precepts and agenda pushed, amongst other things, for equality amongst all human beings with total disregard regard for gender, age, class, profession and race.

Elizabeth Hooton's thus becomes an act of commitment with the rule of engagement geared towards debunking the present socio-political system stifling womankind. It is a conscious reflection and appeal to societal conscience to allow the individual woman and her private self to flourish without entrapments. It is also a spell for her to partake in the making of history. Hooton's lifelong struggle with its messianic thread connects memory, sufferings and her past into an exposition of societal ills against which she fought; especially the outward display of wisdom without an internal/personal experience of wisdom. This willingness to take the heat and be serviceable to mankind and womankind alike, led her not only to fighting against the social, racial, political, judicial and gender injustices of her time but to take the risk to effect the dangerous crossing to the New World where she hoped to continue and win her fight.

Exporting the Rebellion

Elizabeth Hooton did not quarantine her rebellion to England alone. Drawn by the *inner light* to more challenging and adventurous display of her rebellion, she chose to export the struggle to the New World. And she must be remembered for even dying at 72 in Jamaica during one of her missions with George Fox. Before leaving for New England, Elizabeth Hooton made sure she had pressured the King well enough to obtain from him a permit to acquire land in New England. This permit was not only to her benefit as a Quakeress but that of women in general. Also, it was to establish an eternal resting place for Quakers who for the sake of their conscience and beliefs were deprived of any such facility. It must be remembered that during this time in New England, there were laws prohibiting anyone from helping Quakers under the pain of imprisonment and/or heavy fines. Hooton's struggle is therefore one against all forms of privation.

She chronicles her departure to the New World with her daughter and talks about the laws preventing Quakers from coming into the New England colonies with her saving grace being the fact that the shipman who brought her along declared that she'd been with King and that she had the King's authorization. Her imprisonment at Piscatua is an example of a case in which her ministry brought upon her such gruesome sufferings documented in the letters about New England. Her memories of what she lived in the New World are carefully documented in letters addressed to "The King and Council" and her "Lamentation for Boston and her Sister Cambridge" and another letter addressed "To the Rulers and Magestrats of this Island that ought to Rule for god". In the *Letter* addressed to the King and council, she writes:

> O King,
>
> [...] What reason is there to carry us into other lands, and thrust many into an old vissited shipp wch was rotten, & leaked water, whose blood will be laid to the charge of them that did it, for many of them are dead, and the rest wee know not what is become of them, Except they bee took by the Hollanders, as some of them are. And in three shipps before this was there more carryed away into other lands both old and Young from wives & Children & other relations & their owne Native Country....

This letter is not a typical address from an ordinary citizen/subject to the King. It comes across as an injunction from a superior to a subordinate (the King) to give explanation as to why he allows such persecution and wanton abuse of authority and power to be exerted upon innocent and well-meaning subjects. She does not hesitate to rebuke the King for allowing his fellow countrymen to be taken into other countries or leaving them at the mercy of ruthless Dutch seamen who would take them captive.

Elizabeth Hooton equally points out the category of people who suffered this plight. Amongst them were "old and young, wives and children and other relations carried away from their native country." The themes of desolation and displacement that this letter explores are informed by Elizabeth Hooton's life experiences of witnessing the truth about English people for requesting basic freedoms and being persecuted for that reason. In this vain, Quaker writings such as Elizabeth Hooton's instead of becoming the lamentation of an individual's plight, and streaming from his/her memory of personal sufferings and pains, thus tend to address the predicament of a group or subgroup within the society in general. They also bring to mind the famous Chaucerian rhetorical question seeking what iron will do if gold rust. Elizabeth Hooton as a result, appeals straight to the conscience of these leaders, rulers, jailers and people in position of authority. This appeal seeks to instill a bit of individuating awareness in this category of people who seem to be oblivious to their own ills and their effects on the masses. She exhorts those in authority to see for themselves the nefarious effects of their devious administration on their fellow countrymen viz. family break-up; as such, grounds Hooton's and Quaker call for institutional clean up.

Rebellion and Memory for Institutional Clean Up

It was however from this experience, this wholesale incarceration of people who were not themselves members of the criminal classes, that the honourable Quaker commitment to prison reform sprang. It has been pointed out that in her letters from prison Elizabeth Hooton herself anticipated by 150 years the demands of the nineteenth century Quaker reformer Elizabeth Fry. (Fraser 359-360)

The above quote substantiates the *raison d'être* of this subheading. Again, from every indication, Elizabeth Hooton's rebellious attitude in the face of adversity in both worlds parallels Quaker insubordination to anything human authority with the sole purpose of cleansing the institutions of oppression and documenting their sufferings for fear they don't get lost. Elizabeth Hooton's *Letters* elucidate and validate the close knit ties between rebellion and memory. Hooton, as a Quaker *journalist* in quest of *truth* and out to *proclaim* & *publish the truth*, discredits the present socio-political system and does what a later Quaker poet, James Russell Lowell, would highlight in his poem "L'Envoi" saying

> Who speaks the truth stabs falsehood to the heart;
> And his mere word makes despots tremble more
> Than ever Brutus with his dagger could.

She mentions the persecutions and torture endured in the hands of such despots and acolytes such as Nathaniel Hawthorne's ancestors; a story which Nathaniel Hawthorne in his famed novel, *The Scarlet Letter*, remembered hundreds of years after with the same vividness that abound in Quaker colonial literature. Hawthorne informs the reader of what a persecutor of the Quakers his forebears had been. And E. Hooton confirms this in the following lines:

> [...] wth besides 12 bussheles of wheate & provision in his house wch was for himself & children & threatned to take away his Children & sell them for ten pounds wch they demanded, where also they imprisoned me, & at Salem Haythorne[5] ye ruler whipped foure ffrds, & Sought also for me, though afterwards J was moved to cry through ye towne, but had noe power to hurt me at y^{t} time, So at Dover in Piscatua there ffor asking Priest Rayner a question when he had done they put me in ye stocks Richd Walden being (deputye)[2] Magistraite (for Dover) (his wife begged the office in mischeife to friends) & put me in prison 4. dayes in ye cold of winter but ye Lord upheld & preserved my life, where my service to ye Lord was profitable for strengthning of friends & leaving ye other wthout excuse, So more could Stormes did J endure & more persecution then J can expresse, so afterwards J returned to Cambridg, where they were very thirsty for bloud because none had been there before y' J knew of & J cryed repentance through some part of ye towne, [...]

Elizabeth Hooton seizes the opportunity of this repression in New England to refresh the memory of her persecutors of the reason why they find themselves in New England in the first place. She points out the practices of oppression they execute with virulence are far worse than that prevalent in England and from which they had escaped to the New World. This subtle reminder comes after she has highlighted the sole purpose of her writing which is the documentation of memory for Quakers and all to know the evil against which Quakers were waging their war to *proclaim* & *publish truth*. Elizabeth Hooton, in one of her frequent confessions of her motives, writes in a letter which best explains all of the aforesaid:

This is to lay before freinds or all where it may come of the sufferings & persecutions which we suffered in newe England I Elizabeth Hooton have tasted on by the prefessours of Boston & Cambridge, who call themselves Independants who fled from the bishops formerly, which have behaved themselves, worse than the bishops did to them by many degries, making the people of God to suffer much more than ever they did by the bishops which causeth their name to stink all over the world becaus of cruelty.

Elizabeth Hooton emphasizes here the fact that acts of persecution are not worthy of praise. Yet, they help to drag down the reputation of the persecutor. This letter addressed to both "friends and all" and its concern with something of greater and deeper import, the history of persecution, (traced from the Bishops in England as persecutors to the New Englanders now turned persecutors themselves and oblivious to their own past of victims of persecution) thus become a discourse removed from the pragmatic in the sense that it does not read like a note left by a postman for a letter/parcel pick-up to serve an immediate practical purpose but attempts to have a far reaching effect. As is the case here, the writing sends back to the general state of sufferings in the hands of forces external to the "self". Elizabeth Hooton so far gives another illustrative example of using memory as a central "concern" in an attempt to right the wrongs of the present. She does this with such reminder of the wrongs of the past which are easily forgotten. This key issue which early Quakers made a duty to lay or display as evidence before all left its mark on future generation of writers in the English language. Even Samuel Beckett in *Waiting for Godot* would have one of his characters (Vladimir aka Didi) highlight, "Extraordinary the tricks memory plays."

Quakers prise words loose from their everyday use and immediate context and thus initiate writings that capture memory of their own marginalization specifically and marginalization in general. This is especially the case with Elizabeth Hooton who stands on top of the shoulders of her epoch to make of the plight of the poor old widow one of her central thematic concerns of choice with which she avoids the tricks of memory on her, on her offspring, on her persecutors and on future generation of Quakers and all who shall read her works.

Elizabeth Hooton's life struggle for equality at all levels and for all hammers home the more too familiar aspect of societal cruelty directed at women in particular and minorities in general as well as the discrimination women were and are too often victim of. Is it not true that in Elizabeth Hooton's writings, she initiates a conversation with the King and all those in position of power for the reforms of the system that has total disregard for women? Is it not also true that she pursued the reforms of the penitentiary system as a result of the fact that she experienced men and women packed in the same jail cell which ought not to be the case? Is it not equally true that these facts seem to dispel assertions by scholars of feminism such as Guerin et al. who identify three historical phases of women's struggle on behalf of women's rights and interests whether organized or not while completely disregarding Elizabeth Hooton's struggle as a feminine voice within the Quaker struggle that sought the same rights and interests? (185) Does the assertion of these scholars not ignore the Quaker endeavor to prove the worth of women equal to men's in every aspect of life and that there is need for mentality change? These questions can go on without end. However, Fraser, highlights this Quaker endeavor and points out how George Fox "never ceased to push the view that there was work for Quaker women to do as well as men" (358-361). And Quaker women as a result stuck out their necks against Hobbesian pragmatism which views truth as "that which civil government under which we live instructs us in and directs us to believe..." (qtd in Shorthouse 67). Quakers and their women rejected civil government and its instruction. Official History is dismissed and the symbolism of biblical narrative becomes the sole source of human history, truth and law.

Conclusion

From Hooton's very first letter addressed to Noah Bullock, it is evident that she is not only out to make an historical footnote of her unjust imprisonment and those suffered by many others in England and the New World at the time. She seizes every opportunity to transcribe in her *Letters*, her rebellion against dignitaries who failed to do what was right and would rather turn their minds towards pleasing men and not God. She points out the cause of her rebellion as being the "[...] drunkenness, swearing, pride & vanity [which] ruleth from the teacher to the people & this set up. O friend, mercy & true judgment and justice is cried in your streets." And she goes on to warn of the nefarious consequences that await the authorities if nothing is done to remedy the situation. She is vocal and decries in no small terms the arrogance and immodesty of those in power. She thus writes: "O take heed of the woes: woe be to the crown of pride; woe be unto them that drinketh in bowls & the poor is ready to perish." Hooton's *Letters* warrant a visit to a place or site of memory. This is done both through description of place, persons and occurrences as well as through their constant appeal for the debunking of persecution and ills (directed against the *convinced*) of those in power that plague the society.

Through a series of carefully juxtaposed descriptions, Elizabeth Hooton succeeds in bringing out what calls for the rebellion she is willing to die for. The deeds of the oppressors sharply contrast with those of the poor who are "ready to perish." She does not hesitate to call upon the magistrate to mind these things. She crowns her rhetoric with questions which mark her courage, determination and willingness to pursue her rebellion until the oppressors have changed their wayward ways to guarantee equal rights and justice are granted to all without any consideration of gender, age, race, class, religion, profession, etc.. Fearless in her approach, she questions: "Would you have me put in jail, which have not transgressed your law nor misbehaved myself? Consider, is the good old ways that you was taught?" Moreover, her resilience is demonstrated throughout the letters and even in those addressed to the King and Council. Her pursuit is for justice as she writes in a letter addressed to the Duke of York:

"[...] hath waited for Justice agen J went [...]to the bench and followed them whether they went both day and at nights when they met to gether to know whether they would do me justice or no justice to which they hardened there harts and stifened there necks against the widows complaint and Regarded no just law . . .

Through her *Letters* and their accounts shaded with the spirit of rebellion and desire to preserve memory for future generation of Quakers and all that may come by them, it would only be logical to draw a conclusion that contextualizes Elizabeth Hooton in the greater rebellion that shook revolutionary England in the 17th century leaving the world "Upside-Down" (Hill 1977). Her *Letters* chronicling social, moral, political, economic and judicial conundrum in 17th Century England and the New World at that time and above all in a defiant tone transform the experience of reading them into a journey through the memory of an individual whose graphic representation of the ills of her time, tells not only of her rebellion but her desire not to see the memory of this rebellion besmeared by neither time nor tide and drowned into the mire of history. Isn't it for this same reason that almost twenty years after her death, and during a commemorative ceremony to celebrate her life, that George Fox,

(Manners 74) had to remember her with vividness? Fox's remembrances of this *"valiant Sixty"* point to a life of rebellion directed at priests, professors, magistrates, apostates, politicians and backsliders. These remembrances also show Elizabeth Hooton's willingness to impress upon people the truth she had received; which she did till her death in Jamaica in 1672. The remembrances thus mentioned bring together Elizabeth Hooton's rebellion and impression of memory upon people. Fox Stated that,

> ... in her Life she was very much Exercised with priests outward professours Apostates Backsliders and Profane, for she was a Godly Woman & had a Great Care Lay upon her for people to walk in ye Truth that did Profess itt, and from her receiving y Truth she never turned her Back of itt but was fervent & ffaithfull for it till Death.

Elizabeth Hooton's rebellion thus laid a foundation for an even greater rebellion which was illustrated centuries later in the "Declaration of Sentiments" adopted by the 1838 Peace Convention in Boston. Quakers and their rebellion strove at establishing world peace and at the cost of rejecting every human government. It therefore comes as no surprise that the first commendation in the "Declaration of Sentiment" should read thus: "We do not acknowledge any human government." This declaration shatters the hopes and aspirations of the power hungry while attributing recognition of any form of authority only to the divine almighty. Finally all forms of human politics, worldly honors and stations of authority are repudiated as does Elizabeth Hooton in her petitions to the governing bodies of her time. In short Elizabeth Hooton's *Letters* give to the future generation so powerful and eloquent an expression of vivid memory of rebellion against established human institutions at variance with the condition of women and minorities that one would have expected Elizabeth Hooton to be resting in the Pantheon of the torch bearers of feminism.

However, having pointed out most of Elizabeth Hooton's activism, rebellion and documenting of memory it would be worthwhile to allow this soldier of peace, equality and social justice, have the last word in her remembrances of her own rebellion for the great cause. Elizabeth Hooton with the same unwavering insubordination, in her final words, sums her life of rebellion and documenting memory in these words:

> All this and much more I have gone thorugh and suffered, and much more could I for the Seed's sake which is Buried and Oppressed, and as a Cart is laden with Sheaves and as a Prisoner in an inward Prison-House; Yea, the Love that I bear to the Souls of all Men, making me willing to undergo whatsoever can be inflicted

Elizabeth Hooton's refusal to submit, from start to finish, to any vicious attempts at silencing the voices of women, the poor and other minority religions, and "for the seed's sake which is Buried and Oppressed, and as a Cart is laden with Sheaves and as a Prisoner..." is an act of rebellion par excellence documented to constantly remind humanity of what it meant in Elizabeth Hooton's time to be a woman in a world dominated by men who cared little for womankind. As a rebel she was persecuted for standing by her conviction. By documenting, first hand her memory of all that which took place in her time, Elizabeth Hooton and the Quakers seemed to have found a panacea for the tricks memory would have played on all were these memories not carefully recorded. What thereby closes and marks the rebel's language and memory is nothing other than the very thing that birthed them: a fascination and love for change, one for which Hooton was ready to and did stake her life.

Works Cited

- Fraser, Antonia. *The Weaker vessel,* New York, Alfreda Knopf, 1984

- Hawthorne, Nathaniel. *The Scarlet Letter.* New York: Penguin Classics, 1986.

- Hill, Christopher. *The Experience of Defeat: Milton and Some Contemporaries.* London, Faber and Faber, 1984.

- Hill, Christopher *The World Turn Upside-down.* (1977) London, Penguin, 1984.

- Beckett, Samuel. *Waiting for Godot,* London, Faber and Faber, 1955

- Manners, Emily. *The First Woman Preacher,* 1915

- George Fox, *The Journal of George Fox,* London, Penguin, 1998

- Ndi, Bill F. *Hooton, Elizabeth: Une Guerrière de la paix,* Mankon-Bamenda, Langaa-RPCIG, 2011.

- Russell Lowell, James. *L'Envoi* : To The Muse (poem Of The War)

- J. H. Shorthouse, *John Inglesant: A Romane,* 6th ed. London, Macmillan, 1887.

- Fleishman, Avron. *The English Novel: Walter Scot to Virginia Woolf,* Baltimore and London, The John Hopkins Press, 1971.

Chapter 6

Memory and Resistance in the Poetry of Gcina Mhlophe

Adaku T. Ankumah

"The black women in South Africa have shown outstanding tenacity against great odds. We shall never give in to defeat. Today we remain determined, like the women of our community of previous generations, who have left us a living example of strength and integrity"

(Ellen Kuzwayo)

Introduction

For many black South Africans, apartheid laws may have been repealed in 1991, but the memory and the trauma from three centuries of separatist laws that were institutionalized in 1948 into official apartheid policy, are not easily forgotten. Maybe white South Africans and those whose skin colors allowed for tolerable existence may wish to forget a not-so-shining period in their history, but not so the people who had to live under this system, who endured harassment, torture and even murder to uphold this unjust system of government. For some South Africans, the painful memories are deep and not easily dealt with in Truth and Reconciliation Commission hearings to bring out some of these issues from the past to allow for healing and mutual understanding.

In a collection of essays titled *From the Kingdom of Memory*, Elie Wiesel, the 1986 Nobel Prize for Peace winner and a holocaust survivor himself reminisces about his obsession with memory and why he writes. In the opening chapter, he explains his motivation for writing: "Perhaps in order not to go mad. Or, on the contrary, to touch the bottom of madness. [...] I am duty-bound to serve as an emissary, transmitting the history of their [victims'] disappearance, even if it disturbs, even if it brings pain" (13, 16). Indeed, this desire to bear witness to the horrors of the past, to never forget what they and their ancestors went through, motivates writers who use the past as material for present works. It is in this vein that some South African writers (and other writers who have emerged from horrid pasts and/or brutally oppressive regimes) eschewed art for art's sake for a more militant type of writing, resistance literature not just aimed at informing the rest of the world about life under these brutal systems but most importantly at resisting the oppressive structures established by the Afrikaans government to maintain its power over other races. Both black and white artists alike engaged in this type of writing: the long list includes writers like Athol Fugard who has written plays like *Blood Knot*, *Sizwe Banzi is Dead*; Dennis Brutus, Ingrid Jonker and Mazizi Kunene, poets; and novelists and story tellers like Miriam Tlali, Bessie Head, Nadine Gordimer, For some of these artists, though, their engagement would bring them in conflict with the apartheid regime that did not want the rest of the world to get an insight into life in South Africa. The surveillance and harassments led to exile for some.

Resistance literature has been defined by Barbara Harlow as "literature that calls attention to itself, and to literature in general, as a political and politicized activity. The literature of resistance sees itself further as immediately and directly involved in a struggle against ascendant or dominant forms of ideological and cultural production" (qtd. in DeShazer, *A Poetics* 9). For DeShazer, though, resistance is not just "mere opposition" to the powers that be, with participants viewing themselves as helpless victims of an oppressive system; on the contrary, resistance is also "an active quest for justice, and as a means of collectively empowering a particular group of activists" (2). Thus these writers are seeking to dismantle an unjust system and to seek justice for themselves and the oppressed.

Many writers from Africa are familiar with this type of literature from the early stages of contemporary African writing. At an African-Scandinavian Writers' Conference as far back as 1967, participants dealt with the issue of the writer's individuality and social commitment. Nobel Prize winner and author Wole Soyinka sparked no small controversy about the nature and extent of the social involvement of the modern writer when he made a comment about poets who have taken to gun-running and writers who hold up radio stations—charges leveled against him by the Nigerian government and for which he was detained. Alex La Guma, a South African writer supports the involvement of the writer in social matters, making his or her writing relevant to the realities of citizens. He concludes that "all human activity [like literature] which does not serve humanity must be a waste of time and effort" (qtd. in Wastberg 24).

These artists were not only concerned with getting a message across to the outside world; sometimes their artistic creations were to encourage those involved with this internal resistance to an oppressive and brutal regime. To encourage especially the young to be involved in the struggle for freedom, writers sometimes dug into their past to help motivate the youth. As one writer notes, "'calling back on the past' is a precondition for 'the forging of the future'" (Gwala, qtd. in Bhekizizwe 44). Even South African artist, Gcina Mhlophe has not escaped criticism for not being political in her well-known play *Have You Seen Zandile?* This semi-autobiographical play published in 1986 was considered frivolous as it dealt with the protagonist's quest for identity after she was abducted as an eight-year old by her mother. In an interview justifying her use of English as language for the play, Mhlophe calls the play "a very universal story. It could have happened to anybody in any part of the world" ("Interview").

Given the post-apartheid environment in South Africa, some are questioning the significance of memory of anti-apartheid struggles. Some South African writers have noted that apartheid is not going to be the only narrative in post-apartheid South Africa. In his book *African Pasts*, Tim Woods notes that the controversy about the new direction for literature in post-apartheid South Africa continues as prominent members of that society add their voices to the debate.

Albie Sachs, a white South African and well-known judge who comes from an anti-apartheid family that supported the rights of blacks is noted to have said that "writers and artists should surrender their arsenal of artistic weapons and get on with the concerns of writing, freed from the obligations of writing about apartheid" (qtd. in Woods 202). Indeed, discussions on the role of the writer have been ongoing from apartheid period well into the post-apartheid era, and the camp is generally divided into two: there are those who want to use literature in the service of politics and those who feel the goals have been achieved and South Africa must revert to "normalcy." The ANC did advocate the use of literature to aid the struggle for freedom, and so did other writers, including Sachs himself. However, Sachs wants post-apartheid writers to "sit on the fence," a position that he admits is uncomfortable and carries negative connotation but is necessary to "plumb into the deep emotions, the sense of history, the personality, being and significance of people," as Sachs puts it, to see people as "human beings. . . [not as] stereotypes and classes and groups of people" ("Dogs"). In fact, Dennis Brutus, the South African poet and anti-apartheid activist who fought for a ban against his country in sporting activities notes that Albie Sachs has taken a position asking South Africans to forget the past, a course of action that he considers a "blight on South African literature" (qtd. in Sustar and Karim 290-1). Brutus does not believe that the anti-apartheid struggle has produced significant difference in the lives of the disadvantaged South Africans. On the contrary, he is of the opinion that the South African ruling class has aligned itself with the global agenda of the West, to the detriment of its people. His opinion is that the past is what motivates the ordinary citizens to fight in the present, what "revives [their] connection to it" (292) and to lose that memory is to lose the fight for "change [they] can believe in."

One such writer who has used the past to encourage women in their resistance to oppression and their desire to build better tomorrows is Nokugcina Elsie Mhlophe, an actor with the Market Theatre in Johannesburg, activist, a poet, a playwright, storyteller, composer and director—in a word, a performer. Born in 1958 to a

Xhosa mother and a Zulu father, she lived for more than three decades under the dreaded system of apartheid. Mhlophe is known world-wide for her performances and literary output, including children's literature. Among her published works are plays such as *Zandile*, and a number of published poetry, most of which she has performed before live audiences at home and in the west. These poems, which rely on oral tradition, dig into the history of black South Africa, using the past not only to inform but to encourage resistance to the ugly past and a forging of a future which includes the voice of women.

In her book on resistance poetry, Mary DeShazer notes that poetry is a medium of choice for resistance writers from different regions such as South America and South Africa. She refers to South African Nadine Gordimer's response to the question that poetry offers a more covert rather than overt expression of opposition (14). While this observation is true, oral tradition also offers a response to this question. The performing arts in the oral tradition have been both functional and collective, generally relevant to the concerns of society. Praise songs, called *izibongo* in traditional Zulu/Xhosa society and *lithoko* among the Sotho, are composed to honor meritorious accomplishments of individuals, especially chiefs. These poems are used to celebrate achievements of these rulers, as the poems repeat their titles, history, ancestry, and victories on the battle field, and as one author notes, even when there is no war these poets still boost morale "in preparation for a time when war broke out" (Cory, qtd. in Opland 57). Again, deviant behavior can be singled out in a song of ridicule in traditional societies. In some African countries, political leaders acquired their own praise poets to boost their egos. In fact, in defining the *imbongi*, the praise poet, one writer refers to him as "the poet who walks before the great chief" (Deakin, qtd. in Opland, 57). For instance in Ghana, Kwame Nkrumah, first president of the republic, also became the first to employ a poet and spokesman who used to work in a royal court as his personal praise poet. Before he spoke, this poet borrowed titles from various chiefs in Ghana to apply to Kwame Nkrumah. Thus Nkrumah became "Osagyefo":

(Savior from war), "Oseadeeyo" (one who keeps his word) (Yankah 45). This emphasis on the use of praise poetry in politics is supported by Liz Gunner, who sees praise poems as having a significant role in nation building in South Africa: "The ability of praise poetry to exploit the symbolic capital of a particular culture has long been recognized, but its ability to collapse the heroic past into a heroic present, and in this way make memory work for it, had been underestimated" (*Remaking the Warrior?* 52). Gunner notes how this borrowing from the heroic past to the present was used in praise poems comparing Chief Albert Luthuli, president of the ANC in the 1950s to the renowned nineteenth-century Xulu ruler Shaka. Thus the past is not treated as history, far removed from the present, but as easily incorporated into the present to create what Gunner refers to as a "more hybrid history" synthesized from the various past leaders of the many cultures in contemporary South Africa (*Remaking the Warrior?* 54). Moreover, in an atmosphere of suppression of the truth, exiling of writers, intolerance to opposition and in some cases assassination of opposition members, using a traditional poetic form could easily accommodate alternate views and as another author notes, also be used to re-educate and regenerate an audience of activists subject to feelings of discouragement, fear, and internalized oppression" (Shava, qtd. in DeShazer 133).

Praise to Our Mothers / Women & Protest

South African women have played an important role in the dismantling of apartheid in that country, just as other women in different parts of the world have been involved in liberation movements. In 1913, Charlotte Maxeke, the first black South African woman to earn a Bachelor's degree from Wilberforce University, Ohio, led a group of women in Orange Free State to protest the government law demanding women to carry the dreaded passes. These women burned passes in front of government buildings to show their displeasure with this requirement. Maxeke would form the Bantu Women's League of the South African Native National

Congress in 1918 to continue protests over passes for women. The Women's League became the Women's arm of the African National Congress. In 1913, Indian women in Traansvaal, using what later became Mahatma Gandhi's philosophy of *satyagraha*, civil, non-violent resistance, sold goods in the streets without obtaining permits. White women like Sarah Carneson, Sonia Bunting; Indian women such as Phyllis Naidoo and black women like Dorothy Nyembe, Lillian Ngoyi were involved in the struggle against unjust laws. In 1956, there was a large scale protest of the infamous pass-carrying law across the country, with the protest getting violent in places. On August 9, about 20,000 women from a coalition of various women's groups nationwide, known as the Federation of South African Women, protested this pass law for women in Pretoria, and beginning what became known as National Women's Day in South Africa. Mary DeShazer notes that for these demonstrations in 1950s, the women came up with their own slogans to protest the police's attempt to stop them and control their use of language and to also affirm their power: "You have tampered with the women / You have struck a rock. / You have dislodged a boulder. / You will be crushed" (*A Poetics* 11). As recent as February 19, 2012, South African women wearing miniskirts took to the streets of Johannesburg to protest sexual harassment of women who wear these short skirts ("South African Women").

Mhlophe's praise poem celebrates the accomplishments of women in dismantling apartheid and their contributions to nation building. In "Praise to our Mothers," the speaker begins her poem by invoking a tone of pride in her subject matter. In the past, women have not necessarily been the subject of praise poems and few have even been acknowledged as performers of this art form. In fact, in some parts of southern Africa, women singers considered beyond the control of men were referred to "loose women, as prostitutes" by men (Chitauro, Dube, Gunner 117). Being a woman and celebrating women in her poem is therefore a way of breaking traditional barriers which limit female performers, subverting the normal male arena. In addition, it is an opportunity for women to speak for themselves. In her interview with Tyrone August, Mhlophe notes that in the past, white people spoke for blacks, and men spoke for women. Now women have to tell men: "Okay, the men have spoken too much; let's speak" (Interview 277). It is not surprising to note that the speaker has a "proud form" because she has challenged history and tradition's marginalization of women and women performers. The speaker's "proud form," however, cannot be observed since it is a moonless night, but the pride is nevertheless there. She wants her praise to resonate to far-away places, for these women in South Africa are not the only ones struggling with marginalization. With a wider audience in mind, the persona will like to stand on a hilltop to sing her praises to the women of her country and for their altruism, which extends not just to South Africa, but to the whole of Africa.

> If I were to stand on top of a hill
> And raise my voice in praise
> Of the women of my country
> Who have worked throughout their lives
> Not for themselves, but for the very life of all Africans
> Who would I sing my praises to?
> I could quote all the names Yes, but where do I begin?
> (lines 5-12)

Though the history books may mention a few prominent women who have played significant roles in anti-apartheid struggles, Mhlophe notes that there are names omitted, names which are too numerous to mention. Thus she attempts to rectify this omission of women and their contributions to society by creating her own list of women covering the spectrum of races in South Africa - Black, White, Indian and Colored - religious affiliations, languages. In "The Black Writer's Use of Memory," an essay contributed to a seminar on History and Memory in African American culture, Melvin Dixon notes that "[m]emory becomes a tool to regain and reconstruct not just the past but history itself" (19). Mhlophe details for younger South Africans and the rest of the world who may be oblivious about the history of women in South African, the contributions of these women.

As if in a debate with herself, the speaker is at a loss as to where to begin her praise poem: "Do I begin with the ones / Who gave their lives / So that we others may live a better life / . . . Or the ones who have lost their men / To Robben Island and their children to exile" (lines 13-15, 18-19). Again, the speaker interjects the idea that the suffering under apartheid was not limited to men like Nelson Mandela, imprisoned on the infamous Robben Island where he spent eighteen of his total twenty-seven years of jail time. Women suffered too, not just losing husbands but also children like the Mandela children who were separated from father but also from their mother who was imprisoned intermittently. These children experienced the horrors of apartheid and were deprived a semblance of normalcy in their childhood. In addition, some women "marched, suffered solitary confinement / and house arrests" just like the men did. Then there are the women who have had the resilience / And cunning of a desert cobra" (lines 24-5). This reptile, a venomous type, is known to remain relatively inactive during day time, to even stay underground or hidden in a cool place, but come night time, it is active. It will not normally attack first, but when it is attacked, it will strike back with vengeance. This metaphor is an apt description for these women who have been "dormant" in society, normally confined to domestic spheres, but can strike when needed. Next, the speaker mentions women who have used their academic backgrounds to help transform the lives of their fellow citizens: the ones who turned deserts into green vegetable gardens / From which our people can eat" (lines 27-29). She mentions the names of Mamphela Ramphele, a woman of diverse academic background—medical doctor, anthropologist, activist, college professor and administrator, business woman—which she uses to uplift her people. Ellen Kuzwayo, a teacher, social worker activist and MP, is another woman singled out for her contribution to ameliorating life for her people. In her autobiography *Call Me a Woman*, Kuzwayo notes the many contributions black women have made to the resistance movement in South Africa, including their participation in the 1960 Sharpeville Massacre where 48 of the 69 protestors killed were women and children.

The resistance to apartheid includes the 1952 Defiance Campaign when the leadership of the African National Congress and other colored organizations like the South African Indian Congress and the Coloured People's Congress united in a multi-racial collaboration to fight unjust laws under apartheid. This multi-racial collaboration demonstrated to the authorities that citizens would not quietly submit to unreasonable laws. Even if they were unsuccessful in their protest, they would not be silenced. There is also the reference to Soweto and the 1976 protest by school children and those concerned about quality education for their children when the speaker seeks "alternative schools away from Bantu Education" (line 38). Black children received education that was inferior to that of whites, keeping them further down economically.

This poem subtly turns the mirror on relationships in black families. As DeShazer notes in her book *A Poetics of Resistance*, resistance poetry is not limited to anti-apartheid sentiments but also to resisting patriarchy, sexism, etc. The speaker calls attention to alcoholism and its devastating effects on the black male. As the speaker notes, there were women who fought" "against Beer Halls that suck the strength of our men" (line 37). Spending hard-earned money on alcohol deprived women and children of staples needed to survive. The implication of the speaker's initial dilemma is that contrary to what little has been recorded of women's accomplishments, they, in fact, have accumulated many to resist apartheid and make positive contributions to their society. The speaker is not limited to one or two activities by these women; on the contrary, she has many options to use in creating her praise poem to their mothers.

Thus in creating this praise poem to these women, the speaker reveals her lucidity, her clear awareness of the contributions of these women to the fight against apartheid. However, Mhlophe singles out one woman referred to by former President Mandela as "Mother of the nation" to vicariously represent all these women whose contributions have been marginalized by society. The poem is supposed to have been performed in 1989 in honor of Mama Nokukhanya Luthuli, wife of ANC leader chief Albert Luthuli, president-general of the ANC in the 1950's and Nobel Peace Prize winner in 1961, and an important pillar in the movement for freedom, working alongside her husband. She was the leader of the women's wing of the ANC. In that same tribute, Mandela speaks glowingly of this woman's contribution to the liberation struggle: "Mama Nokukhanya was one of those leaders who contributed to our struggle away from the limelight. But she will go down in history as a member of the battalions of resilient women whose spirit could not be broken by the pain and suffering which the apartheid government imposed on them. She was a woman of rare and distinct qualities" ("President Mandela's Speech"). Mandela recognizes in this tribute that women contributed to the struggle, but they did so "away from the limelight." It takes a woman like Mhlophe to turn the lights on these mothers of the movement to reveal their place in history.

In reconstructing the history of women, though, Mhlophe agrees with other women of color that writers cannot look just high for women whose works are obvious and known to many. Barbara Christian, using Alice Walker's idea of searching for black women artists in the south among lowly, ordinary women like her mother who planted gardens, reinforces the idea of not only looking high but also looking low, supporting the idea of not leaving behind women of lower status (qtd. in DeShazer, *Women's Anthology* 352). In writing the history of South African women, Mhlophe includes those whose names do not appear in anybody's history books:

Maybe my voice would be carried by the wind
To reach all the other women
Whose names are not often mentioned
The ones who sell oranges and potatoes
So their children can eat and learn
The ones who scrub floors and polish executive desktops
In towering office blocks

While the city sleeps
The ones who work in overcrowded hospitals
Saving lives, cleaning bullet wounds and delivering new babies

And what of the women who are stranded in their homelands
With a baby in the belly and a baby on the back
While their men are sweating in the bowels of the earth?
(lines 48-57, 62-64)

The list will not be complete without including these nameless women who are distinguished more by their roles than by their names. In real life, they have been overlooked and their contributions marginalized; in her recollection of the past, they will not be forgotten but "celebrated and made to shine." Mhlophe subtly critiques classism where women of a particular class or economic background assume the right to advocate for these women because they lack wealth or education to speak for themselves. These women cannot be excluded because they "scrub floors and polish executive desktops." To assign worth to the contributions of the named women and ignore those of the nameless women will be to perpetuate the injustices inflicted on women in society, or in other words to continue apartheid for these women.

Say No

Mhlophe takes protest to another level in her poem "Say No," a poem that chronicles the history of apartheid, especially in relation to the treatment of blacks, the lowest on the color pole. Using a belligerent tone, the speaker employs repetition and a digging up of painful historical images associated with apartheid to fire up black women to resist apartheid. In the words of Barbara Christian, Mhlophe has to "'rememory'—reconstruct [their] past" (qtd. in DeShazer, *Women's Anthology* 352). It is interesting to note that the oppressors are not identified specifically except with the pronoun *they*: "*they* rape your daughter" but *they* is not reserved for white oppressors alone, for in the last stanza, *they* refers to patriarchy of the liberation movement in South Africa who confined women to the back seat of the liberation movement. In her introductory remarks on "Resistance and Transformation," DeShazer observes that resistance is not merely a response to abuse of power but also "an active quest for fairness" (*Women's Anthology* 1079). Thus Mhlophe's poem is her attempt to empower women to seek an end to these various forms of oppression under apartheid. Both colored men and women have suffered under this racist regime, for as she writes, their sons who are jobless because of limitations on black employment have been insulted with demeaning words like *tsosti*, a term in South Africa that means "young black urban criminals," and their husbands, grown men who are in their 60s, have been humiliated by being called "boys." This type of degradation of grown men is familiar to black men during slavery in the southern states of America:

>   Say No, Black Woman
>   Say No
>   When they call your jobless son
>   a Tsotsi*
>   Say No
>   *young black urban criminal, used as a racial insult
>   Say No, Black Woman
>   Say No
>   When they call
>   Your husband at the age of 60
>   a boy
>   Say No

In contrast to the negative appellation given to black men and youth, white women and white men are referred to as "madams" and "Baas" respectively. An Afrikaner word which means "boss," baas was the term used by blacks and coloreds in referring to their white masters. Black South Africans who fight oppressive laws and demand better working conditions in the work place are referred to as "terrorists," but among non-blacks, these people are "trade unionists." The speaker calls on black women to refuse using such monikers for the very people who disrespect them.

The memories that the poet goes back to are painful ones, but to build a better future, a future devoid of the horrid events of the past, the poet must dig up the pain and bring it up to be dealt with and healed. One area of struggle uniquely experienced by women under various forms of oppression is sexual assault by their masters. Slave women experienced rape at the hands of their masters who believed the women's bodies were to be at their disposal. The notable example is the case of Harriet Jacobs (Linda Brendt in her autobiography *Incidents in the Life of a Slave Girl*) who resisted the advances of her married slave master to the extent that she lived in a crawl space for seven years. She refused to have no agency in making her choice of a partner; in fact, she would choose to sleep with a white attorney to have that agency rather than be forced to sleep with her boss. Mhlophe calls on mothers whose daughters are raped while in detention and then called "whore" to resist this type of violence against their children.

In the last stanza of her poem, Mhlophe addresses one of the difficult issues in liberation struggles—gender, patriarchy and sexism. Generally, political activism, civil rights and liberation struggles are considered predominantly men's sphere, even when women have participated in resistance movements. When books are written about liberation enterprises, women's roles are minimized, their contributions appearing negligible. As to leadership roles, women seem to be barred from assuming them in such organizations. There may be a Mama Nokukhanya Luthuli, but she is the wife of one of the leaders of the movement and a "mother" of the nation—a designation which limits her sphere of influence to women and youth. Thus she oversees other women, not men. Even women who have risen to prominence like Mamphela Ramphele are still remembered in their relationship to men, so Ramphele was the "political mistress" of Steve Biko, the anti-apartheid activist who died in police custody in 1977. This situation is not limited to women from developing countries but to women all over the world. In the United States, for example, African American women also complained about getting a "back seat / in the liberation wagon" (lines). During the Civil Rights Movement of the mid-twentieth century, for example, names like Ella Baker, Septima Clark, Amelia Boynton Robinson or Fannie Lou Hamer were not household names, and still today, remain unfamiliar to the majority of Americans of any color.

For Mhlophe, though, if there is one area which calls for resistance from women, it is this very one of gender inequality in the freedom struggles where black women are not treated as equals to black men. This particular "apartheid" calls for a "BIG NO" as opposed to the smaller "Say No" repeated over twenty times in the poem. She has little tolerance for this kind of treatment and reserves the harshest protest to its manifestation in liberation struggles.

One way to underscore the oppressors' negative treatment of black South Africans is through the use of irony. In the opening sentence of her book on irony, Gloria Onyeoziri notes that in African literature irony is a "response to an oppressor convinced of his superior wisdom" (1) a way of challenging his preconceived notions about the oppressed. For example by juxtaposing "rape" which is what the speaker calls the treatment of black women and "whore," which is the white men's name for these black women, the speaker challenges the morality of these white men who rape these women and in a twist of logic call them immoral!

Mhlophe calls on these women to resist on the behalf of men because they are deeply committed to the liberation of South Africa from under the grips of apartheid. Black women, as Kuzwayo notes, have shown "outstanding tenacity against great odds" (qtd. in DeShazer, *Women's Anthology*, 1116), thanks to the legacy of strong black women in their history who have paved the way, sometimes with their blood.

The Dancer, Sometimes When It Rains & Sitting Alone Thinking

Not all poems by Mhlophe are explicit in their resistance to apartheid. Sometimes the protest comes in the form of a recollection of a primeval past that juxtaposes the Edenic with the crude realities of the present. At other times, protest is lodged in a poem that seems to be a simple recollection from her childhood, but the poet is able to weave in resistance to the oppressive system of apartheid even in these poems.

One such poem is "The Dancer," a more personal poem where a daughter remembers her mother's past. This poem is said to have been performed in front of the Truth and Reconciliation Committee (TRC) on July 28, 1997, after two women complained about the absence of women's voices at these hearings (Singh & Chetty 63). The women's complaint was that given the traumatic nature of women's experiences under apartheid and given the format of the hearings, women were not going forward to testify. Thus special hearings were conducted for women, and Mhlophe, whose poetry addresses women's concerns, was asked to perform at such the hearings. Singh & Chetty correctly remark that "The Dancer" is a poem which has "as much to do with the narrative of communal loss as it does with the narrative of loss between mother and daughter" (63). The speaker begins by recalling her mother's past, nostalgically looking back to a time of relative peace, allowing her mother to be a wedding dance, shuffling her feet in the sand as she helped couples celebrate the beginning of their lives together. "Mama / they tell me you were a dancer / they tell me you had long / beautiful legs to carry your graceful body" (lines 1-4). Unfortunately, these times are part of history, a memory of things lost in the midst of apartheid: "o hee! how I wish I was there to see you / they tell me you were a pleasure to see" (lines 24-25). The daughter has to be told about her mother's past because she is ignorant of that lifestyle in her present, and their diametrically opposed worlds create what DeShazer refers to as "a terrible irony that connects mother and daughter" (*A Poetics* 209). The reality for the speaker is far from what used to happen in the past, for the weddings have given way to funerals, and unlike her mother, a wedding dancer, she has become a funeral dancer: "I don't know for sure what a wedding dancer is / there are no more weddings / but many, many funerals" (lines 29-31). The would-be brides and grooms are the ones being buried in the violent atmosphere of apartheid. The singing, dancing and fast runs with coffins at these funerals are nothing like the slow, graceful dances at weddings, and the joys and smiles at weddings are replaced by "eyes full of vengeance" (36), to fight the system that produces funerals and robs them of joyous occasions like weddings.

In "Sometimes When it Rains," the reader may assume the poem will focus on childhood remembrances and the naïve questions that ran through a child's mind, such as "when will I grow?" or wondering why people wear clothes. But the questions progress from "easy" to "complex," ordinary to political when the speaker starts wondering about societal issues like the homeless and the poor:

I think of people
who have nowhere to go
no home of their own
and no food to eat
only rain water to drink
(lines 36-40)

In apartheid South Africa, these conditions were aggravated by government policies that denied access to decent accommodation for Black people who worked in the cities and were not allowed in certain areas because of their skin color. Even a child knew something was wrong when people went hungry and had nowhere to live.

Again, race issues come to her mind as she remembers "illegal" job seekers (mainly blacks), being chased in the rain and "dodging police vans" since they do not have the right to be in the city looking for jobs to take care of themselves and their families. Putting *illegal* in quotation marks reveals the speaker's challenge of designation for jobless men looking for honest work. From her concern for South African racial situation where jobless people cannot even look for jobs without harassment from the police, the speaker broadens her concern beyond the borders of South Africa to show her solidarity and commitment to those who are "life prisoners / in all the jails of the world" (lines 58-59). These are not necessarily political prisoners like Mandela and other men on Robben Island; these are people who are trapped by the workings of race, class and gender and cannot see "the rainbow at the end of the rain" (line 61). There is nothing to smile about in their lives.

Gender issues also occupy the speaker's thoughts as she thinks of mothers "who give birth in **squatter** camps / under **plastic** shelters / At the **mercy** of cold angry winds" (lines 45-47). The situation of these pregnant women contrasts sharply with that of their white counterparts who generally give birth in sanitized rooms, attended to by trained health personnel. These black women don't even give birth in homes or in rooms but in make-shift shelters. Mhlophe's focus on gender issues is clearly illustrated in another poem she read before the special hearings for women at the TRC, "Sitting Alone Thinking." As Singh and Chetty note, Mhlophe has the ability to insert the "narrative of women's experience into the literary and political arena" (64), and this poem intertwines the personal with the political. In the midst of a hectic schedule, this "busy woman" finds the time to sit for a short time to think and keep up with the "fast world" around her. In the world of the speaker, thinking about the larger issues of the world is not the prerogative of men only but also of women who have to deal with the "hustle and bustle" of the day's activities. The question she ponders in her mind has nothing to do with domestic activities of her day; her thoughts turn to politics: "Would Mr. President be a better man / If he had a womb and breasts full of milk?" Lodged in this question are issues of male leadership, especially that of the apartheid regime and its violent impact on society. Under this regime, the number of children jailed in the name of "peace, law and order" has gone up; even ten-year olds are not exempt from tear gas and bullet wounds, leading the speaker to ask whether a womb and breasts full of milk would mollify a male president and bring humanitarian consideration to the political process.

Conclusion

These poems of resistance, as Tim Woods notes in his book, are not meant to merely chronicle the evils of apartheid. Indeed, Mhlophe and other South African writers are not listing these to inform the world of the many sufferings black people underwent: Writing about the poetry of Es'kia Mphahlele, another South African writer, Tim Woods states that the significance of protest poetry "lies in the ways that the poetry strives for a new organic link between the past and the future that has been arrested by apartheid; and the significance of this 'future' lies in its political [visualization] of a remembered past. The poetry of writers under apartheid, such as Gcina Mhlophe's, has been referred to as "a cultural necessity. It is a political necessity. It is also a psychological necessity" (Woods 197). These poets have to go back in memory to relieve their past to help them shape their future. Even in post-apartheid South Africa, protests have not completely disappeared. As recently as November 2011, the South African government decided to impose limitations on freedom of expression as its way of "protecting information." The government will criminalize any leak of sensitive information, including leaks by journalists, sentencing violators to twenty-five years in prison. Groups opposed to this move by the government, like the National Press club, called for a protest on a day called "Black Tuesday." The protestors go back to the past to recall a similar situation from the apartheid era in 1977, after Steve Biko had died in police custody, when the government took two newspapers out of circulation and banned 19 black consciousness movements. Protestors wore black then to express their indignation at the apartheid government. They plan to use same tactics against their own government. Miners have been fighting over wages with management as of this writing and have taken to protests, and on August 16, 2012, 34 miners were shot and killed by police. One of the trade union leaders makes this observation about protests: "Protests in South Africa, not only trade union protests but community protests as well, have been getting increasingly violent and angry. [...] We're sitting on a ticking time bomb. And what happened on the 16th of August is the bomb exploded" (Craven, qtd. in Wilson). Sachs correctly notes that for the writer to sit on the fence, the fence must be metaphorically speaking, stable ("Dogs"). So long as the fence is wobbly, writers like Gcina Mhlophe will not sit down passively and watch the abuses to freedom.

Works Cited

- August, Tyrone. "Interview with Gcina Mhlope." In *Politics and Performance: Theatre, Poetry and Song in Southern Africa*. Liz Gunner, ed. Johannesburg: Witwatersrand UP, 1994. Print.
- Christian, Barbara. "The Highs and Lows of Black Feminist Criticism." In DeShazer. *The Longman Anthology of Women's Literature*. 347-352. Print.
- DeShazer, Mary K. *A Poetics of Resistance: Women Writing in El Salvador, South Africa and the United States*. Ann Arbor: U of Michigan P, 1994. Print.
- ___. "Resistance and Transformation." *The Longman Anthology of Women's Literature*. Ed. Mary K. DeShazer. New York: Longman, 2001. Print.
- Dixon, Melvin. "The Black Writer's Use of Memory." *History and Memory in African-American Culture*. Eds. Geneviève Fabre and Robert O'Meally. New York: Oxford UP, 1994. Print
- "The Dogs Bark and Bite, even in Cartoons: Justice Albie Sachs on Free Speech and Dignity." AfriCartoons.com.April 2011.Web.14 Sept.2012.
- Gunner, Liz, ed. *Politics and Performance: Theatre, Poetry and Song in Southern Africa*. Witwatersrand: Witwatersrand UP, 1994. Print.

- Gunner, Liz _ _ _."*Remaking the Warrior?* The Role of Orality in the Liberation Struggle and in Post-Apartheid South Africa." Brown, Duncan, ed. *Oral Literature and Performance in South Africa.* Oxford: James Currey, 1999, 50-60, Print

- Onyeoziri, Gloria. *Shaken Wisdom: Irony and Meaning in Postcolonial African Fiction.* Charlottesville: U of Virginia P, 2011. Print.

- Opland, Jeff. *Xhosa Oral Poetry: Aspects of a Black South African Tradition.* Cambridge: Cambridge UP, 1983. Print.

- Peterson, Bhekizizwe. "Apartheid and the Political Imagination in Black South African Theatre." *Journal of Southern African Studies* 16.2 (June 1990): 229-245. *Academic Search Premier.* Web. 01 Sept. 2012.

- President Mandela's Speech at Funeral of Nokukhanya Luthuli. Issued by ANC. 22 Dec. 1996. Web. 02 Sept. 2012.

- Singh, Jaspal K. & Rajendra Chetty, eds. *Trauma, Resistance, Reconstruction in Post-1994 South African Writing.* New York: Peter Lang, 2010. Google Book Search. Web. 01 Sept. 2012.

- Smith, David. " 'Black Tuesday's' Protests to Mark Likely Passing of South African Secrecy Bill." *Guardian.* 21 Nov. 2011. Web. 10 Sept. 2012.

- "South African Women Protest in Miniskirts." *3News.com.* 19 Feb. 2012. Web. 14 Sept. 2012.

- Sustar, Lee, and Aisha Karim, eds. *Poetry & Protest: A Dennis Brutus Reader.* Chicago: Haymarket Books, 2006. Print.

- Wiesel, Elie. *From the Kingdom of Memory. Reminiscences.* New York: Summit Books, 1990. Print.

- Wilson, Gretchen. "Four Wounded in South African Gold Mine Protest." *Marketplace.* 4 Sept. 2012. Web. 10 Sept. 2012.

- Woods, Tim. *African Pasts: Memory and History in African literatures.* Manchester: Manchester UP, 2007. Print.

- Yankah, Kwesi. "The Making and Breaking of Kwame Nkrumah: The Role of Oral Poetry." In *Ghanaian Literatures.* Richard K. Priebe, ed. Westport, CT: Praeger, 1988. Print.

Section Four

Trauma

Chapter 7

Veiling the Past: Memory and Identity in Edwidge Danticat's *The Dew Breaker*

Adaku T. Ankumah

Introduction

The past has presented a challenge to postmodern writers, a paradox of some sort. For some the past has its glorious achievements, its high points that define individuals, cultures, nations. Various groups and nations celebrate centennials and millenniums, as individuals celebrate anniversaries to mark the progress made from one point in time to the next. In 1976, for example, America celebrated 200 years of her existence, proud of her achievement to finally reach the pinnacle of success. Though there may be low points, the overall feeling is about the accomplishments of the period. In recent years, many writers and nations have taken an interest in examining the past in relation to the present and in the formation of identity. For instance, in the 1990's, French historian Pierre Nora, edited several volumes titled *Lieux de Mémoire,* a monumental undertaking using events and locations in French history to build what one writer refers to as the "collective consciousness on a national scale" (Vidal-Naquet, qtd in Ivry). Even Pope John Paul II, known mainly for his writing on religious topics, joined in the on-going discussions about memory and identity in his 2005 work with identical title: *Memory and Identity: Conversations at the Dawn of a New Millennium*. In this book, the Pope recalls attending a symposium on Identity and Change, where Paul Ricœur discussed the two major poles of remembering and forgetting.

Indeed, this interest in the past follows on the heels of some major rumblings in the twentieth century - from two major wars and hundreds of other smaller wars, to holocausts, genocides from civil wars, etc. For survivors of such atrocities like Elie Wiesel, the resilience of the victims comes from the desire never to forget what he refers to, in the case of the Jewish people, as their obsession with memory (9). Indeed, that obsession with memory comes through the entire corpus of Wiesel's works, both fiction and non-fiction. He makes an important reference to memory in a 1987 speech he gave in the Reichstag, Germany, at a conference to plan a museum in Wannsee, the very town where Nazis decided to wipe out Jews: "We remember Auschwitz and all that it symbolizes because we believe that, in spite of the past and its horrors, the world is worthy of salvation; and salvation, like redemption, can be found only in memory" (200-1). The emphasis on learning from the past has led to many studies even in atrocities of the past. For example, there exist some graduate programs including a PhD program in Holocaust and Genocide Studies and a Psychology of Genocide program (Clark University, Worcester, MA). The goal of such programs is preventative: "Never again!" Such atrocities never happen again and the way to ensure this is to nip them in the bud before they get out of control.

For Africans in the Diaspora, remembering plays a huge role in dealing with the present. The past includes traumatic events like slavery, colonialism and internal conflicts which have deeply impacted and continue to affect the lives of many. In writing about the African situation, Tim Woods notes that colonialism left such "indelible and distressing memories - memories to which the nation, continent and its subjects or citizens continually return" (7). In fact, the main contention in his book is that "African literatures represent history through the twin matrices of memory and trauma... [and] are continually preoccupied with exploring modes of representation to 'work-through' [the] different traumatic colonial pasts" (1). The past, then, becomes a site of contestation as writers confront the fragmentation and disintegration, the things-fall-apart conditions left behind by colonizers and dictators around the world to help forge a future that is "whole." In fact, the literatures produced by Africans in the diaspora are greatly impacted by these two occurrences. From the early writings of slaves in America, like Phyllis Wheatley's "On Being Brought to America" to slave narratives of the nineteenth century to even the works of Nobel Prize winner Toni Morrison, slavery underscores the works of these authors. Indeed, her 2008 publication of *A Mercy*, a novel which revisited slavery with a different emphasis, was a surprise to some of her critics who think she has exhausted the topic with publications like *Beloved*. In a speech first given in honor of Martin Luther King, Jr., Day at Washington and Lee University in January 2008, critic Charles Johnson provoked audience (and later readers alike) with his suggestion to novelists (like Toni Morrison) to "consider leaving slavery and its long aftermath behind" since in his view, a constant focus on the past, "[emphasizing] the experience of victimization" (1) is outmoded in the twenty-first century. After all, we are almost five centuries removed from these events. Why beat on a dead horse? Toni Morrison, however, is of the opinion that dealing with the horrible past, instead of repressing it, is exactly what minorities relegated to the fringes of society need to do in order to move forward. Unfortunately, veiling these painful issues is also what the perpetrators want to see happen. In an essay on memory, Morrison notes: "My job becomes how to rip that veil drawn over 'proceedings too terrible to relate.' The exercise is also critical for any person who is black, or...marginalized...for historically, we were seldom invited to participate in the discourse even when we were its topic" (191). The writer's task, then, is to expose the evils of the past because such exposure is vital, essential for the mental health of victims of such atrocities. To keep the veil in place, to use Morrison's metaphor, is to side with the perpetrators and to deny the victims an opportunity to deal with this trauma.

In the same way, African writers have explored colonialism and its aftermath in works from earlier works like *Things Fall Apart* by Achebe, Nugi wa Thiong'o's novels like *Weep Not, Child, Devil on the Cross* and *Matigari* more recent works like Chimamanda Adichie's *Half of a Yellow Sun*, a work based on the civil war in Nigeria - the Biafran War. Asked about why she wanted to write a novel on the Biafran War, Adichie connects her writing this novel on issue of identity: "because I wanted to engage with my history in order to make sense of my present... because the brutal bequests of colonialism make me angry [...] because I don't ever want to forget" (Interview). After publishing his signature novel, Achebe was able to articulate the role of the novelist in the emerging independent nations. Using the language of the colonizers, he answered the distorted versions of colonial discourse from writers such as Joseph Conrad in *Heart of Darkness* and Joyce Cary in *Mister Johnson* with a description of an Igbo community, the imaginary Umuofia. He does not allow the redefinition of that culture by the colonizers to deter him from tapping into the historical memory of his society to write their version of their story in such novels as *Things Fall Apart* and *Arrow of God*. Ngugi wa Thiong'o has also used colonialism, the armed resistance against the British appropriation of Kenyan lands more commonly known as the Mau Mau uprising, and the neocolonialism of post-independent Kenya as material for his creative work. His novel *Matigari* examines the dichotomy between the goals of the Mau Mau freedom fighters and those of the new elite who had reaped the harvest of what the 1950's fighter fought for. Having survived the struggle for independence, Matigari whose name literally means "the patriots who survived the bullets," returns from his hide-out in the mountains to search for his family and claim the material things he thought belonged to the workers after the struggle for independence.

Other writers in the African Diaspora, like Haitian-American Edwidge Danticat, have tapped into the collective memory of their people to write their stories. Danticat concurs with Morrison's view about ripping the veil on the past, for she believes, like Robert Stone, that our problem today is that we suffer from "de-storification", disconnecting from our past which leads to lives which are less meaningful. Speaking about her dad at the Bucknell University Forum at Lewisburg, Pennsylvania, on April 12, 2011, Danticat comments about his terminal illness and the power of remembering in storytelling that helped him cope with dying: "Because he told these stories at an important point in his life, his heart was lighter.... We tell our stories to become whole. We tell stories to live, to connect with one another and to build community" ("Storytelling").

As a novelist, she revisits her home country in most of her works, allowing her characters to relive painful experiences of the past to allow them to deal with the present. Her highly celebrated first novel, *Breath, Eyes, Memory* examines memory at two levels: the individual and the collective. The novel centers around twelve-year old Sophie Caco, whose mother, after being raped twelve years earlier in her native country Haiti, leaves her to go to New York Martine's rape shows the intersection between the personal and the collective, for the rapist was a tonton macoute, one of the militia men of former president Francois Duvalier ("Papa Doc"), ready to carry out gruesome acts of violence and not answerable to any established legal system in the country. Martine eventually escapes the physical location of her rape, Haiti, but unfortunately, she is unable to escape the emotional baggage she carried from Haiti to the United States. She relives her rape every night, making it hard for her to settle down with her lawyer boyfriend. When she finds herself pregnant, she tells her daughter that it feels like "getting raped every night" (190). Unable to deal with this situation, she liberates herself through suicide.

Danticat further elucidates on the significance of memory in the lives of Haitians in her book *Create Dangerously*.

Grappling with memory is, I believe, one of many complicated Haitian obsessions. We have, it seems, a collective agreement to remember our triumphs and gloss over our failures. Thus, we speak of the Haitian revolution as if it happened yesterday but we rarely speak of the slavery that prompted it. Our paintings show glorious Eden-like African jungles but never the Middle Passage. In order to shield our shattered collective psyche from a long history of setbacks and disillusionment, our constant roller-coaster ride between saviors and dictators, homespun oppression and foreign tyranny, we cultivate communal and historical amnesia, continually repeating cycles that we never see coming until we are reliving similar horrors. (63-4)

In this excerpt, Danticat reveals one of the complexities associated with memory: what we choose to remember and what we choose to forget. Human beings tend to be selective in what they remember. To evoke pleasant memories helps us to feel good about the present, and so we capitalize on the positive memories. Unpleasant ones, however, are tucked away so as not to remind us of past failures. The attempt to bury the unpalatable past or to manipulate it in the present to relieve guilty consciences raises a number of problems for memory studies. There are those who deny that horrific deeds like the Holocaust actually happened, and there are writers and editors of history books who sanitize unpleasant events from their works. As Edward Saïd notes, people "refashion" memory to "give themselves a coherent identity, a national narrative, a place in the world, for national history, is "never neutral" (179).Thus we develop what Danticat refers to as "communal and historical amnesia," a deliberate repression of painful memories.

In her novel *The Dew Breaker*, Danticat examines this issue of cultural amnesia. In the real world, scientists know what happens to individuals who suffer from memory disorders like dementia or amnesia and therefore cannot remember their stories. Unfortunately, life starts deteriorating, moving towards disintegration. For those who deliberately choose not to remember the past because of the pain associated with it, voluntary amnesia does not erase the past, but it leads to a present that is even more painful and fragmented, and the dew breaker and his family learn this painful lesson in Edwidge Danticat's *The Dew Breaker*.

Memory and Identity

Memory has become a significant issue in our time because of its close ties to identity formation. In fact, several authors have delved into the issue of recollecting the past to help forge an identity in the present. John Paul II notes from his participation in the Identity and

Change Symposium that he left with an understanding that "it is through memory that our sense of identity forms and defines itself in the personal psyche" (144). John Paul II recollects some painful events in Poland's history, but he also notes that the "beginnings of renewal" or the "seeds of rebirth" (141) lie in bringing up the past and its failures and opening a path to recovery. Tim Woods reinforces the connection between memory and identity in *African Pasts: Memory and History in African Literatures* when he writes that "[m]ost invocations about memory are part of a discourse about identity. [...] Memory and identity serve to reinforce one another, as people's sense of who they are is closely linked to what they think about memory" (30). From these authors, it is clear that without a recollection of the past, it is impossible to operate in the present.

In Danticat's works, some of these are shared memories connected to the painful history of her country of birth, Haiti. *The Dew Breaker* is made up of 9 stories with the unifying character being the dew beaker, the former Macoute torturer who murdered many people in Haiti, including his wife's preacher stepbrother, his last victim. Having escaped from Haiti to New York, the dew breaker sheds his identity as a "fat" prison guard who killed many people and forges a new identity for himself as a former prisoner, husband, a father, a landlord, a barber in East Flatbush, New York. Ka, the daughter born in America, is frustrated as a child of Haitian immigrants who knows very little about Haiti; in fact, she has never been there. She has no connection to her past to help her understand her present. When she introduces herself at the beginning of the first story, she immediately remarks that she has never been to Haiti, the birthplace of her parents. As she puts it, "I was a part of them. Some may say I belonged to them. But I wasn't them" (25). She cannot fully identify with them because she is disconnected from their past in Haiti. Ka cannot fully construct her identity because of this missing link from her parents' past. She has been successful in constructing an American identity: she is an educated single woman who teaches school and also an aspiring sculptor attempting her first sculpture. Thus when her father requests to talk to her but falls into the habitual silences she associates with him, she starts to wonder: "Is he going to explain why he and my mother have no close friends, why they've never had anyone over to the house, why they never speak of any relatives in Haiti or anywhere else, or have never returned there or, even after I learned Creole from them, have never taught me anything else about the country beyond what I could find on my own, on television, in newspapers, in books?" (21).

What Ka does not know is that the habitual silences of her father is an attempt to repress his memory, the secrets of his past life in Haiti as a member of the feared Tonton Macoutes, the military arm of the dictatorship controlled by father and then son, the Duvaliers. In 1959, François Duvalier, "Papa Doc," established his own militia, inflicting all kinds of pain on citizens- from rape, torture, murder - in order to shore up his regime that was failing the people. In fact, it is impossible to recount Haiti's history without recalling the ghosts of its political history: Papa and Baby Doc and the dreaded Tonton Macoutes are described by Abbott as the "bogeymen of Haitian folk belief who prowled at night in search of bad little boys and girls whom they thrust into their *macoutes*, the straw satchels peasants carry" (qtd. in Chancy 94). These macoutes do not simply exist in folk imagination and are not throwing people in straw satchels. They are real live people armed with guns and who leave devastation and death after their nocturnal activities. In *The Dew Breaker*, an octogenarian who left Haiti 30 years ago and was a prisoner of the dew breaker, is still haunted by memory of this man whose face she could no longer recollect and who "thought he was God" (198-9).

Remembering and talking about these traumatic events, we are told by health professionals, is the best approach towards healing. In his book *The Spirit of Mourning*, Paul Connerton supports this position with a quotation from Judith Herman: "Remembering and telling the truth about terrible events are prerequisites for the restoration of social order and for the healing of the individual" (33-34). In the section "The Funeral Singer," three Haitian women who find themselves as immigrants in NYC narrate their stories of how they ended up in NYC as they seek restoration from this nightmare, and in each case, the hated macoutes were involved. Mariselle, the wife of a painter left after her husband painted "an unflattering portrait of the president," and he was not allowed to walk away from the show but was shot dead (172). Freda, who refused to accept an invitation to sing, lost her father as the macoutes carried him away one day. For her family, he returned, but as a changed man with no teeth left and "a mouth full of blood." As the daughter puts it, "In one night, they'd turn him into an old, ugly man" (172). Ashamed of himself, he went out to sea the next night, vanishing forever. Rézia, the third woman, was raped by one of these uniformed men. Thus for these women who have suffered in various degrees at the hands of the macoutes, they share their stories, laugh and cry together as they attempt to put those "terrible days" behind them and face a future still uncertain without their certificates to find good jobs. In remembering, these women dig up their pain, their hurt, their loneliness and fear; in their mutual sharing, they understand each other—who they are and what they have been through. They find community in their shared suffering, an identity with others who have gone through similar experiences in Haiti.

Living the Past in the Present

For those who have been victims of such brutality sanctioned by their governments, constructing a new life and forgetting the past is easier said than done. Having physically escaped the painful *lieux de memoire* as Nora terms it, they cannot escape the mental and emotional trauma and the memory of the perpetrators, like Martine couldn't in *Breath Eyes, Memory*. They still hope for justice to be served and so cannot let go. Berber Bervenage, a researcher in the area of history and memory notes that for these people the past gets "stuck" in the present, retaining a "haunting presence" (217). Indeed, for the victims of the atrocities of the Duvaliers' Haiti, abandoning the lieux de memoire and relocating to a new country and city does not erase the pain of the past. Having left Haiti to escape the terror and nightmares of the past, they find their thoughts and focus on the perpetrators, looking for them on the faces of the many Haitians in their new communities in New York. As Anne and her family sit through a Christmas Eve church service watching the priest burn incense, the daughter, who does not have faith in God like her mother and is a self-declared atheist, starts talking to her dad. Anne, wanting to shut her daughter down, finds out from her husband that her daughter believes she has spotted a Haitian man, Emmanuel Constant, wanted for crimes against the Haitian People, and whose picture has been on flyers stapled to lampposts a month before for "torture, rape and murder of 5,000 people" when he ran a militia called Front for the Advancement and Progress for Haiti (78). After the ouster of the Haitian president, Constant and his followers torched neighborhoods with gasoline, shooting residents, skinning faces of the dead to make it hard for them to be identified. He fled to New York after the president returned from exile. For Anne and her dew breaker husband, looking at the "Wanted" flyers in front of their store is difficult; they can only cast cursory glances, for fear the next poster on a lamppost will be one of the husband, whose thirty-seven-year old crimes have followed him to his new country. This desire to keep his anonymity is reinforced by his weight loss (80 pounds), change in name, birthplace and their decision not to get close to any of the Haitians who may ask too many questions. Ka is aware that the father lies constantly, choosing different provinces as his birthplace to hide his identity as he did when they visited the Fonteneaus to deliver the sculpture.

Unfortunately, the perpetrators of evil cannot always hide their past. After World War II, though many Nazi war criminals were successful at escaping justice, fleeing to other countries around the world, (South America, for example) and changing their identities, a few like Adolf Eichman and Josef Mengele, were captured. Through the hard work and determination of people, especially victims of the Holocaust who chose never to forget because they were haunted by the cries and torments of the dead, these men were forced to confront their ugly past. Thus "memory," notes Wiesel, "restores absence to presence and the dead to the living" (200). The apprehension and trial of these men were one way to unveil the past and redeem the future from such horrible past. The process is not without pain for the victims, but it is in this very painful process that they find closure and healing.

The dew breaker cannot hide his past. His picture may not have been on poster, but the victims' families have not given up on breaking the silence and helping "the dead vanquish death" (Wiesel 21). They are haunted by the memory of their loved ones, brutally silenced by the weapons of these perpetrators of evil and so they seek liberation from their painful past and the possibility of rest after these many years of mental torment and anguish. The Haitian who identifies the dew breaker is Dany, the child and nephew of 3 victims. He is on a quest for a vacant room in the dew breaker-turned-barber's basement (105). The dew breaker tortured and killed his parents in a fire and blinded his aunt, his dad's older sister, some 25 years ago when he was 6 year old. Ten years after he left Haiti, Dany makes the long trip back to his village to tell Aunt Estina: "I found him. I found him in New York, the man who killed Papa and Manman and took your sight" (97). Dany has been focused on the parents, "not the way [they] had lived but the way they had died" (99). This present encounter brings the past back so powerfully and so painfully that Dany cannot sleep for months and yet he cannot stay away from the barber's shop - to get a good look at his face and confirm his suspicion. Dany's restlessness makes him sneak out 2 nights before leaving for Haiti, when the dew breaker's wife is away at a religious event, into the bedroom of the couple, to take a look at the murderer and choke him to death as he heard political prisoners were treated in the past or at least to find a reason for the gratuitous killings. Yet given this opportunity to kill his enemy, he freezes, not wishing to kill the wrong person or cause unnecessary grief for his family by killing the wrong person. Going back to Haiti is his attempt to deal with his inability to confront the killer and his present.

Reconciling the Past with the Present

The tension between the past and the present is so powerfully present in the dew breaker, the perpetrator of evil in the past. In a sense, he has committed the "perfect crimes" and escaped Haiti to live a new life in Brooklyn, New York - or so he will like to think. Though he is in a new environment, he cannot escape his past; thus he avoids any reproduction of himself. Ka informs us that her dad does not like his picture taken. Because of the scar on the face, he considers himself "ugly." When his obsessive wood-carver daughter attempts to capture him in a sculpture that she agrees to sell to the Haitian-born TV star Gabrielle Fonteneau, he steals the sculpture early one morning to dump it into a Florida lake. As he tells Ka, "I don't deserve a statue . . . not a whole one, at least. You see, Ka, your father was the hunter, he was not the prey" (20). The sculpture, which is the daughter's way of capturing the father's pre-American life in Haiti, is based on this lie that the father was a prisoner in Haiti. The daughter carves a naked figure kneeling, with downcast eyes - her representation of her dad's humiliation in a notorious Haitian prison. However, it was the dad who was humiliating others in prison

Another evidence of the tension between past and present is in his attraction towards museums. As Ka analyzes him after receiving the shattering news about his past, she ponders the contradiction in a man who does not want to be "permanently documented in any way" yet he enjoys the "permanent markers" about Egyptian civilization found in museums (34). Ka notices that he "[comes] alive Saturday mornings [...] mesmerized by the golden masks, the shawabtis and schist tablets" (13). Why is he so fascinated with these monuments to the past, when he is so desirous to forget his own past? In an examination of museums in a culture that tends to forget, Andreas Huyssen has this to say about the growing interest in museums: "Fundamentally dialectical, the museum serves both as a burial chamber of the past, with all that entails in terms of decay, erosion, forgetting - and as site of possible resurrections, however mediated and contaminated, in the eyes of the beholder" (15).

In the Ancient Egyptian rooms of the Brooklyn Museum, Ka's father can identify with the Egyptians: "They was like us," he tells Ka (12). He identifies with the statues too because they have missing body parts, and though he does not have missing body parts physically, morally he is not whole. He is missing some parts because of his wicked past as a Macoute. Among the dead, he is at home because of his evil past, but he is also concerned about his future in the world of the dead. If his heart is put on the scales of heaven, as the ancient Egyptians believe happens in the afterlife, will the weight be too heavy because of his evil past and thus prevent a resurrection into another life? In the Egyptian *Book of the Dead* and in his visits to that room in the museum, the dew breaker is seeking redemption. Before weighing the hearts, the dead are given a last chance to assert positively that they have done only good things in their lives. Thus the dead will say such things: "I am not a violent man .... I have made no one weep. I have never been angry without cause. I have never uttered lies. I have never slain any men or women. I have done no evil" (23). Ka's father loved to read this particular chapter to her as a girl, but he did not have a clear conscience, as Ka reminds him when she asks about "those nightmares" he used to have. As "contaminated" as he is, the dew breaker is looking for redemption and resurrection from his horrible past, from what he did to others. In finally telling Ka his story, he concludes with these words: "Ka, no matter what, I'm still your father, still your mother's husband. I would never do these things now" (24). This last statement is his confirmation of a "good life," that he has done only good things later in his life. He has shed the horrible past like a snake sheds its skin and thus he has hope of attaining a resurrection.

But there are physical connections to awaken the past he wants to forget, making him a prisoner of his past. The most obvious is the vicious scar, the "ropelike scar that runs from [his] right cheek down to the corner of his mouth, the only visible reminder of the year he spent in prison in Haiti" (5). The cut has been inflicted by his last victim, the bold, fearless critic of the government and his later to be brother-in-law. It is a scar he wishes he could rub away, to conceal with his hands to avoid the stares of strangers or to fabricate a lie to explain its existence, but he can't (32). His last victim, suspicious of the dew breaker's smile as he tries to explain his impending release, seizes a piece of wood from his disintegrated child's seat, throws it at the fat man with the intent of blinding him. He misses his target, but he leaves an indelible mark on his face. With his waning consciousness, the preacher is still satisfied with the mark he is leaving on the fat militia's face. The preacher prophesies, "Whenever people asked what happened to his face, he would have to tell a lie, a lie that would forever remind him of the truth" (228).

The most powerful physical reminder of his lurid past is the very presence of his wife, the half-sister of his last victim. They meet by accident, on the very night that the "fat man" arrests her older brother and later kills him. She dashes out into the streets in a white satin nightgown to enter Casernes prison, only to be stopped by the dew breaker who is bleeding from his wound. Her question, "What did they do to you?" is like music in his ears, the "most forgiving question he'd ever been asked" (237), setting him free from any responsibility. The question implies he is a victim, not a perpetrator, the hunted, not the hunter, the prisoner, not the brutal guard and allows him to hide his identity as a murderer: "I'm free," he said. "I finally escaped" (237). Later on when Ka hears about her father's violent past while on their Florida trip, her question to her mother is this: "Manman, how do you love him?" (24). The relationship between the couple, the narrator tells us, started as a "benevolent collaboration, a conspirational friendship" which metamorphosed into "love . . . a strained kind of attachment" (240-1). They have become a "society of two," in Ka's words, "sharing a series of private codes and associations, a past that even if I'd been born in the country of their birth, I still wouldn't have known, couldn't have known, thoroughly" (25). Initially, they needed each other: the dew breaker needed assistance for his bleeding wound and Anne needed help locating her preacher brother. It is a relationship which operates on a "Don't-ask don't-tell" principle, after her husband lied about the situation, claiming he had only arrested the preacher, handed him over to another, and the preacher killed himself. Anne does not believe the story, but she does not challenge it either. Instead, they settle into silence, what Connerton refers to as the "silence of suspicion . . . the silence before the unspeakable" (54). The break in this silence is from the birth of their daughter, for it is hard to maintain silence with a baby around.

A Fragmented Future

In the end, the dew breaker realizes that '[f]reedom could be found only in acknowledging the scars of one's history, not in escaping from it" (Roth, qtd. in Woods 73). After keeping this secret from his grown daughter, he chooses what his wife considers the perfect setting - a trip to sunny Florida with Ka to deliver a sculpture to the Haitian TV star - to ask her for "Yon ti koze, a little chat" (13), a conversation he conducts mainly in Creole because his tongue "is too heavy in English to say things like this, especially older things" (17). As the father unveils the past to his daughter, Ka finds herself unprepared for this avalanche of evil from his past. Hearing the dad's declaration that he will not do such things in the present gives Ka, whose identity has been threatened by this confession, hope and gives her a *tell-me-that-it-ain't-so moment*: "It was my first inkling that maybe my father was wrong in his own representation of his former life, that maybe his past offered more choices than being either hunter or prey" (24). Ka is not ready to claim a new identity as the daughter of a former murderer.

This feeling of hope does not last long, for as she calls her mother in Brooklyn from Lakeland, Florida, and processes the revelation from the past, she feels frustration, anger, resentment, a feeling of not being in control anymore: "As my mother is speaking, this feeling comes over me that I sometimes have when I'm carving, this sensation that my hands don't belong to me at all, that something else besides my brain and muscles is moving my fingers, something bigger and stronger than myself, an invisible puppet master over whom I have no control" (25). She is not prepared for this revelation, and her mother's explanation that the two of them, "[y]ou and me, we save him... You, me, we make him take root" (25) does not make any sense at all to her. She cannot reconcile her life at present with this gruesome past; her fairly comfortable, middle-class, respectable existence has been shattered and she feels "betrayed" (26): first by her mother for not understanding her confusion and secondly, her mother failing to understand that this revelation this late in her life was totally unnecessary. It affects her identity. As she notes, her "life could have gone on fine without [her] knowing these types of things about [her] father" (26). Kaka's inability to accept this new identity leads her to disconnect from her mother: first physically when she hangs up the telephone. All the mother hears at her end is "a strange mechanical voice . . . telling her "to hang up and try again" (241). The physical is quickly connected to the metaphorical. Her mother immediately feels the alienation the silence on the other end brings. The narrator tells us that Anne had hoped to end the conversation with "something like 'You are mine and I love you'" (242). Instead of the two talking, Anne feels instantly that "her daughter was already gone, lost, accidentally or purposely" (241).

Ka's relationship with her dad is now similar to that of the missing art work lying at the bottom of "muddy and dark" waters of a Florida lake. It was not a perfect art work, "rough and not too detailed, minimalist at best" (6). This description can be applied to their relationship—not perfect, with a few cracks. Unfortunately, the cracks absorb too much water, splitting the wood and causing it to sink to the bottom. Their relationship too has absorbed too much of the murky past, causing it to disappear. On their short drive to the hotel, her father, who normally comments on her driving is silent; communication is impossible under these circumstances. Ka, though, doesn't close the door permanently to a restoration with her parents. She convinces herself that she can pick up the conversation with her mother "at will, in a few minutes, a few hours, a few days, even a few years. Whenever I'm ready" (26). Will it be that easy? Could her shattered identity be put together again or as in Humpty Dumpty's situation, "All the king's horses and all the king's men" can't put this family back together again. Her dad's refusal to open up to his past earlier, his closing the door on his past for over three decades has helped hoist a curtain of silence.

Conclusion

The end of this text raises questions about the "blessing" of memory, as some writers consider memory. Elie Wiesel, in his Preface to his book *From the Kingdom of Memory*, writes passionately about the benefits of memory: "It creates bonds rather than destroys them. Bonds between present and past, between individuals and groups. It is because I remember our common beginning that I move closer to my fellow human beings" (10). The family of the dew breaker is very far from that bond at the end of the story; thus one may question the revelation of his gory past as extraneous - at least Ka feels that way. However, refusing to disclose the past only complicates the present. Edwidge Danticat certainly presents a strong connection between past occurrences and present identity. As Paul Connerton notes, "past history is a rich resource for my conception of myself, my self-knowledge, my view of my character and potentialities" (*Modernity* 141). When that history is erased, wholeness is erased too. Embarrassed by his past role as a member of the dreaded Tonton Macoutes, the dew breaker refuses to open up his past, even to those closest to him. The curtain he draws on his past for three decades also obscures his present; the silence of the past becomes the silence of his present, and his only and beloved daughter, her identity shattered, is also disconnected from her parents. Thinking he is protecting his daughter from this terrible narrative, she ends up fragmented, broken, and unable to trust both mother and father.

Works Cited

- Adichie, Chimamanda N. "The Story Behind the Book: Q & A with the Author, *Half of a Yellow Sun*." Interview by Daria Tunca. 2006. Web. 20th July, 2012.
- Bervanage, Berber. *History, Memory, and State-Sponsored Violence: Time and Justice.* New York: Routledge, 2012. Print.
- Chancy, Myriam J. A. *Framing Silence: Revolutionary Novels by Haitian Women.* New Brunswick: Rutgers UP, 1997. Print.
- Connerton, Paul. *How Modernity Forgets.* Cambridge: Cambridge UP, 2009. Print.
- _ _ _. *The Spirit of Mourning: History, Memory and the Body.* Cambridge: Cambridge UP, 2011. Print.
- Danticat, Edwidge. *Breath, Eyes, Memory.* New York: Vintage Books, 1994. Print.
- _._._.Create Dangerously: The Immigrant Artist at Work. Princeton: Princeton UP, 2011, Print.
- _._._. *The Dew Breaker.* New York: Vintage Books, 2004. Print.
- Ferrante, Julia. "Danticat: Storytelling Keeps Memory, Tradition Alive." Bucknell Forum. Bucknell University. Lewisburg, PA.13 April, 2011.Web. 11 Mar. 2012.
- Huyssen, Andreas. *Twilight Memories: Marking Time in a Culture of Amnesia.* London: Routledge, 2005. Print.
- Ivry, Benjamin. "Building a Collective Consciousness on a National Scale: Jewish Historian Pierre Nora Defined What's Quintessentially French." *The Jewish Daily Forward.* 8 June 2011. Web. 2 July 2012.
- John Paul II, Pope. *Memory and Identity: Conversations at the Dawn of the Millennium.* New York: Rizzoli, 2005.Print.
- Johnson, Charles. "The End of the Black American Narrative." *The American Scholar* 2008: 1-11. Print.
- Morrison, Toni. "The Site of Memory." *Inventing the Truth: The Art and Craft of Memoir.* Ed. William Zinsser. New York: Houghton, 1998. Print

- Nora, Pierre, ed., *Lieux de Mémoire*. Paris: Editions Gallimard, 1984, Print.
- Said, Edward. "Invention, Memory, and Place." *Critical Inquiry* 26.2 (2000): 175-192. JSTOR. Web. 15 Aug. 2012.
- Wiesel, Elie. *From the Kingdom of Memory. Reminiscences*. New York: Summit Books, 1990. Print.
- Woods, Tim. *African Pasts: Memory and History in African literatures*. Manchester: Manchester UP, 2007. Print.

Chapter 8

Memorizing the Dark: Margaret Walker and Toni Morrison Compress African American Time and Space in Poetry and Fiction

By Eleanor J. Blount

Clocks slay time... time is dead as long as it is being clicked off by little wheels; only when the clock stops does time come to life."

William Faulkner, *The Sound and the Fury*

In the twenty-first century, both science and literature inflict upon us a more taxing concept of memory than was standard at one time. Earlier notions of time have been agitated, stretched, revised by modern and post-modern theorists. Owing to the dicta of Albert Einstein, William Faulkner, Marcel Proust, Sigmund Freud, and many less luminary others, today's literate thinkers are aware that mental rumination tends toward fragmentation and non-linearity. Yet, it yields fully comprehensible narratives. When the rumination centers on events we perceive as "past," it becomes a story we refer to as a memory.

When seeking an exegesis of African American slavery, not merely as history dissociated from life of the present day but as literary text vital to the identity of contemporary Americans, applying some investigation into the nature of the time-space continuum may be helpful. It is certainly so if the novels and poems of Toni Morrison and Margaret Walker are selected as exemplary (and they are) of well-grounded African American historical literature. These two writers present as highly significant the need to pay tribute to ancestors whose determination to survive the peculiar institution built and endowed today's society, and the ability to resurrect seminal narratives by *re*-membering testimonies which have unfortunately and incorrectly been relegated to a kind of false nothingness called the past. Before looking at their respective works, however, let us acclimate the discourse to concepts of time and space that differ from those used more routinely.

Physicist Einstein's special and general theories of relativity dissolve the layperson's stock belief in "time."

He often referred to the separation of past, present, and future as a persistent illusion[6]. He refutes the moment of now. With $E=MC^2$ he proved that though the speed of light is universally constant, time is relative and, therefore, not an absolute. It depends on a changeable thing with which it enjoys mutuality–space. This coexistence leaves time malleable to the human subconscious, and for that reason, humans have manipulated it into segments labeled past, present, and future for ease-of-life's sake. As soon as we stretch our imaginations to align with Einstein's that shows us why/how there is no such thing as time, in the colloquial sense of that word, literature and psychology step in to add another dimension to our effort. In addition to the two African American subjects, Faulkner, Proust, and Freud convince us that time and memory are interlaced, codependent. Furthermore, they teach that to give short shrift to conscious or unconscious memory is to diminish time, especially if time is viewed as commodity. Memory must be honored lest dire consequences be suffered. After all, amnesia, the absence of memory, is a disease.

To the rescue, Morrison and Walker endeavor through fiction and poetry to rekindle, or instill for the first time, storied memories of African American life through time by re-membering the forgotten or intentionally dismembered histories of silenced people. Time spent with them reveals that rumination occurs less absent mindedly and

---

[6] The statement made by Einstein to Besso's widow is often misquoted or incorrectly translated. Definitive citations appear in *Correspondance avec Michele Besso 1903-1955* (Paris: Herman, 1979) 327 pages and *Albert Einstein-Michele Besso Correspondence: 1903-1955* (Paris: Herman, 1949), pp. 537-538.

less temporarily than we ought casually assume. Occurrence is recurrent, so it behooves present readers to pay closer attention to the ways in which these poets/novelists have ordered what looks like the past and brought memory to the fore. At this juncture in our examination, a new rhetorical wrinkle emerges. Finding language to assert that that which must exist but in actuality does not, requires care. Let us remain cognizant that the mind's fragmented thoughts we are scrutinizing form a meandering stream, not a rigid line, of consciousness. The resulting disregard for chronology and spatial sequence creates a linguistic strain on discourse such as that which is undertaken here. Phrases already used here-- centuries, early vs. late, modernity, and bring from memory (the back) to the fore (the front)-- are from the vocabulary of time and space, and this disregard renders them as garbled as the concocted ideas they were invented to communicate. So familiar and resonant of a viscerally felt sense are these terms, we should maintain a careful use of them here; we will not need to dismiss our prior concocted ideas of time and space. Instead, let us attempt for the time being to impose a more philosophical filter onto the notions of time and space human beings have resorted to as a means of making daily necessary routines more navigable.

To further complicate the modern understanding of the phenomenon we seek to define as memory, consideration must be given to sensory perception as it differs from conscious thought. Few of us have escaped unexpectedly hearing a forgotten tune or happening upon a once-common fragrance and being transported instantly in the mind's eye to the time, place, or person with whom the sensation was last experienced, perhaps many years ago. Regarding sensation, Proust says:

> It's no use trying to evoke our past, all the efforts of our intelligence are futile. The past lies hidden beyond the mind's realm and reach, in some material object (in the sensation that material object gives us). And it depends entirely on chance whether or not we encounter that object before we die. (Web 10/21/2012)

Additionally, Freud's dream work indicates that when processing information as memory, much of the activity is not only involuntary but takes place during sleep. All the bits of data which constitute our daily lives cannot be adequately manipulated by the very busy conscious mind while awake, so stories are contextualized during our sleep into situations we *should* recognize readily. In the *Freud Reader*, he further states that "The content of dreams, however, does not consist entirely of situations, but also includes disconnected fragments of visual images, speeches and even bits of unmodified thoughts," (157). Through psychoanalysis it may be determined that a dream is a peculiar form of expression from memory,

> a psychical complex of the most intricate possible structure. Its portions stand in the most manifold logical relations to one another: they represent foreground and background, conditions, digressions and illustrations, chains of evidence and counter-arguments. Each train of thought is almost invariably accompanied by its contradictory counterpart. This material lacks none of the characteristics that are familiar to us from our waking thinking. (157)

There is no cause, then, to find fault with writers whose themes and characters take advantage of the multilayered attributes of consciousness that are, according to scientific evidence, ever-present in real people in the real world. This is what literature is expected to do. Yet, when Faulkner in his day and, in later years, Morrison embraced the nonlinear aesthetic in their fiction, they were frequently critiqued disapprovingly for ignoring readers' preset paradigms and making themselves inaccessible by subjugating chronology or resorting to the paranormal. To the contrary, their cutting edge stratagems laid open to readers a fuller sampling of the plethora which is the human condition, and a greater, more introspective range of human reaction and emotion. Morrison finds Faulkner resonant of her own literary impetus, and many find evidence of his influence in her work. A noted Morrison scholar, Carolyn Denard, includes in her edited collection of Morrison's interviews (Denard, *Conversations* 25) one in which Morrison reveals that "there was for me not only an academic interest in Faulkner, but in a very, very personal way, in a very personal way as a reader, William Faulkner had an enormous effect on me, an enormous effect."[7]

Faulkner's disposition on memory and time is sharp and is deeply felt by his readers. He succinctly reveals his attitudes in his famous quotation: "The past is never dead. It's not even past." (Faulkner 73) He works his theory to capacity in his magnum opus, *The Sound and the Fury*. In this novel he utilizes the device of stream of consciousness to tell the same historical story of a white southern family from the three viewpoints of its sons and a narrator who focuses on its racially oppressed black servant family. He chooses to open the book with the world as seen by Benjy, a man born with mental handicaps so severe he has no comprehension of time. To him, everything is the moment of now. He cannot distinguish yesterday from today from tomorrow. He cannot place things or thoughts into any discernible order, yet he knows what he remembers of his daily life and communicates it to those who spend enough time figuring him out. He cannot be educated, and his mental process is driven largely by sensual triggers like odors. It seems as if his whole life is just one jumbled memory. Conversely, his brother Quentin who goes north to be educated at Harvard is preoccupied with propriety and order. These are outmoded proprieties of the old order, slave era South. He fixates on time and is obsessed with clocks and watches. Ultimately, he loses his mind and commits suicide. Speculation about the motive behind these authorial parallels and paradoxes is not difficult.

As did Faulkner's, Morrison's new aesthetic favorably impressed a Nobel Prize committee. Hers exhibits a decidedly feminine posture in the masterpiece, *Beloved*, in that it privileges the voice of a woman

---

[7] See Taylor-Guthrie page 152 where Morrison states she does not object to being compared to Faulkner and others though she is not *like* them.

who is consumed by the concerns of nurture and motherhood in a society that prevents her from enacting nurture and motherhood due to her blackness which imposes upon her the condition of servitude. *Beloved* reinforces the notion that, at its core, memory is fleeting but repeated. It is so ethereal, so involuntary that forgotten events and people who have important life lessons attached to them will *insist* upon being re-membered, assembled once again. Human beings, in attempts to avoid what they fear will be painful, may try to suppress the mental remnants of dismembered identities they would prefer to leave behind, but this serves to ignore or negate whatever necessary or useful axioms accompanied the experience, and haunting consequences ensue.

In the novel, Sethe, the major character, is based on a real woman who had escaped slavery with her beloved children but later murdered one of them at the moment it became apparent that the child was about to be repossessed by its southern owner rather than allow her to be taken back into captivity. For years, Sethe gets on with her life as best she can without acknowledging that the morbid action she took earlier may not have been as altruistic as she chose to believe. A degree of uncharitable selfishness might have been involved, and, without question, it quashed the voice of an autonomous being which had, itself, manifested as a life entitled to choices of its own. The child's essence had no intention of staying nullified; it reappeared as a ghost wreaking havoc in her mother's house for all the live inhabitants. The apparition's presence forced Sethe to re-member what she had not adequately memorialized in the first place: slavery and the memories of its "sixty million" and more. Until the woman worked through her myriad anxieties about her nation's and her personal pasts, the associated pain could not help but rear its hideous head without warning, as haints do.

According to Morrison who spoke about the multiple motives she had in mind during the two years she spent contemplating *Beloved* and additional three writing it, "The past until you confront it, until you live through it, keeps coming back in other forms. The shapes redesign themselves in other constellations, until you get a chance to play it over again" (qtd. in Taylor-Guthrie 241). Attention is focused, both literally in the book's dedication and figuratively all throughout the story, to the sixty million and more. Those to whom she refers are the people whose lives were lost during the Middle Passage from Africa and early days of transplantation onto American soil. The "more" are their black descendants who cannot help but live the legacy of oppression which lingers after slavery's ostensible end, and their white descendants to whom the fruits of forced labor accrued. Morrison wants this remembered. In her essay, "The Site of Memory," she likens the urgency to review and acknowledge slavery in her work to the fervency of moving water. "All water has a perfect memory and is forever trying to get back to where it was," she says (qtd. in Denard, *Margin* 77).

Memory is potent. Not only do individuals live within its confines, but so do the cultures and nations that individuals comprise. Few forces synergize as powerfully as do the subconscious thoughts and consciously crafted images that combine to establish a national memory. What results, in a nation that indemnifies race, is a database of stereotypes and pejorative definitions designed to impugn a targeted racial group *into perpetuity*. Placing these false images and definitions into America's memory bank is more pernicious than the physical pain inflicted upon actual slaves in that it lives longer than they did. Memory does not end with the physical death of a slave or with signatures on a treaty saying a war has concluded. Memory is regenerative and therefore insists on the recurrence of prejudice. It is not logical to maintain that a *pre*-judice can exist purely in the so called past.

In the years since *Beloved's* 1987 debut, Morrison has said multiple times that she envisioned the book as an aid for the remembrance of slavery. Her view of many modern Americans is that they would prefer to forget about slavery, especially if white, because the memory bites so embarrassingly. Blacks can also be susceptible to a wished for amnesia, though usually because of a pain more pernicious than embarrassment. She, like a psychologist, deems amnesia unhealthy and believes that refusing to countenance the impact slavery made on the culture creates a warped national consciousness. She and psychology both suggest that the root causes of pain, when suppressed, emerge inevitably, fiercely, and counterproductively. She makes a protracted argument in *What Moves at the Margin*, another volume edited by Denard, a series of essays, that covers what she calls the "Gothic ignorance" that was cultivated in America after the Civil War and into the 20th century through concerted white efforts to lump all blacks together and portray them the same as they would "funny, but barely verbal, animals" in the press, music, and literature. She expresses incredulity at how careless white people were of what they were admitting about themselves through their practices:

Surely they knew that intelligence was judged by the ability to tell the difference between one thing and another. Surely they knew that intellect itself was the skill in determining the difference between one blood cell and another, between one molecule and another, between one leaf and another. That the finer the distinctions, the higher the intellect. The inability, then, to tell one black person from another was tantamount to a public admission of brain damage. (47)

Were it not for the pervasive and intentional misrepresentation of the Negro through coon trading cards, sheet music covers and jokes, and depictions as apes after Charles Carroll's popular 1900 book, *The Negro a Beast*, minstrel shows, Mammy and Sambo pictures in advertising, widespread, automatic disdain for the African American, even in areas of the country where slavery had never been practiced, could not have been instantiated into America's national memory so successfully, necessitating that it be overcome 100 years after emancipation. When malevolent forces use memory to their advantage, it is crucial that opposing entities exploit all opportunities to refashion subconscious pictures with sanity. Morrison notes over and over how relentless whites have been in preserving and perpetuating unfounded information onto the American public. Academics are entitled to much of the credit for it. She points to a professor who asked W. E. B. Dubois in 1905 to assist in a study of whether colored people cried as an expression of emotion as did whites. She recounts others in a similar vein and concludes this about scholars and other professionals as they have beleaguered the African American since abolition:

> If sociologists applied the same values to Ulysses (that classic absent father) as they do to black families, Penelope, a welfare mother, would have been damned for not getting a job while Telemachus would have been persecuted in school as a product of a broken home and tracked into a class for slow readers with social adjustment problems. (49)

Required sanity sufficient to counter the disrespect cannot be attained, however, if the sane are busy retreating from the memory of slavery's brutality. So in *Beloved*, Morrison did not recoil from delineating it graphically. Her sustained metaphor of mother/child abandonment is as clear in its referrals to modern diasporic blacks who turn their backs on Mother Africa as it is in those that highlight the present blight in so many black communities, which is a direct offshoot of the dearth of nurture imposed upon black progeny whose mothers were not allowed to mother them, so that the maternal energy would be saved for white progeny instead. Morrison realizes that allowing ourselves to receive and host the brief snatches of awareness of slavery as they periodically present themselves can be instructive if we will do so without fear and histrionics. So where her text invokes the scathing memory of dehumanization, she is not just conjuring up the past but illuminating the present. Shedding some light on a problem is always an excellent step toward solving it.

Once again, Margaret Walker's *Jubilee,* another female neo-slave narrative, popular and critically acclaimed in its heyday, decades before Morrison's *Beloved,* explores this thematic concern of the dearth of the nurturing of Black progeny. It received constant comparison to Margaret Mitchell's *Gone with the Wind*, to Walker's consternation. Walker, who was primarily a poet and also a sharp critic, may be best known for this novel. Not unlike *Beloved*, it is the saga of a former slave and the family she loves unquestionably, and it, too, is based on the life of a real woman. The protagonist is Vyry who imitates Walker's own great-grandmother and has been likened to the more iconic Scarlet O'Hara. She never met her great-grandmother but felt as if she knew her just the same. Walker grew up in a family that took pride in commemorating the efforts of their enslaved and newly freed ancestors that were undertaken to enable the continuation of the line into which she was born in early 20th century Alabama. All her life she had heard the folk tales about Vyry and how her perseverance under adversity saved her family. Few poets can effectively linger, as Walker did, on the imbedded though often neglected memories that are capable of infusing us with the African American experience. Significantly, she recreated the experience with equal aplomb in *Jubilee* and in the well-known poem, "For My People." Another poem, "Memory," is also worthy of observation here.

Whereas Morrison explores the supernatural world of a dead slave to highlight the presence of slavery in the real world, Walker's approach is to direct subconscious attention in the poems to ancestors' lives and struggles. There are bits and pieces of them that resonate with the memorabilia—the hundreds of mundane activities and images performed and recognized routinely without any particular acknowledgment—of our own lives. She celebrates them as history in *Jubilee*.

It is as if Walker uses a cutlass, not a pen, to carve from words the vivid descriptions which are the novel's opening. It is extremely poignant, largely because of the astounding success she achieves at evoking music and other sounds to trigger auditory memory, in writing. She starts the story with lines from the familiar Negro spiritual, a sorrow song, "Swing Low Sweet Chariot," to signal that death is approaching for Hetta, who at age 29 has already birthed 15 children (mostly as result of rape by her master) but is now dying in childbirth and setting the stage for Vyry, her favorite and remaining child (the others were sold off), to become the heroic motherless child who, in real life, was Walker's great-grandmother. Equally heart wrenching is the scene in which Vyry, who becomes a too young personal servant to the plantation's mistress, has the contents of the woman's chamber pot dashed in her face as chastisement for incorrectly carrying out an order. The girl's physical resemblance to the woman's husband is the cause of the heightened degree of mistreatment inflicted upon this child. In time, the woman, now old and sick, is shown as bereft of family or other servants to administer to her needs except for Vyry whose goodness and strength of character is intestinal despite adversity.

Walker is devoted to the careful exploitation of sensory memory elicited through music, not only because of its deep and immediate effect on readers, but also because she views it as an essential part of African American existence, past and present, that should not be neglected. She knows that for slaves, music and religion were inextricably linked and that these were often the only two things that outfitted them for the endurance test which was their institutionalized bondage. Vyry and other *Jubilee* characters are frequently described as having melodious or resonant or amazing voices as the author lavishes attention on song lyrics of the period, and she creates numerous times for slaves and newly freed Americans to break into song while traversing treacherous territory. They teach their children to sing, and the children never tire of joining in the choruses. At one point when shortly after their emancipation, Vyry and her family "wander in the wilderness," apprehensive and perilously intent on happening upon suitable new land for new lives, they propel themselves by singing jubilant songs. "Time always seems to go faster when you sing," Vyry says. "Don't it though," answers her husband. And then they go on to discuss how they hope to start a church for more and better singing and proper preaching, first thing, just as *soon* as they find somewhere to settle.

The profundity of the role played by sensory memory, particularly in regards to sound and rhythm in the African American experience, can be likened to theorist and culture critic, Marshall McLuhan's, late 20th century pronouncement, "the medium is the message." His intention at that time was to inform the public of the unexpected ways in which a new media device, television, unlike previous, less invasive technology had not only captured, but permeated, the attention of its viewers. He went on to explain that the device, after a while, became as much at the center of the messages it imparted as was the originally planned content of those messages. How many viewers could truthfully say, by the 1960's, that they had never read credibility into a television news story simply because that story was on the TV? More importantly, could such a viewer identify that moment—no telling how long ago it had been—at which s/he began to conflate the thing and the thing's message?

If McLuhan had been a reader of Walker, would he, with his heightened awareness of how symbiotically things can conflate outside our conscious awareness, be able to put his finger on the phrase, the line, or the page that started him to see the African American and his/her culture as the personification of rhythm and all else that is musical? How far through the book would he have made it before it unintentionally occurred to him that lyricism, sometimes jubilant, sometimes doleful, provided a necessary accentuation to Walker's tale? How long before he would have realized that the cadence of Walker's prose rendered it more than a mere chronicling of events that took place during the protracted slave era. Rather, her subtle lilt, in its undulations, created a felt sense of life lived both tragically and triumphantly by people who were not deaf to the recurrent cycling of sounds that emanated from within them, symbolizing the ebbs and flows of life. Repeating and imitating spirituals feeds Walker's pronounced sense of rhythm. It is not lost on her that her enslaved ancestors lived and worked largely in an agrarian environment that focused on the rhythms within nature: crop sowing and reaping as the seasons changed, the ebbs and flows of tides along with the phases of the moon. People who lived that way possessed a felt sense of nature and sound as intimate as their own pulse.

Many times, Walker stated that the poem "For My People" had so much become her signature that it might as well have been her name. Once its facility for extracting sensory memories has been aroused, there is no wonder. Its opening section, for instance:

> For my people everywhere singing their slave songs
> repeatedly: their dirges and their ditties and their blues
> and jubilees, praying their prayers nightly to an
> unknown god, bending their knees humbly to an
> unseen power; (Walker "For My People")

To say that these lines possess the mirth necessary to qualify them as music would be an understatement. To add that they simultaneously possess misery sufficient to qualify them as tale of woe would be equally lacking in heft. Of course they are homage to mirth and misery. But the degree to which they are, on account of their ariose structure, is what is so much more appealing. In the beginning, the sing-song cadence is what pulls us into the language without our having exerted any effort at all toward understanding it. Before we realize it, we do not only start to read the words on the page, but respond to them auditorily as if having meandered into a concert hall by accident. The coupling of sound (even if the sound is heard only as hint from the writer that it *should* be heard) to the visual, strengthens our focus on the harder job of analyzing the message. But we would have difficulty escaping the message because the medium is so fully engaging. Up to a point, we almost sing each successive line (though there is not a single note there) because music is so strongly suggested by the tempo. The brio, as a composer may describe this state, is what resonates within us for a while, but in short order we realize we are listening to a death chant. We are plucked, pizzicato style, from complacence about the nature of African American life. Like the old spirituals, the poem honors life *and* death while seeking to explain the extraordinary uniqueness and simultaneous run-of-the-mill routineness which is the cruelty that accompanies daily existence for black people. It is important to note that the message does not end on a doleful motif. The exposition leads to a rendition of day-to-day regular occurrences that comprise, simply, life. Again, like the spirituals, the poem is written to be vocalized, but reading it silently allows us to linger over more of the subtleties, such as the turn of events from harmless children's games to costly adult daliance in the exposition. Then, with great pathos, the final section is a loving and inspiring benediction:

> Let a new earth rise. Let another world be born. Let a
> bloody peace be written in the sky. Let a second
> generation full of courage issue forth; let a people
> loving freedom come to growth. Let a beauty full of
> healing and a strength of final clenching be the pulsing
> in our spirits and our blood. Let the marshall songs
> be written, let the dirges disappear. Let a race of men now
> rise and take control.
>
> (Walker "For My People")

To those who are dark, these pieces of literature embody vindication in the face of vindictiveness, while portraying the exaltory and the desultory, the brutal, beautiful, loathsome, loving legacy that slavery and racism have provided. The respect for the full spectrum of memory, conscious and unconscious, is in that legacy, and it can no more be ginned from the black experience, as if seeds from cotton, than it could be combed from Toni Morrison's or Margaret Walker's writings. And most especially in the case of Margaret Walker whose poem "Memory" (fully qtd below for the readers' appreciation) both sums this discussion and shows that to remember is, first, to observe.

Memory

> I can remember wind-swept streets of cities
> on cold and blustery nights, on rainy days;
> heads under shabby felts and parasols
> and shoulders hunched against a sharp concern;
> seeing hurt bewilderment on poor faces,
> smelling a deep and sinister unrest
> these brooding people cautiously caress;
> hearing ghostly marching on pavement stones

and closing fast around their squares of hate.
I can remember seeing them alone,
at work, and in their tenements at home.
I can remember hearing all they said:
their muttering protests, their whispered oaths,
and all that spells their living in distress.
Margaret Walker

Works Cited

Denard, Carolyn, ed. *Toni Morrison Conversations.* Jackson: University Press of Mississippi, 2008. Print.
——————————. *What Moves at the Margin.* Jackson: University Press of Mississippi, 2008. Print.
Freud, Sigmund. *The Interpretation of Dreams.* Kessinger Publishing, 2004. Google eBook. Web. 3 Sept. 2012.
Morrison, Toni. *Beloved.* New York: Knopf, 1987. Print.
Proust, Marcel. *In Search of Lost Time, Volume 1: Swann's Way.* Random House Digital, Inc., 1992. Google eBook. Web. 3 Sept. 2012.
Taylor-Guthrie, Danielle.,ed. *Conversations with Toni Morrison.* Jackson: University Press of Mississippi, 1994. Print.
Walker, Margaret. "For My People." The Poetry Foundation. Web. 3 Sept. 2012.
——————————. *Jubilee.* New York: Houghton Mifflin, 1966. Print.

Section V

Cultural Identity

Section-V

Critical Issues

Chapter 9

There's No Place Like Home: Cultural Memory in Toni Morrison's *Tar Baby* and Edwidge Danticat's *Breath, Eyes and Memory*

Rhonda Collier

> *I wandered lonely as a cloud*
> *That floats on high o'er vales and hills,*
> *When all at once I saw a crowd, --*
> *A host of golden daffodils*
> *Beside the lake, beneath the trees,*
> *Fluttering and dancing in the breeze.*
>
> William Wordsworth - *Daffodils* (1804)

Unsuccessful during its film-debut in 1939, it is surprising that the film based on L. Frank Baum's best-selling children's book *The Wonderful Wizard of Oz* (1900), written 112 year ago, is more than familiar to today's television and movie audiences. Around the globe, *The Wizard of Oz* represents the magic of self-discovery and cultural memory. Extrapolating from Homi K. Bhabha's use of the term in *Locating Culture* (1994), "cultural memory" refers to the dichotomy that exists as a person or group experiences "historical" events in relation to one's interpretation of "historical" events. *The Wizard of Oz* is after all a multi-layered tale about a young girl, Dorothy, who runs away from home, only to be reminded that home is where she belongs. The film version of Baum's book, now over 70 years old, is listed as one of the top 100 films of the twentieth century. No less surprising is that Salman Rushdie, famed author of *Midnight's Children* (1980) and *Satanic Verses* (1989), claims "*The Wizard of Oz* as his very first literary influence" (9). This explains why Rushdie's first story written, at the age of ten, is entitled *Over the Rainbow* (9). Given the film's influence on contemporary culture, it seems more than appropriate to draw upon *The Wizard of Oz* to discuss the idea of cultural memory in literature. For Dorothy, as with the characters Jadine Childs in Toni Morrison's *Tar Baby (1982)*, and Sophie Caco in Edwidge Danticat's *Breath, Eyes, Memory (1994)*, the power to embark on the journey homeward lies within words and the knowledge of important historical elements. As the post-colonialist writer Jamaica Kincaid warns, interpreting historical events is almost impossible without being able to perceive the past, to appreciate the present and to anticipate the future. This chapter explores how Toni Morrison and Edwidge Danticat reflect on the connection between place and cultural memory.

Jamaica Kincaid's *A Small Place (1988)* provides an interesting post-colonial framework in which to view cultural memory. Kincaid's Antigua, a nine-by-twelve-mile island in the British West Indies, has a confused identity that has yet to attain the secure, self-assured existence that independence promised. She suggests that the decolonization and the true independence of Antigua is complicated by a cultural tradition which does not make distinctions between the past, the present, and the future. Kincaid notes:

> To the people in a small place, the division of Time into the Past, the Present, and the Future does not exist. An event that occurred one hundred years ago might be as vivid to them as if it were happening this very moment. And then, an event that is occurring this very moment might pass before them with such dimness that it is as if it had happened one hundred years ago. No action in the present is an action planned with a view of its effect on the future. When the future, bearing its own events, arrives, its ancestry is then traced in a trancelike retrospect, at the end of which, their eyes wide with astonishment, the people in a small place reveal themselves to be children being shown the secrets of a magic trick. (54)

Here, Kincaid describes self-discovery as an act of magic seen through the eyes of a child. More importantly, she implies problems of identity lie with the interpretation of "events." For example, in the film version of *The Wizard of Oz*, Dorothy experiences the Land of Oz as a dream. But in her mind's eye, she actually experiences the Land of Oz as a real place. Upon her return to Kansas, Dorothy adamantly comments to her Aunt Em:

No, Aunt Em, this was a real truly live place. And I remember that some of it wasn't very nice—but most of it was beautiful!! But all the same, all I kept saying to everybody was, 'I want to go home.' And they sent me home!!

(She waits for a reaction; they all laugh again.)

Doesn't anybody believe me? (Langley 131-132)

For Aunt Em, Uncle Henry, Zeek, Hunk, Hickory, and Professor Marvel, what is real to Dorothy is seen as the result of her unconsciousness after being hit in the head by flying debris from the twister. Dorothy was traveling in the Land of Oz for days and days: "But I did leave you, Uncle Henry—that's just the trouble!! And I tried to get back for days and days—" (Langley 131). In the end, Dorothy accepts her experiences as a dream that only she and Toto share. The memory exists for the individual, but the place is not available for the group or the individual. The experience benefits the culture as a whole. Thus, the connection between "cultural memory" and place is that what happens to Dorothy. This is becomes more important than the place, Oz. Dorothy's journey to Oz is a heroic journey to self-knowledge. The people of Kincaid's *A Small Place* are in many ways like the child Dorothy who magically learns secrets about herself : courage, wisdom and love through the actions of the Lion, the Scarecrow and the Tinman.

Toni Morrison's Jadine Childs, as her last name "childs" symbolizes, is an adult "child" in search of herself. As Kincaid notes about people in *A Small Place*, Jadine "cannot give an account, a complete account, of herself" (53). Jadine has no memory or knowledge of herself. *Tar Baby* chronicles Jadine's diasporic journey to self-discovery. For American readers, the title "Tar Baby" is a *signifying* title that situates Jadine as a character in a Brer Rabbit folk tale. The Brer Rabbit folk tales are tales about a smart rabbit who outsmarts a farmer, who tries to catch him with a tar baby. The rabbit gets the vegetables and never gets stuck to the farmer's black tar baby. The historical term "tar baby" has many implications. One is a subtle compliment to the "trickster" nature of the African American—"the rabbit," who is able to survive the white man's farm. The other is often seen as an insult to the beauty of African Americans' skin as black as "tar." The "tar baby" can also be viewed as beautiful figure of attraction, which gets the rabbit's attention. However, in American English, "tar baby" is often used to refer to a situation that is difficult to get out of, and this use of the term is considered a racial slur. Morrison's use of the *signifying* term "tar baby" signals readers that Jadine is a part of a game involving a *trickster* figure. Who is he or she?

Jadine is a fair-skinned black fashion model in Paris, who also holds a degree in Art History from the prestigious Sorbonne. Upon first meeting Jadine on the mythical Caribbean island, Isle de le Chevaliers, readers assume that the Caribbean is Jadine's home; perhaps, she is the rabbit. On the Isle de le Chevaliers, Jadine, like the orphaned Dorothy in Kansas with Aunt Em and Uncle Henry, appears safe with her Uncle Sydney and Aunt Ondine, who have cared for her the majority of her orphan life. Yet readers soon learn that Jadine is unable to reconcile her responsibilities to her family, white society's expectations, and her quest for independence. This imbalance keeps Jadine constantly searching. It appears she is a rabbit escaping many "tar babies" set before her, trying to capture her and keep her in one place.

In Paris, as a model, Jadine is an exploited black body symbolically like the nineteenth-century Sarah Bartnam, known as the Venus Hottentot (Gilman 239). The French exploited Hottentot as a sexual object as they were fascinated by her genitalia and buttocks. Indeed, it became common to purchase engravings of her image, as well as to purchase bustles to enhance white female buttocks. Morrison's Jadine invokes the cultural memory of another historical figure, the fair-skinned African-American dancer Josephine Baker (Ross 260). About Baker, one critic comments "modern audiences see her as a rebel, black audiences see her as a thankless child" (Baker 189). Tellingly, the outline of Jadine's character is much like that of Baker's, who migrated to France where she felt she was not discriminated against, and where she was free to explore her career in dancing. "Most of the blacks said, 'Look at her, she thinks she's white, and she's acting like a white woman, a French white woman at that...'" (Baker 189). Maybe, Jadine is a "tar baby" figure and not a "rabbit."

While Jadine strives for independence, she is trapped in the duality of her racialized body because she economically profits from her own self-commodification. In many senses, she is a black person wearing a white mask. She is seemingly connected to place, but disconnected to its cultural memory. A place can only exist as a function of its experience and the memory of its own history; thus Jadine has no real connection to Paris. Her connection is as false as the mask she wears. "Morrison restores the dialectical potential in fashion to unmask the very process of masking while simultaneously deploying fashion's ideological power to create woman as middle-class objects of desire" (Emberly 406). Morrison creates a possible "tar baby" scenario for Jadine. Jadine's occupation in fashion serves to illustrate the complexity of her "otherness" and her struggle for self-identity. Jadine's photographed image of beauty represents an entity that is devoid of past or future.

Similar to Kincaid's Antigua, Jadine's body is just a little island that lacks history. Kincaid observes about the little island:

> The unreal way in which it was always beautiful now is the unreal way in which it is beautiful. The unreal way in which it is beautiful now that they are a free people is the unreal way in which it was beautiful when they were slaves. (80)

The beauty that Kincaid describes lacks a distinction between past, present or future; it has no place in time. Historically, Jadine might as well be Venus Hottentot or Josephine Baker. While she is free to move around and pursue a lucrative career in Paris, is she really free? That is to say, is she the rabbit? In reality, she is not free. Jadine is merely an identity that has adapted the mannerisms of the colonizer and has no history or home of her own. Albert Memmi notes that the colonized "is in no way a subject of history, and has forgotten how to participate actively in history and no longer asks to do so" (92). In post-colonial terms, Jadine is a cultural orphan who enjoys her homelessness. She chooses to be an exile. She chooses to forget her origins.

After migrating from Paris to the Isle, Jade notes that the Isle is a place where there is "no fear." In addition to her aunt and uncle, Jadine enjoys the emotional and financial support of Valerian and Margaret Street, the wealthy white couple that employ Jadine's aunt and uncle. Instead of a servant's child, she is treated like a close friend and a daughter. Yet, Jadine chooses to run away from the Isle with Son, her stowaway black lover. Edward Saïd notes that "no matter how well they do, exiles are always eccentrics who feel their difference (even as they frequently exploit it) as a kind of orphanhood" (360). After fleeing the once "safe" Isle for New York, Jadine notes:

After two months of stingless bees, butterflies and avocado trees, the smart thin trees on Fifty-Third Street refreshed her. They were to scale, human-sized, and the buildings did not threaten her like the hills of the island had, for these were full of people whose joints were oiled just like hers. This is home, she thought with an orphan's delight; not Paris, not Baltimore, not Philadelphia. This is home. (221-2)

Again, Jadine claims yet another place as her home. With "an orphan's delight," she identifies herself as a New Yorker. She finally has a home. However, as Jadine runs from her financial responsibility to her aunt and uncle, who wish to retire from their work as servants on the Isle, she begins to realize that she has no home. Her visit to her lover's all black hometown of Eloe, Florida, frightens her, and further confirms her homelessness.

In Eloe, she dreams, but is not quite sure if she is dreaming:

> They looked as though they had just been waiting for that question and they each pulled out a breast and showed it to her. Jadine started to tremble. They stood around in the room, jostling each other gently, gently—there wasn't much room-revealing one breast then two and Jadine was shocked. This was not the dream of hats for in that she was asleep, her eyes closed. Here she was wide-awake, but in total darkness looking at her own mother for God's sake and Nanadine!! (258)

Morrison uses Jadine's "wide-awake" dream to confirm Jadine's status as a "tar baby." Jadine is with her lover, Son, in his hometown Florida, when she realizes that she has no place. Much like the child Dorothy, the dream state becomes a real place where Jadine must face her fears. Moreover, it is in Son's real place that Jadine realizes that she lacks the experience that makes her a real woman and not a "child."

In the Caribbean, in Paris and in Eloe, Jadine faces images of women and breasts, some which surface from trees. Particularly, the breasts have haunted her. These images are her ancestral and familial past that are magically trying to reach her. Her cultural memory has the power to free her, but she refuses to embrace it. Before Jadine leaves the Isle, her Aunt Nanadine comments:

> Jadine, a girl has got to be a daughter first. She has to learn that. And if she never learns how to be a daughter, she can't never learn to be a woman. I mean a real woman: a woman good enough for a child; good enough for a man—good enough even for the respect of other women. Now you didn't have a mother long enough to learn much about I and I thought I was doing right by sending you to all them schools and so I never told you it and I should have. You don't need your own natural mother to be a daughter. (Morrison 281)

But Jadine continues to run; she ignores her Aunt, as well as her dreams. She refuses to connect with her past.

Later, as Jadine finally prepares to return to Paris, she admits to herself that:

> New York was not her home after all... Every orphan knew that and knew also that mothers however beautiful were not fair. No matter what you did, the diaspora mothers with pumping breasts would impugn your character. And an African woman, with a single glance from eyes that had burned away their own lashes, could discredit your elements. There is no home... (Morrison 288-9)

Ironically, this passage ends with the opposite of what Dorothy learns upon returning from Oz. Jadine sees no value in place in that "there is no home." She runs to escape the images that have chased her throughout her migrations. In particular, she notes the African woman, dressed in a canary yellow dress, who initiates her flight from Paris by chasing her away with a single glance. She criticizes the woman's appearance commenting, "The skin like tar against the canary yellow dress" (Morrison 45). Jadine also characterizes the woman as a "woman's woman-that mother/sister/she; that unphotographable beauty" (Morrison 45). Jadine behaves, as Saïd classifies it, like a "jealous exile." Saïd explains that "exiles look at non-exiles with resentment. They belong in their surroundings, you feel, whereas an exile is always out of place" (362). Jadine questions her own reaction to the African woman. She wonders "Why she had wanted that woman to like and respect her. It had certainly taken the zing out of the magazine cover as well as her degree" (Morrison 47). There is no home for Jadine who refuses to listen to the breasts and to accept the magic of her ancestral past. Unlike Dorothy, Jadine's quest for self is not heroic. Instead, she abandons her family and the man she loves. In the end, Jadine returns to her modeling career in Paris. In contrast, Son, her lover, embraces the magic of his past and becomes one of the mythical blind horsemen on the Isle de le Chevalier. Son is the true rabbit of the "Tar Baby" story. He is at home; he is free. For Jadine, migration allows her to remove herself from what she calls her "diasporic mothers," and thus, prevents her from being a real woman. She remains a "child." Morrison dedicates *Tar Baby* to women who know their true and ancient properties, these women include her mother and grandmothers. The character, Jadine serves to show readers that sometimes in the diasporic journey "there is no home" because home is complex while exile is often comfortable. There is not always enough magic to bring all the jagged pieces together.

Like Morrison, Edwidge Danticat addresses "becoming a woman and defining what that means in terms of a mother who may have been there in fragments" (Shea 382). In *Breath, Eyes and Memory*, Sophie is reunited with her birth mother, Martine, who migrates from Haiti to New York. This forces her from her "motherland". Here, Sophie, twelve, has already invested in terms of cultural tradition and familial past. In New York, French-speaking Sophie is alienated as a Haitian in exile and a child separated from her motherland. Sophie calls herself her mother's daughter and her aunt's child (Danticat 49). In Sophie's case, it appears as if "migration creates the desire for home, which in turn produces the rewriting of home" (Davies 113). She is constantly remembering the place that she calls home. In *Breath, Eyes and Memory*, the Haitian myth of doubling, Marassa, becomes a way of conceptualizing place and cultural memory.

Danticat notes that in the tradition of the Ibegi in Africa, Marassa twins are very special, and frequently have special powers. For Sophie, the myth of Marassa creates two people inside of one body: one to deal with the bad, and the other to enjoy the good. By accepting the African tradition of Marassa, Sophie is able to create a space for herself in spite of the realities of New York and Haiti. Danticat's use of Marassa correlates with Homi Bhabha's description of Janus-faced ideology. Bhabha explains that "the Janus face of ideology is taken at face value and its meaning fixed, in the last instance, on one side of the divide between ideology and 'material conditions'" (*Nation and Narration* 3). He calls the Janus-faced:

> a figure of prodigious doubling that investigates the nation-space in the process of the articulation of elements: where meaning may be partial because they are in media res; and history may be half-made because it is in the process of being made; and

the image of cultural authority may be ambivalent because it is caught, uncertainly, in the act of 'composing' its powerful image. (*Nation* 3)

Comparable to Morrison's use of fashion with the character Jadine Childs to unmask its ideological power implicit in the discourse of commodification, Danticat employs doubling to illustrate the conflict that may exist within an individual. To illustrate this duplicity, Sophie's mother explains how the twins function. She notes, "When one went to the stream, the other rushed under the water to get a better look. When one looked in the mirror, the other walked behind the glass to mimic her" (Danticat 85). Doubling creates the opportunity to rewrite home in that "events" may be interpreted in a space that does not necessarily exist. For example, one Dorothy sleeps in Kansas, while the other Dorothy is lost in Oz. Could it be that Dorothy has a twin? The possibilities for place and cultural memory are two-fold, and the ability for communication can either be amplified or destroyed. Which Dorothy is free? Is the Dorothy in Oz really trapped in a place that does not exist? Or is she enjoying a supernatural experience? Is it a good dream or a nightmare?

In the 1996 interview, Danticat notes that "going back to the mother-daughter relationship, the idea[Marassa] is that two people are one, but not quite, they might look alike and talk alike but are, in essence, different people"(qtd. in Shea 385). Sophie's mother tells her, "The love between a mother and a daughter is deeper than the sea. You would leave me for an old man who you didn't know the year before. You and I we could be like Marassas" (Danticat 85). As Sophie gets older, her mother initiates her into the Haitian tradition of testing. "She would put her finger in her very private parts and see if it would go inside" (Danticat 60). This according to her mother, Martine, was to keep Sophie pure until she was married. However, Sophie never links these painful and humiliating tests with her own childhood experiences of Haiti; she ties them solely to her mother. When she speaks of Haiti, she recalls Tante Atie's stories. She notes, "There was magic in the images that she had made out of the night.

She would rock my body on her lap as she told me of fishermen and mermaids bravely falling in love..." (Danticat 110). On the contrary, when she speaks of her mother's stories, Sophie notes that they are used to mask the horror of testing:

> Like Tante Atie, she had told me stories while she was doing it, weaving elaborate tales to keep my mind off the finger, which I knew one day would slip into me and condemn. I had learned to double while being tested. I would close my eyes and imagine all the pleasant things that I had known. The lukewarm noon breeze through our bougainvillea. Tante Atie's gentle voice blowing over a field of daffodils. (Danticat 155)

In this sense, storytelling provides a vehicle in which a person may initiate the doubling process. Doubling allows the character Sophie to gain strength as she pictures fields of daffodils. As a writer, Danticat is a skilled storyteller, who passes on the Haitian tradition in a wonderful tribute to her Haitian mothers.

Interestingly enough, Danticat's images of the daffodil recall Wordsworth's nineteenth - century poem of the same title. The daffodil recalls the longing for home. In the first stanza, the poet wanders lonely as a cloud until he is greeted by dancing daffodils. These "golden daffodils" greet him besides the lake and become the crowd that make England's Lake District his home. Yet, for Haitians, the image of the daffodil epitomizes the presence of the European colonizer. In *Breath, Eyes and Memory*, Tante Atie describes the significance of the yellow daffodil in Haiti:

They were really European flowers, French buds and stems, meant for colder climates. A long time ago, a French woman had brought them to Croix-des-Rosets and planted them there. A strain of daffodils had grown that could withstand the heat, but they were the color of pumpkins and golden summer squash, as though they had acquired a bronze tinge from the skin of the natives who had adopted them. (Danticat 21)

For the character Sophie, the yellow daffodil may signify the presence of the colonizer, but the bronze tinged daffodil symbolizes a re-appropriated past that is uniquely Haitian. As doubling tradition implies the daffodil can serve two-fold as a cultural reminder of triumph and survival.

A compelling cultural connection may be made in terms of the color yellow with respect to journeys for self-discovery. For Dorothy, the yellow brick road leads her to the Wizard of Oz, who supposedly can help her return home. For Morrison's Jadine, yellow represents the African authenticity that she rejects, particularly in the figure of the African woman who wears a yellow dress. Conversely, Sophie embraces the color as a symbol of strength. As Sophie and Tante Atie discuss Sophie's first journey to the United States, Tante Atie reminds Sophie that everything she owns is yellow (Danticat 21). Following the "Oz" motif, "yellow" seems to suggest a path to wisdom, courage and strength. Each woman faces a journey that may be expressed as a dream in that it may seem unreal. Tante Atie expresses to Sophie: "I was going to put you to sleep, put you in a suitcase, and send you to her. One day you would wake up there and you would feel like your whole life here with me was a dream." (Danticat 17) Indeed, Tante Atie is correct; Sophie's childhood experiences in Haiti become like a dream. The fact that the virginal testing takes place in the U.S. allows Sophie to idealize Haiti, and makes her yearn for the place of bright colors, good food, wonderful stories, and her Tante Atie. As a young adult, Sophie eventually ends the testing by faking her own deflowering; essentially, she rapes herself. She breaks the Marassa bond that her mother wants to share with her and as her mother predicts, Sophie leaves her for a man. Her mother will no longer test her. Sophie not only destroys her virginity, she destroys a symbol of her own cultural tradition. She is free from the traumatic experience, but not from the memory.

When Sophie journeys back to Haiti, she connects the past and the present, realizing that the test of her 'virtue' is a part of the Haitian cultural tradition. She learns that outside of the space she creates while doubling, the realities of Haiti are no better than those of New York. Thus, the idealized Haiti of her dreams is not the real Haiti. Sophie's grandmother notes at the end of *Breath, Eyes and Memory*, "there is always a place where, if you listen closely at night, you will hear your mother telling a story and at the end of the tale, she will ask you this question: 'Ou libéré?' 'Are you free, my daughter?'"(Danticat 234). For Sophie, "home is a contradictory, contested space, a locus for misrecognition and alienation" (Davies 113). She has created a space in her mind that does not exist. Only when she journeys and then revisits home does she realize that home is a myth. Once she realizes this misinterpretation, she is free to return to doubling, but with a new self-awareness informed by a knowledge of her past.

Morrison's Jadine Childs proclaims "there is no home." But Morrison, as a writer, has made it known that home is a space available in fiction. Rushdie argues that the secret to the magic slippers is that "there is no longer such a place as home; except, of course, for the home we make, or the homes that are made for us, in Oz: which is anywhere, and everywhere, except the place from which we began" (57). Danticat implies that home is a place that you construct. Is there truly, as Dorothy phrases it, "no place like home?":

> Tin Man: What have you learned, Dorothy?
> Dorothy (thoughtfully): Well, I... I think that it...that it wasn't enough just to want to see Uncle Henry and Aunt Em...and it's that if I ever go looking for my heart's desire again, I won't look further than my own back yard. And if it isn't there, I never really lost it to begin with.
> (Langley 128)

After the journey to Oz, Kansas will never be the same again. All journeys home do not begin in our backyards as Dorothy suggests. They begin in our dreams and in the continual reflection of our pasts that, like magic, allow humans to be strong like daffodils and to double when tested.

Works Cited

- Bhabha, Homi K. *Location of Culture*. New York: Routledge, 1994. Print.
- _____. ed. *Nation and Narration*. New York: Routledge, 1990. Print.
- Bake, Jean-Claude and Chris Chase. *Josephine: The Hungry Heart*. New York: Random House, 1993. Print.
- Danticat, Edwidge. *Breath, Eyes Memory*. New York: Vintage, 1994. Print.
- Davies, Carolyn Boyce. *Black Women Writing and Identity: Migrations of the Subject*. 113.
- Emberley, Julia V. "A Historical Transposition: Toni Morrison's *Tar Baby* and Frantz Fanon's Post Enlightment Phantasms." *Modern Fiction Studies* 45.2 (1999): 406.
- Gilman, Sander L. "Black Bodies, White Bodies: Toward and Iconography of Female
- Sexuality in Late Nineteenth-Century Art, Medicine, and Literature." *"Race," Writing, and Difference*, ed. Henry Louis Gates, Jr. Chicago, IL: U of Chicago P, 1986. Print.
- Kincaid, Jamaica, *A Small Place*. New York: Plume, 1988. Print.
- Langley, Noel, Florence Ryerson, and Edgar Allan Woolf, *The Wizard of Oz: The Screenplay*, 1939. New York: Dell, 1989.
- Memmi, Albert. *The Colonizer and The Colonized*. Trans. Howard Greendfeld. New York: Beacon, 1991.
- Morrison, Toni. *Tar Baby*. New York: Plume, 1981. Print.
- Rose, Phyllis. *Jazz Cleopatra*. New York: Doubleday, 1989.
- Rushdie, Salman. *The Wizard of Oz*. London: British Film Institute, 1992.
- Said, Edward. "Reflections on Exile." *Out There: Marginalization and Contemporary Cultures*. ed. Russell Ferguson, Martha Gever, Trinh T. Minh-ha and Cornel West. Cambridge, MA: MIT, 1991.

- Shea, Renee H. "The Dangerous Job of Edwidge Danticat: An Interveiw." *Callaloo* 19.2 (1996): 382.

Chapter 10

"Go Back and Get It:" Spirit Possession as Rite of Passage and a Medium of Self-reinvention in Contemporary African Diasporic Literature

Festus Fru Ndeh

One ever feels his two-ness,—an American, a Negro; two souls, two thoughts, two unreconciled strivings; two warring ideals in one dark body, whose dogged strength alone keeps it from being torn asunder.... The history of the American Negro is the history of this strife — this longing to attain self-conscious manhood, to merge his double self into a better and truer self. In this merging he wishes neither of the older selves to be lost. He does not wish to Africanize America, for America has too much to teach the world and Africa. He wouldn't bleach his Negro blood in a flood of white Americanism, for he knows that Negro blood has a message for the world. He simply wishes to make it possible for a man to be both a Negro and an American without being cursed and spit upon by his fellows, without having the doors of opportunity closed roughly in his face. (Dubois 3)

Through the invocation of "two-ness," Dubois launches the dialectic of double consciousness which to him delineates the African diasporic people's constant struggle to reconcile an African heritage with a European upbringing and education. This ambivalence, or ethnic dualism, occasions the need for African diasporic people to define themselves not only by the identity of the land in which they are born, but also by their Africanness. To elucidate this, Rampersad argues while commenting on Dubois, that African Americans are "American by citizenship - political ideals, language, and religion –

and African as a member of a 'vast historic race' of separate origin from the rest of America" (61). Dubois, therefore, reminds society that the "soul" of black folks is not a coherently unified one, but rather "two souls" - American and African. This is not only true of African Americans, but of all African diasporic people. Informed by this perspective, it could be said with certainty that any understanding of the black diasporic self must be framed by the subtext of this dualism, for, as Ron Eyerman contends, contemporary African diasporic people will need a certain transitioning cushioned on "being modern, forgetting slavery and the past, looking to and even returning to Africa ... these would characterize this generation's search for identity and reworking of collective memory" (88).

In this vein, the life of one great, but often ignored African American scholar's struggle through memory to understand himself and to construct his own identity forms the center of this chapter. Hoyt W. Fuller was born on September 10, 1923 in Atlanta, Georgia, and later became an editor, educator, critic, and author during the Black Arts Movement.

Fuller attended Wayne State University and graduated in 1950 with a bachelor's degree in literature and journalism. During his time in Michigan, he met Fred Williams, an amateur historian of Detroit's black community, who became his mentor. Williams introduced Fuller to a myriad of readings about Africa and African Americans, and also took him along as he went about interviewing older members of Detroit's black community. Upon graduation, Fuller pursued a career in journalism between 1949 and 1957 with the *Detroit Tribune*, the *Michigan Chronicle* and *Ebony Magazine*.

In his autobiographical work *Journey to Africa*, Fuller recounts that he became dissatisfied with the gap between *Ebony*'s content and the fight for black freedom, so he left his editorial position in 1957. After quitting *Ebony*, he became very distraught at the racially overbearing culture of America; consequently, he, like many of his contemporaries, moved to Europe where he lived in France and Spain between 1957 and 1960. While living in Spain, Fuller traveled to Africa where he spent three months in Algeria and Guinea, and contributed articles about West Africa for the *Amsterdam Hasage Post*. These visits were transformational experiences and became his motivation for writing *Journey to Africa*.

As Fuller explains in the work, his experiences in Africa led him to return to the United States in 1960 with a fuller understanding of his *raison d'être*. He resolved to stop concerning himself with trying to alter white American racial tenets, instead focusing his attention on black America with the aim of fostering the understanding of the black self as the key to the formulation of individual as well as collective identities. To the new Fuller, an understanding of African and African American culture would be crucial to African American's indefatigable struggle against racial tyranny, and foreground their resolve to assertively express their own identity.

In 1961, he became editor of *The Negro Digest*, which transitioned to the *Black World* in 1970. *Negro Digest*, like *Black World*, was dedicated to black culture and arts, and it became a home for many Black Arts Movement writers. With the cessation of the journal in 1975, he returned to Atlanta and founded the *First World*. Later on in his life, Fuller taught at numerous universities, including Cornell, Northwestern, and Columbia College. In 1965-66, he again visited Africa as a John Hay Whitney Opportunity Fellow. Upon his return, he helped organize quite a few Pan-African festivals and formed the Chicago Organization of Black American Culture — a writers' guild that later became more radical in its struggle for black emancipation.

The story of Fuller is that of many blacks in the diaspora. It is a recurring story that constitutes the consciousness of a society and in obeisance of Marxism's reflection theory; contemporary black diasporic writers have resorted to narrating such epic journeys of adventure, spiritual rebirth and revitalization, return and coming of age in their works. This is the case in Johnson's *The Middle Passage* where Rutherford Calhoun, though an educated freed slave, is at first narcissistic, therefore initially unable to comprehend the privations of his life. As a result, he escapes from New Orleans on a ship called the *Republic* to avoid being coerced into marriage by Isadora Bailey, a schoolteacher who persuades Calhoun's creditor, Papa, to request that Calhoun pays him all he owes if he continues refusing to marry her. In this mix-up, he resorts to alcohol as an escape. During one of his drinking bouts, he meets the drunken cook of the *Republic*, a slave ship. Calhoun stows away and is only discovered later after the voyage has begun. The ship sails to Africa to capture members of the Allmuseri tribe to take back to America to sell as slaves. In the course of the expedition, Calhoun becomes humbled by his experiences and circumstances, at the end of which he learns lessons in appreciating and respecting humankind. He is transformed entirely, making it possible for him to identify with his own country, America. It is fascinating that Rutherford Calhoun has to return to Africa to locate his American identity, to gain a sense of self and purpose. It is only after this journey that he becomes man enough to marry his sweetheart, Isadora. Such transatlantic journeys of discovery are common especially amongst those created by the African holocaust called slavery.

This chapter explores such returns for empowerment, knowledge and self-discovery, a concept which Michael A. Gomez calls Reversing Sail in his work by the same title: *Reversing Sail: A History of the African Diaspora*. The metaphor of 'reverse sail' is even more powerful because it echoes the Akan (Ghana) concept of '*sankofa*'— literally, to return in order to move forward. As used by writers, characters could embark to the ancestral homeland physically and/or psychologically, which Gomez describes as "reversing sail in their minds and hearts, if not with their bodies" (162). In valorizing this concept, this chapter will concentrate on the mythical dimension of the reversing sail, rooted in sprit possession, a constituent of what Mircia Eliade calls "shamanism." It will show how black diasporic writers draw memories from their indigenous African consciousness to reenact moments of spirit possession by which they cast spells on characters. The result of such spells is that the characters embark on a journey towards self-discovery. Primary works by Derek Walcott (*Dream on Monkey Mountain*) and Haile Gerima (*Sankofa*) will illustrate this concept, and some theoretical considerations will also be borrowed from the dialogic musings of Mikhail Bakhtin who, in *The*

Dialogic Imagination, insists that "In order to forge a self, I must do it from outside, I author myself" (29). The chapter recognizes that this paradigm is also prototypical of another journey: "that to the American South, a landscape of contradiction and continuity, cast as a repository of cultural memory in twentieth-century African American literature. Many writers recuperate the American South," like they do Africa, "as a site of reconnection with ancestral history, as this symbolic geography bears witness to what Jean Toomer labels the 'pain and the beauty' of African American history" (Wardi 35).

Given this background, the concept of spirit possession can be understood as a very catholic concept explored by anthropologists from various cultural contexts. In fact,

> ...notions of what constitutes possession and the paths by which possession concepts and practices are transmitted, even across vastly different cultural environments and historical periods, are informed and constrained by recurrent features of cognition that guide perception, representation, thought and action. (Cohen 3)

Consequently, there is no one-size-fits-all definition as it remains varied, with some more encompassing than others. With the understanding that possession is a pattern of experiences, Janice Boddy convincingly argues that

> Spirit possession commonly refers to the hold exerted over a human being by external forces or entities more powerful than she. These forces may be ancestors or divinities, ghosts of foreign origin, or entities both ontologically and ethnically alien. Some societies evince multiple spirit forms. Depending on cultural and etiological contexts such spirits may be exorcised, or lodged in relatively permanent relationship with their host (or medium), occasionally usurping primacy of place in her body (even donning their own clothes and

speaking their own languages) during bouts of possession trance (Boddy 407).

Boddy's definition ties in with other analogous perspectives, including that of Raymond Firth. According to Firth, spirit possession is "a form of trance in which the behavior actions of a person are interpreted as evidence of a control of his behavior by a spirit normally external to him" (129). This phenomenon is generally manifested in two ways: in a trance and in what E. G. Parrinder in *African Traditional Religion* calls "mediumistic possession" (103). In the case of a trance, when a spirit is believed to have possessed someone, it induces a certain ecstasy, and the rapt person transcends into a euphoric state characterized by culturally and socially sanctioned dissociation, automatisms and involuntary utterances (Alembong 130). In his *Introduction to African Traditional Religion*, J. S. Mbiti states that a person who is possessed is often attached to medicine men or diviners who cast a spell on her under which she may "jump about, beat herself, bang her head, walk on fire and thorns, and do other things which she would not do when in her normal self" (156).

Derek Walcott's *Dream on Monkey Mountain* (hereafter *Dream*) makes effective use of spirit possession. The play is about one man's search for identity, and how the loss of his African heritage, the ruthless realities of slavery and his feeling of utter rootlessness or displacement in the world have made that search all but impossible. It is obvious that related feelings of dislocation and hopelessness seethe in the souls of young blacks everywhere in the Americas and the diasporic world. For Makak, the main character in *Dream*, that journey begins by being thrown in jail for drunk and disorderly conduct. Under interrogation, Makak explains that an apparition has summoned him to reclaim his destiny as the descendant of African kings. As Makak falls asleep in a drunken stupor, he begins to dream of his heroic descent from Monkey Mountain and his return to Africa, where he is ultimately crowned king.

Makak's real-life journey is not so grand. As a man of African descent, Makak feels belittled, trampled on and discriminated against.

His pride was drowned long ago in rum, and his opportunities in life have been almost nonexistent. Before the apparition motivates him to salvage his destiny, he was just another fuming African soul wandering through life without purpose or direction, selling coal to survive. Most of Makak's journey toward self-discovery takes place in a dreamlike state of stupor functionally similar to the state of being in a trance or daze characteristic of spirit possession. What Makak exhibits could be described in terms of what Witzel, borrowing from Eliade, denotes as a shamanistic experience. According to Witzel, Eliade argues that "the shaman employs trance-inducing techniques to incite visionary ecstasy and to go on 'vision quests'. This is achieved by music (drumming), dancing, recitation of certain texts, mantras, etc. The shaman's spirit can leave the body to enter the supernatural world to search for answers" (2), and this is exactly what happens in the play.

With an understanding of Mbiti's definition, most scholars of African traditional religions agree that entrancement and dissociation are characteristics of spirit possession; consequently, such an understanding identifies Makak's stuporous trance as a form of spirit possession occasioned by Walcott to effect the psychological journey to Africa, a journey necessary to engender some equilibrium within his unbalanced and destabilized self. In fact, Makak is characterized with an altered state of consciousness, a partial or complete disruption of the normal integration of his conscious or psychological functioning. Given Makak's state of mental dislocation within a deterministic Eurocentric society to whose dictates he must adhere, but to which he has nonetheless been refused admission, it is inconceivable that his journey could be physical considering his impoverished nature. Rather, it can only be psychological, and I do not think there is a better way for a writer to induce that but through such a scheme - a sort of dissociative travel. This mode of spiritual travel becomes very important to Makak, for he completely loses control of his body and mind, yielding to the Cartesian split of body and mind, as it is now controlled by some other force. As Cohen notes,

Such possession concepts, which I propose to label 'executive possession' concepts, may be defined as minimally entailing the following features: (a) the presence of an incorporeal intentional agent in or on a person's body, that (b) temporarily affects the ousting, eclipsing or mediation of the person's agency and control over behaviour, such that (c) the host's actions are partly or wholly attributable to the intentions, beliefs, desires and dispositions of the possessing agent for the duration of the episode. These features collectively represent the basic causal structure of *executive possession*. (Cohen 9)

An obvious question from reading *Dream* is: why must Makak travel to Africa? This could be definitively answered by drawing on Mikhail Bakhtin's notion of linear time and history as a progression of steps or stages toward a state of enlightenment, wisdom, or vision as is the case with *Dream*. Walcott's *Dream*, like Charles Johnson's *Middle Passage* and Toni Morrison's *Song of Solomon,* emphasizes personal and collective memory and the continuous interplay of past and present as an alternative to chronological linear time. Makak, like his friends, is so ravaged by the horrors of rootlessness and displacement that his present becomes inconsequential to him. He has to reconnect with his past in a Bakhtinian dialogic manner to bring meaning to his existence, and such a reconfiguration of the past is what Morrison envisions as "rememory" and Alice Walker as "dream memory."

In looking at the cultural connection between past and present, the diaspora and the homeland, from a dialogic perspective which enhances self-consciousness, Bakhtin stresses that existence is a dialogue and one must appropriate the vision of others to see one's self. He further argues that "only from a position outside something can it be perceived in categories that fix it in time and place" (31). It is in this vein that an audience would not be wrong to argue that Walcott frames *Dream* around the valorization of whiteness, and the absolute devaluation of blackness, in colonial racist ideological frame, a consequence of which Makak has to return to his roots to locate an understanding of self. In the eyes of Corporal Lestrade, a mulatto, and Inspector Pamphillion, Makak (a monkey of the Macaque breed) and his friends - Moustique (Mosquito), Tigre (tiger) and Souris (mouse) - all French nomenclatures, are inconsequential animals. As Lestrade reminds them, he is different from them in that he has no animal name; in fact, he thinks he is very different because he is a *mulatto* as opposed to Makak and his friends who are all black. In *Ecrits,* Jacques Lacan stresses that personal identity does not translate to some direct and immediate sense of self, but rather is a function of object relation, a "constitution" of the self as a construct of the *other* (1286). Clearly, then, the basis of personal identity is nothing other than social identity negotiated via the "mirror stage": being male or female, white or black (or colored or Indian), European or African (or Asian), Christian or Muslim etc., defines our personal identity as social identity. Whatever one may think of it—whether one finds it a fact to revel or to deprecate—each person begins his/her self-constitution on the basis of a series of social categories which are the result of ascription, not experience, and which locate us in one or more social hierarchies. Equally clearly, such a location is problematic, particularly for those who have been placed in a socially devalued locus. Their basic underpinnings of identity—often indubitable tenets concerning the color of their skin or the nature of their reproductive organs—are not only devalued in themselves, but linked with a series of other devalued features which are either evidently absent from the dominant group or are more capricious and impermanent. Hence, Makak, like his friends, is tied to many animal images in the play. His state of being warrants rebirth of consciousness and that rebirth can only come from connecting with his roots; in fact, by going outside himself. This definition of self-consciousness as the corollary of a negotiation between 'self' and 'others' is a common trope in black literature, especially for characters who pursue the subject of self-consciousness through the web of relationships that constitute their experience. Later in the play, Makak, as a function of an understanding of himself, comes to a realization that the situation of blacks in society is framed around white racism (otherness). In a moment of despair, he says: "We are wrapped in the black air, we are black, ourselves shadows in the firelight of the white man's mind... soon it will be morning... and the dream will rise like vapour" (304).

It is possible that Walcott intended for Makak's state of delirium to be the result of the effect of oppression and mental molestation, as is frequent postcolonial literature wherein *Dream* rightfully belongs. Consequently, there is the use of the mytho-religious exemplar of 'dissociation' otherwise known as out-of-body experience. Makak's alcoholism becomes the biological basis for mediumship, his dreamlike journey to Africa. Such *dissociation* is a psychological experience in which people feel disengaged from their sensory experience, sense of self, or personal history. It is commonly experienced as a feeling of extreme alienation or illusoriness, in which the subject precipitously loses his/her sense of place, identity, and motive of actions. From this definition, Makak's state of ecstasy is almost certainly dissociative because "when mediums become possessed, they describe their own consciousness as being 'asleep.' Moreover, they have amnesia for all that takes place while they are possessed, and they emerge from possession as if 'waking up'" (Seligman 89). When Makak is first encountered in the prologue, he seems disoriented, with no sense of his identity; not even his African ancestry:

> Corporal: Where is your home? Africa?
> Makak: Sur Morne Macaque
> ...
>
> Corporal: What is your name?
> Makak: I forget.
> Corporal: What is your race?
> Makak: I am tired. (218-9)

He further tells Corporal Lestrade, Tigre, and Souris that he is sixty years old and has lived all his life "like a beast in hiding" and, for thirty years, he has not seen his reflection and accordingly does not even know who he is. That same night, while in jail, he has a dream, inspired by an apparition which came to him the night before. In *Nobody's Nation*, Paul Breslin asserts that, at the end of the prologue, "Makak enters the dream world that rules the play until its epilogue" (140). He later transitions into a state of incorporation when he sees himself as an African king ruling over his people. He finally comes out of his dreamlike state in a process known as 'waking up' after gaining an understanding of himself and the power to overcome his social challenges. At this point, his language completely changes and, instead of speaking in a disoriented fashion with delusional responses and incongruous diction, Makak affirms "I will be different." As a product of the transformation, he further says, "my hatred is deep, black quiet as velvet." In the Epilogue, Makak says that his name is Felix Hobain. Through this remembrance, the audience is assured of his transformation. At the end, even the corporal discovers that Makak was not really drunk; rather, he "had a fit," a trance at the end of which he discovers his identity. It should be noted that identity in this play is the result of many factors, including setting. The play's action takes place in several locations, both real and imagined, and the most real place is the jail where the play begins and ends. According to Belalouna et als, in Makak's dream, the action goes from his hut on Monkey Mountain to a country road where he heals a sick man and then to the public marketplace before returning to the jail cell (215). But is the dream just Makak's? Is he the only character who goes through the dreamlike rite of passage?

Towards the end of part two, Lestrade proclaims the dream as communal: it is not only Makak's. When he accuses the revivified Moustique of betrayal, Lestrade says, "You have betrayed our dream" (314). By using the first-person plural, Lestrade seems to suggest his own transformation as he claims the dream for the other characters and the audience. Although it may have begun with Makak's deliriums, the dream no longer resides solely in Makak's mind. While the corporal resists Makak's dream in part one, and Moustique continues to resist it throughout the play, they are also nonetheless participants in the dream for they all end up seeking their own African experiences. So, to assign the dream only to Makak denies their parts as principal characters in shaping the action of the play. At the end of *Dream*, the singing and dancing in the play - very typical of spirited literature - reminiscent of the dramatis personae's African ancestry blends with the playwright's poetic vision and western-inspired creative genius to reveal the dualistic nature of Walcott's Western and African heritage. But, by utilizing the myth of Makak, an ultimately universal figure, he succeeds in achieving some resolution of the conflict between black roots and white culture.

The use of the bizarre as a paradigm in spirited literature is consolidated not only through singing, dancing and drumming, but also through the several apparitions seen in the play. Wearing a dark coat and hat disguised as a cabinetmaker, Basil is a black phantom who materializes each time death is looming for someone in the play. As a mythopoetic character as well, he remains a constant in Makak's journey after he reaches Monkey Mountain. Later he coerces Corporal Lestrade to own up to his sins, occasioning his personal epiphany. Finally, when the scene shifts to Africa, Basil reads the list of the accused, all of whom are classical western personages.

As a memory writer and a militant for a hybridity of thinking informed by his conceptualization of self in the image of a choirmaster's house which is "half shango-chapel and half Presbyterian country vestry" ("Twilight 28), or his lust to "see the word Ashanti ... with the word Warwickshire both separately intimating my [his} grandfather's roots" ("Twilight" 10), Walcott seeks to record the encounters of diasporic blacks with their past to ensure that such a part of their heritage doesn't vanish. He does this by underscoring that these encounters emerge as cultural translations of fixed points of cultural memory which, in effect, are

> Fateful events of the past whose memory is maintained through cultural formation (texts, rites, monuments) and institutional communication (recitation, practice, observance). We call these 'figures of memory' ... in the flow of everyday

> communication such festivals, rites, epics, poems, images, etc., form 'islands of time,' islands of completely different temporality suspended from time. In cultural memory, such islands of time expand into memory spaces of 'retrospective contemplativeness.' (129)

He not only explores such diasporic encounters in *Dream*, but also in his other plays, thereby reconfiguring the subject of cultural discourse, wherein he writes to replicate the way in which the journey out of the self leads to immersions into, and continual re-evaluations of new modes of representation.

Walcott is a Caribbean partly of African ancestry, and it is obvious that African writers in the diaspora cannot escape the call of Africa, and not one of them considers himself or herself truly an African diasporic writer without having confronted Africa in some way. Accordingly, some critics of the play have interpreted Makak's killing of his white goddess when he becomes an African king as "a call to black power" while others have seen his portrayal of Africans within the subtext of animals amidst their violent tendencies as a promotion of the stereotype of a "savage African. " In his defense, Walcott submits that Makak

> achieves nothing, but he completes something. What he does is he sheds an image of himself that has been degraded. When he thought he was white, he did what the white man did. When he thought he was Black, he did what he thought the Black man should do. Both errors. So that moment of cutting off the head is not a moment of beheading a white woman. It is a matter of saying there is some act, some final illusion to be shed. And it is only metaphorical anyway—it's only a dream.

In this vein, in a Janus-like fashion, Walcott uses the past as repository from which he muses a framework around which to build his literary work by invoking a trance-induced journey to self-awareness. In a postcolonial context, a culturally displaced and subordinated group engages a Hegelian struggle for recognition "to rechart and then occupy the place in imperial cultural forms reserved for subordination, to occupy it self-consciously, fighting for it on the very same territory once ruled by a consciousness that assumed the subordination of a designated inferior Other" (Said 210).

A similar paradigm of struggle is negotiated by Haile Gerima's *Sankofa,* a 2003 movie on slavery which was filmed at the former slave castles in Cape Coast, Ghana. In it, Mona, an African American model visiting the Elmina castle, which she does not know historically, was used to store and transport slaves across the Atlantic—a consequently spiritual site symptomatic of what Gerima calls the "genocide on the African continent" framed around western contempt for the African people. Sankofa, a mysterious self-proclaimed guardian of the site who seems to communicate with the spirit world, appears to Mona and commands her saying "Back to your past! Return to your source." He does not end there, but he chases tourists away and commands them to not desecrate the land. With these words, Mona is possessed by a spirit which takes her back to the past where she is captured and transported as a slave across the Atlantic. The film continues with Mona, now Shola, on the plantation working hard with other slaves for the Lafayettes where she is sexually abused by the master.

Through this spiritual transportation, Shola experiences the gruesomeness of slavery: the lashings, the killings, the rapes, the hopelessness, the psychological and physical ills, as well as rebellion and subjugation. She also experiences African solidarity and communality, African spirituality and Christian hypocrisy. She is told to pray by the priest who is a warden of the slaves, but the more she does, the meaner the master becomes. She experiences African spirituality naively portrayed as heathenism in such celebrations, prayers and incantations honoring the spirit of "Asona ancestors." She is forced and beaten into submission to accept Christianity and to rebuke African ancestral worship, and this she does with her lips just to avoid death. Later, the spirit of community and African spirituality unleashes a certain cosmic effect through a mystical carved bird called Sankofa, which Shango (named after the thunder god of the Yoruba culture), a West Indian lover of Shola who constantly resists and rebels against the slave masters, puts around her neck. The bird occasions a transformation as she details:

> Shango trusted me for the first time. He gave me this handmade bird that he had carved out of wood. He called it a Sankofa bird and he put it round my neck. Shango said the Sankofa was passed on to him by his Papa. But I tell you whatever that bird was all about after he put that bird on my neck I became a rebel. No more was I scared of being flogged, burned; even death didn't scare me. And when [chuckle] they got the notion to throw me out in the field suit me just fine. (Gerima)

The bird instantaneously initiates and transforms her as she immediately goes through a rite of passage from docility to rebelliousness. She suddenly starts defying the master, without any fears. At the end, Mona is spiritually transported back to the Elmina Castle where she meets the American photographer who has been looking for her. She is received by the Sankofa bird and a drumming festival to welcome her back in celebration of her new consciousness. Now transformed, she understands her American-ness in an entirely different light.

The movie captures a certain identity formation that Molefi Kate Asante advocates in his Afrocentric philosophy, very similar to that experienced by Makak in *Dream*. From reading the play, one notices that he has been changed by European culture without having been admitted into it; in fact, in the eyes of Europeans, he is only an African monkey (Uhrbach 579). It is only when he becomes enthralled that he reinvents himself in recognition of his African identity. Similarly, when Mona is captured by the slave traders, she disowns Africa which she and her American photographer seemed to romanticize not as her cultural melieu, but as an exotic setting for sexually mundane exhibitions as she screams "I'm an American! I'm not an African!" However, after going through a sort of spiritual rebirth orchestrated through spirit possession, Mona becomes a changed being as she starts celebrating Africa and rejecting the west as captured in her last monologue:

> Guns, Horses, Head Slaves
> I can still hear it all now
> And I heard the guns go off again
> And the dogs I heard them as they scrunched one of us
> I heard his voice
> Keep on runnin' sister
> Keep on runnin'
> The horses' hooves got closer and closer right on our heels
> And suddenly I heard another one go down
> They were right on our heels
> And I knew I was next
> One cried out to me to go on as the dogs feasted on him
> Keep on runnin' sister
> Run! Run! Run!
> My head started getting hot and I wasn't tired no more
> Then I had this feelin' this light feelin'
> And there wasn't no more pains in my feet
> This big buzzard was flyin' next to me and he spread his wings and scooped me up and up and up
> Just like what Shango said
> Next thing I know I'm in the air goin' up and up and up and
> This miserable earth is gettin' smaller and smaller
> Turnin' into somethin' small
> Dogs and Overseers
> Head Slaves
> Horses
> Getting smaller and smaller
> Just like what Shango said
> The buzzard brought me. (Gerima)

Shola is completely extricates herself from her servitude to "dogs and overseers, head slaves and horses" who now in her eyes become smaller and smaller while the "bird," a symbol of her utter liberation "scoops" her "up and up and up."

By the end of the film, each of the main characters has gone through a spiritual rite of passage induced through spirit possession. The dissociation of characters could be a singular event or a group of events. For Mona, her experience as a possessed being spiritually incorporates and initiates her into becoming a sort of shaman. Her departure point is evident when she trails the tour group down into the slave dungeons of the Elmina Castle. She is plunged back into a past life of being netted, branded, and eventually becoming Shola. Notably, naming and renaming is critical in identity discourse in slave stories; her change of name entails a change in identity. This leads to Mona/Shola's spiritual transition on the plantation where her past culture, viz traditions, legends, beliefs etc., is learned. The incorporation phase for Mona cum Shola is when she emerges from the oubliette and Shola is thus reborn as Mona and there is an intertwining of past, present and future. Mona is now a new being who has transitioned from an American Mona, through an African Shola to an African American Mona.

It is also evident from the film that other characters such as Joe, Nunu and Noble all endure some or all of the stages of initiation. Joe, for instance, goes through the departure phase when he is poisoned by Lucy with the help of Shango. Through the poison, he is cast into herbal-induced state of phantasm. He evolves into the transition state through the killing of Nunu, his mother. He then attains incorporation when he brings Nunu's body back to the church to mourn. With this incorporation, he begins to appreciate all that he has done, his abandonment of the spiritual essence of his indigenous African people and the embrace of western spirituality—Christianity. This becomes a turning point for Joe on his journey to becoming a transformed being: he defiantly attacks Father Raphael, the Catholic priest, who is the symbol of his spiritual adulteration and mental incarceration with a newfound understanding of his past. He is renewed and begins to spiritually open up to the values of that past with a full awareness of the need of its incorporation into his future.

Significantly, the message in the film not only radiates from the transformations that the characters experience after being spirit-possessed, but it is also echoed through these words hallucinatorily uttered by the narrator at the beginning of the movie against a backdrop of music and drumming:

> Spirits of the Dead rise up,
> Lingering Spirits of the Dead rise up and possess your bird of passage.
> Those stolen Africans step out of the ocean from the wombs of the ships and claim your story.
> Spirits of the Dead rise up,
> Lingering Spirits of the Dead rise up and possess your vessel.
> Those Africans shackled in leg irons and enslaved,
> Step out of the acres of cane fields and cotton fields and tell your story.
> Spirits of the Dead rise up,
> Lingering Spirits of the Dead rise up and possess your bird of passage.
> Those lynched in the magnolias,
> swinging on the limbs of the weeping willows,
> rotting food for the vultures,
> Step down and claim your story.
> Spirits of the Dead rise up,
> Lingering Spirits of the Dead rise up and possess your vessel.
> Those tied, bound, and whipped from Brazil to Mississippi
> Step out and tell your story.
> Those in Jamaica,
> in the fields of Cuba,
> in the swamps of Florida,
> the rice fields of Carolina
> You waiting Africans step out and tell your story.

> Spirits of the Dead rise up,
> Lingering Spirits of the Dead rise up and possess your bird of passage.
> you African Spirits
> Spirits of the Dead rise up,
> Lingering Spirits of the Dead rise up and possess your bird of passage. (Gerima)

By this virtual roll call of the African diaspora, Gerima seeks to invite all former slaves to rise up and claim their story, to tell their stories. The sounds of the drums and the call of the drummers all blend with the incantatory voice over of the narrator to give the opening a ritualistic feel. Such a feeling and setting is always needed for spirit possession to happen and for liminality to take place.

Of obvious significance to the two works examined in this study are the notions of spirit possession and the value of the past. In fact, 'sankofa' diametrically ties in with the Sankofa Bird, a bird that flies forward while looking backward with the future in its mouth, thus going back and fetching what was left behind. Such a exemplar is vital to the construction of the African diasporic identity. In Gerima's film, everyone needs to look back in order to go forward; the same holds true of the protagonists in *Dream on Monkey Mountain*, for only then are they able to find their peace and achieve their potential as they move forward. To attain this goal of going back to reclaim whatever has been lost, forgotten, or stripped away in order to move forward, otherwise conceptualized as "belonging and becoming," Gerima and Walcott integrate spirit possession, as the characters depart, incorporate and transition (rites of passage) during which they seem to become intermediaries between the human and the spirit worlds, what Mircia Eliade calls shamanism. However, what is the relationship between spirit possession and memory? In *How Societies Remember*, Paul Connerton, in his examination of how the collective memory of groups is expressed and sustained, contends that ceremonies characterized by possession, among others, are more than sites of consciousness-raising about gender relations; they are also more than arenas in which anti-colonialist discourses are constructed. Rather,

> If there is such a thing as social memory... we are likely to find it in commemorative ceremonies; but commemorative ceremonies prove to be commemorative only in so far as they are performative; performativity cannot be thought without a concept of habit; and habit cannot be thought without a notion of bodily automatisms. (5)

This exactly is what Walcott and Gerima do in their works; they mobilize spirit possession, a sort of performative ceremony, to reconstruct collective social and cultural memory. Although not anchored to a particular nation, *Dream on Monkey Mountain* and *Sankofa* are specific to the identity reformation and nation-building process in the black diasporic world, "a process that lends itself to drama, dreams, and delirium" (Josephs 2).

Given the preponderance of critical material that has been published on the dialogism of orature and written literature, African diasporic writers have experimented with such African oral traditional tropes as orchestration, masquerading, song, dance and the use of a myriad of African myths to explore issues of contemporary significance. They have, therefore, tapped into a sacred aspect of African traditional religion rooted in spirit possession. Collective memory therefore becomes a framework for reinventing the self and of formulating a collective identity as highlighted by Countee Cullen's poem "Heritage":

> What is Africa to me:
> Copper sun or scarlet sea,
> Jungle star or jungle track,
> Strong bronzed men, or regal black
> Women from whose loins I sprang
> When the birds of Eden sang?
> One three centuries removed

> From the scenes his fathers loved,
> Spicy grove, cinnamon tree,
> What is Africa to me?
> ...
>
> *Meekly labored in its hair.*
> *One three centuries removed*
> *From the scenes his fathers loved,*
> *Spice grove, cinnamon tree,*
> *What is Africa to me?*
> ...

The poem deals with the slit between contemporary diasporic individuals, who are sensitive to their cultural heritage, and their society which, to them, appears desiccated and fruitless in comparison. From the lavish use of local and nature imagery, it is clear that Africa is much more than bedtime reading or a play subject for the narrator. It is a source of hope. This is framework around which this endeavor has flourished as it is even more true in a postcolonial world, in which writers are resolved to negotiating a polarity of repulsion and attraction inherent to a past which is both traumatic and triumphant.

Works Cited

Bellalouna, Elizabeth, Michael le Blanc, and Ira Mark Milne, eds. *Literature of Developing Nations for Students: Presenting Analysis, Context, and Criticism on Literature of Developing Nations.* Detroit: Gale Group, 2000. Print.

Boddy, Janice. "Spirit Possession Revisited: Beyond Instrumentality." *Annual Review of Anthropology* 23 (1994): 407-434. *Academic Search Complete.* Web. 01 Mar. 2013.

Boyer, Pascal. *Religion Explained: The Evolutionary Origins of Religious Thought.* New York: Basic Books, 2001. Print.

Breslin, Paul. *Nobody's Nation: Reading Derek Walcott.* Chicago: University of Chicago Press, 2001. Print.

Cohen, Emma. "What Is Spirit Possession? Defining, Comparing, and Explaining Two Possession Forms." *Ethnos: Journal of Anthropology* 73.1 (2008): 101-126. *Academic Search Complete*, Web. 02 Mar. 2013.

Du Bois, W. E. B. *The Souls of Black Folk*. New York, Avenel, NJ: Gramercy Books, 1994.

Eliade, Mircea. *Shamanism, Archaic Techniques of Ecstasy*, Bollingen Series LXXVI. Princeton: Princeton University Press, 1972. Print.

Eyerman, Ron. *Cultural Trauma: Slavery and the Formation of African American Identity*. Cambridge: Cambridge University Press, 2001. Print.

Fuller, Hoyt W. *Journey to Africa*. Chicago: Third World Press, 1971. Print.

Gerima, Haile, dir., *Sankofa*. Perf. Kofi Ghanaba, Oyafunmike Ogunlano, Alexandra Duah, and Nick Medley. Washington, D.C: Mypheduh Films, 1993.

Gomez, Michael A. *Reversing Sail: A History of the African Diaspora*. Cambridge: Cambridge University Press, 2005. Print.

Johnson, Charles Richard. *Middle Passage*. New York: Atheneum, 1990. Print.

Josephs, Kelly Baker. "Dreams, Delirium, and Decolonization in Derek Walcott's "*Dream On Monkey Mountain*." *Small Axe: A Caribbean Journal of Criticism* 32 (2010): 1-16. *Academic Search Complete*. Web. 07 Mar. 2013.

Mbiti, J.S. *An Introduction to African Religion*. London: Heinemann, 1975. Print.

Morrison, Toni, *Song of Solomon*. New York: Plume, 1987. Print.

Parrinder, E. G. *African Traditional Religion*. London, 1954.

Rampersad, Arnold. *The Art and Imagination of W. E. B. Du Bois*. Cambridge, MA: Harvard University Press, 1976. Print.

Seligman, Rebecca. "Distress, Dissociation, and Embodied Experience: Reconsidering the Pathways to Mediumship and Mental Health." *Ethos* 33.1, *Special Issue: Building Biocultural Anthropology* (Mar., 2005): 71-99. JSTOR, Web. 15 Feb. 2013.

Stoller, Paul, "Embodying Cultural Memory in Songhay Spirit Possession" *Archives de Sciences Sociales des Religions* 79.1 (Jul. - Sep., 1992): 53-68. *JSTOR*, Web, 02 Mar. 2013.

Uhrbach, Jan R. "A Note on Language and Naming in Dream on Monkey Mountain." *Callaloo* 29 (Autumn, 1986): 578-582. Print.

Walcott, Derek. *Dream on Monkey Mountain and Other Plays*. New York: Farrar Straus Giroux, 1967. Print.

--- "What the Twilight Says: An Overture." *Dream on Monkey Mountain and Other Plays*. New York: Farrar Straus Giroux, 1967: 3-40. Print.

Wardi, Anissa J. "Inscriptions in the Dust: A Gathering of Old Men and Beloved as Ancestral Requiems" *African American Review*, Vol. 36, No. 1. (Spring, 2002): 35-53. Print.

Witzel, Michael E. J. "Shamanism in Northern and Southern Eurasia: Their Distinctive Methods of Change of Consciousness. *Social Science Information* 50(1): 39-61. 2011. Web.

Index

A

Abbott.. 140
Absalom, Absalom................................. 85
Achebe, Chinua 135, 136
African Diasporic Literature............. 187
African Pasts 111, 139
African-Scandinavian Writers' Conference 111
Afro-American 66
Alabama 162
Alexie, Sherman... 73, 74, 75, 80, 81, 83, 84
American Quakers 3
Anabaptists... 8
ANC..............................112, 114, 119
Ankumah, Adaku T................... 109, 133
Antigua...................................... 172, 175
apartheid.. 109, 110, 111, 113, 114, 115, 116, 117, 118, 120, 122, 123, 124, 125, 126, 127
Auld, Hugh.. 60
Auld, Thomas............................. 59, 60
Auschwitz.. 134
Autobiographical Acts.......................... 63

B

Baker, Ella 123
Baker, Houston A. 66, 81, 174, 175
Baker, Josephine 174, 175
Baptists.. 8
Barbara Christian 120
Barbour, Hugh............................. 5, 34
Bartnam, Sarah 174

Baum, L Frank................................. 171
Beckett, Samuel 16, 29, 34, 103, 108
Beloved 135, 158, 159, 161
Bennett, Judge 9
Bervenage, Berber............................ 141
Bhabha, Homi 171, 179
Bhekizizwe, Peterson 111
Biafran War 136
Biko, Steve............................... 122, 127
Bishop, John Peale 45
Black Tuesday.................................. 127
Blood Knot, Sizwe Banzi is Dead........... 110
Blount, Eleanor J................................ 153
Blues, The.............................. 81, 82, 83
Bono 79, 81, 82, 83
Book of the Dead 145
Boston.......................... 99, 102, 106
Breath, Eyes and Memory.... 171, 179, 181, 182
Brendt, Linda................................... 122
Brent, Linda............................... 64, 67
Brewton, Vince............................ 60, 70
Brinton, Howard............................ 7, 22
Brooklyn Museum 145
Brutus, Dennis........................ 110, 112
Bunting, Sonia 115
Bunyan, John 23
Burns, Loretta S. 55

C

Calvin, John.. 8
Calvinist.. 5
Cambridge 7, 8, 23, 34, 99, 102
Canterbury, Archbishop of 6
Carby, Hazel................................ 64, 70

Caribbean 174, 177
Carnal Will 16, 17, 23
Carneson, Sarah 115
Carroll, Charles 160
Cary, Joyce 136
Chancy, Myriam 140, 150
Charles I 6
Chetty, Rajendra 124, 126
Chimamanda, Adichie 135
Chitauro 115
Choctaw 76
Christian, Barbara 119
Civil Rights Movement 123
Civil War, the 160
Clark, G.N. 20, 134
Clark, Septima 123
Coleman, James C. 80
Collective Unconsciousness 22
Colonel Lloyd 58
Coltrane, John 79, 81
communication model 14
Connerton, Paul 140, 147, 149
Conrad, Joseph 136
Conventicle Acts 9
Cory 79, 84, 113
Covey, Mr. 59, 60, 61, 62, 63, 66
Coxere, Edward 4, 17, 18, 19, 20, 21, 22, 23, 24, 26, 27, 28, 30
Craven 128
Create Dangerously 137
Cromwellian Interregnum 8
Cromwellian Protectorate 6
Crystal, David .... See
cultural memory. 63, 171, 172, 173, 174, 175, 177, 179, 180

D

Danticat, Edwidge ... 133, 136, 137, 138, 139, 149, 171, 172, 179, 180, 181, 182, 183

Davies, Carolyn Boyce 179, 183, 184
Dawn of a New Millennium 133
Deakin 113
Declaration of Indulgence 9
Declaration of Sentiments 106
Defoe, Daniel 34
Denard, Carolyn 157, 159, 160
DeShazer, Mary 110, 113, 114, 115, 118, 119, 120, 121, 123, 124
de-storification 136
Dew Breaker, The 133, 138, 139
Douglass, Frederick ... 58, 59, 60, 61, 62, 63, 66, 69, 70, 71
Dreiser, Theodore 73, 86
Dube 115
Dubois, W.E.B. 160
Duvalier, Francois 137

E

$E=MC^2$ 154
Eagleton, Terry 4, 12
Eichman, Adolf 142
Einstein, Albert 153, 154
Elizabeth Stirredge 35
Emberly 175
England ... 91, 95, 98, 99, 102, 104, 105, 181
Established Church 9, 33, 92
Evans, Ifor 14, 34
externalization 23, 24

F

Faulkner, William. 73, 74, 76, 77, 80, 83, 85, 153, 154, 156, 157
Federation of South African Women 115
feminism 103, 106
Fences 74, 78, 80, 83
Fishkin, Benjamin H. 37, 73

Fitzgerald, F. Scott......37, 39, 42, 45, 46, 47, 50
Fleischner, Jennifer................63, 69, 71
Flint, Dr. 64, 66, 67, 68
Fonteneau, Gabrielle....................... 144
Fox, George 5, 7, 8, 9, 10, 26, 33, 89, 98, 103, 105, 106
France 17, 175
Fraser, Antonia............90, 93, 100, 103
Freud Reader....................................... 156
Freud, Sigmund .4, 37, 41, 51, 153, 154, 156, 168
Freudian 12, 13
From the Kingdom of Memory........ 109, 149

G

Gandhi 33, 115
Gender 126
Genocide 134
Ghana 113
Gilman 174
Go Down Moses 74, 75, 76, 83
Gordimer, Nadine 110, 113
Grubb, Edward 7
Guerin 103
Gunner, Liz 114, 115
Gwala 111

H

Haiti 137, 139, 140, 141, 143, 144, 145, 179, 180, 181, 182
Halls, Beer 118
Hamer, Fannie Lou.......................... 123
Harlow, Barbara.............................. 110
Have You Seen Zandile? 111
Hawthorne, **Nathaniel**..................... 101
Head, Bessie 110
Hendrix, Jimi 80
Herman, Judith 140

hermeneutics 12
Herod.. 40
High Church........................... 8, 89, 97
Hill, Christopher.3, 10, 16, 91, 105, 108
hireling priests................................... 92
Hireling priests 8
Holland, Norman 12
Holocaust 134, 138, 142
Hooton, Elizabeth89, 90, 91, 92, 93, 94, 95, 97, 98, 99, 100, 101, 102, 103, 104, 105, 106, 107
Hugh Auld.. 58
Humpty Dumpty 149
Huyssen, Andreas 144

I

Icarus 39, 78
identity ..48, 59, 61, 64, 74, 76, 80, 111, 133, 136, 138, 139, 141, 142, 146, 147, 148, 149, 153, 172, 173, 175
Igbo.. 136
Incidents in the Life of a Slave Girl.... 58, 63, 122
Independents.. 6
Individual Will 16, 23
individuating................................... 100
inner light.....5, 7, 8, 9, 22, 30, 31, 89, 92, 96, 97, 98
inner voice 16
integration 22, 24
internalization 23
Interregnum, Cromwellian 93
Intimate Relationships, Marriage, and Family 80
Ireland 13
izibongo 113

J

Jacobs, Harriet 58, 63, 64, 65, 66, 67, 68, 69, 70, 71, 122
Jamaica 98, 106, 172
Janus 179
Johannesburg......................... 113, 115
John Paul II, Pope 133, 138, 139
Johnson, Mister 136
Johnson, Robert 83
Jonker, Ingrid 110
Joyce, James.........................29, 34, 136
Jubilee 161, 162, 163
Jung, C. J. 22

K

Karim, Aisha 112
Kincaid.. 172
Kincaid, Jamaica 172, 173, 175
King Lear.. 74
King, Jr, Martin Luther 135
Kunene, Mazizi................................ 110
Kuzwayo, Ellen 117

L

La Guma, Alex 111
Langley, Noel 173, 183, 184
Lapham, Lewis H............................... 73
Laud, William 6
Levelers 6
Lewis.. 78, 79
lieux de memoire 141
Lieux de Mémoire........................... 133
lingering memory........................ 40, 42
Literature. 4, 6, 9, 10, 12, 13, 14, 15, 21, 22, 23, 29, 30, 31, 50, 76, 78, 90, 91, 92, 96, 101, 110, 111, 112, 113, 123, 153, 154, 156, 160, 166, 172

lithoko... 113
Lone Ranger and Tonto Fistfight in Heaven, The.. 74, 81, 84
Lover's Discourse, A............................. 93
Lucifer... 40
Lurting, Thomas 4, 13, 26, 27, 29, 30, 31, 32, 96
Luther, Martin 5, 8, 135
Lutheran.. 5
Luthuli, Albert 114, 119
Luthuli, Mama Nokukhanya..... 119, 122

M

Mandela, Nelson 117, 118, 119, 126
Mangum, Bryant 46
Manners, Emily.................. 89, 97, 105
Marassa 179, 180, 182
Marvell, Andrew 29, 33
Marxism 25
Mastering Slavery 63
Matigari... 135
Mau Mau 136
Maxeke, Charlotte.................... 114, 115
Maxson, Troy 78, 80, 82, 84
McCaslin, Isaac 77, 81, 83
McLuhan, Marshall 163, 164
Memmi, Albert 176
Men of the Fifth Monarchy................ 6
Mengele, Josef 142
Mercy, A... 135
Meson-Furr 82
Meyerstein, E. W. H........................... 20
Mhlophe, Gcina.......109, 111, 112, 113, 115, 116, 117, 118, 119, 120, 121, 124, 126, 127, 128
Milton, John 5, 16, 33, 95, 108
Mississippi 73, 77
Mitchell, Margaret........................... 161
Modernity 149

Morrison, Toni 135, 136, 153, 154, 156, 157, 158, 159, 160, 161, 162, 166, 171, 172, 173, 174, 175, 177, 178, 179, 180, 182, 183
Mphahlele, Ezekiel 127
Muddy Waters 39, 42
Muggletonians 6
Murray, Albert 55, 71
music 74, 75, 78, 79, 81, 82, 83, 146, 160, 162, 163, 165

N

Naidoo, Phyllis 115
Nazi 142
Ndeh, Festus Fru 187
Ndi, Bill F. 3, 89
Negro spiritual 77, 162
New England 95, 98, 99, 102
New Model Army, the 6, 26
New World. 3, 93, 98, 99, 102, 104, 105
New York 35, 84, 108, 137, 139, 142, 143, 144, 176, 177, 179, 182
Ngoyi, Lillian 115
Ngugi wa Thiong'o 136
Nkrumah, Kwame 113, 114
non-conformists 9
Nora, Pierre 133
Norcom, Dr. James 64
Nyembe, Dorothy 115

O

Oedipus 78
Of Time and the River 45
Onyeoziri, Gloria 123
Osagyefo 114
Oseadeeyo 114
Othello 78
Oxford 7, 8, 23

P

paradise 37
Paradise Lost 33
Paris 154, 174, 175, 176, 177, 178
Pattison, George 29
Pearlstein, Mitch 84
Pepys 14
Pereira, Kim 40, 47, 49, 50, 78, 80
philosophy 78, 115
Picower Institute 41
Pilate 40
Piscatua 99, 101
power .. 58, 66, 69, 79, 97, 99, 101, 103, 104, 106, 110, 115, 121, 136, 165, 172, 175, 177, 180
Preston-Patrick 9
Proclamation of Truth 8
Proust, Marcel 38, 46, 153, 154, 155
psychology 154
Publishing of Truth 5, 7, 96
Puritan Revolution 4, 91
Puritans 5

Q

Quaker Acts 9, 95
Quaker communication model 14
Quaker memory 3, 4
Quaker rebellion 92, 95, 96, 97
Quakerism 3, 4, 7, 13, 15, 18, 19, 22, 25, 90, 91, 92, 94, 97
Quakers ... 15, 89, 90, 91, 92, 93, 94, 95, 96, 98, 99, 101, 102, 103, 104, 105, 106, 107

R

Raleigh, Sir Walter 23
Ralph Ellison 55

Ramphele, Mamphela 117, 122
Ranters 6
realization 22, 25, 26, 50
Rebellion 89, 92, 94, 96, 98, 100
Reforms 5
re-membering 154
resistance 62, 84, 97, 110, 111, 112, 113, 115, 118, 121, 122, 123, 124, 127, 136
Resistance 87, 109, 110, 118, 121
Restoration 5, 93
Rite of Passage 187
Robben Island 117, 126
Roberts, A 5
Robinson, Amelia Boynton 123
Ross 174
Rushdie, Salman 171, 172, 183, 184
Russell Lowell, James 101
Russell, Bertrand 11, 101

S

Sachs, Albie 112, 128
Saïd, Edward 138, 176
Saillens, Émile 5
Saint Louis 38
Sam Fathers 76, 77
Samuel Tredwell Sawyer 66
Sands 66, 67, 68
satyagraha 115
Scarlet Letter, The 101
Seekers 6, 8, 9
self-actualization 22, 33
self-denial 83
Seven Guitars 39, 43, 47, 49, 50
Shaka 114
Shakespeare, William 74
Sharpeville Massacre 118
Shava 114
Shea 179, 180
Shorthouse 104

Singh, Jaspal 124, 126
slave narratives 55, 57, 58, 70, 71
Small Place, A 172, 173, 184
Smith, Bessie 80, 82
Smith, Nigel 3, 13
Society of Friends, The 9
Sola Scriptura 5
Sophia Auld 58
Sotho 113
Sound and the Fury, The 153, 157
South Africa 109, 110, 111, 113, 115, 116, 118, 121, 123, 125, 126, 127
Southwark 19, 20
Soyinka, Wole 111
Spain 18
Spalding, John Lancaster 37
Spirit Possession 9
St. Margaret's Hill 20
Steeple Houses 8
Stepto, Robert 57, 71
Stirredge, Elizabeth 12, 26, 35
Stone, Robert 136
Supra-individual Will 23
Sustar, Lee 112

T

Tar Baby 171, 172, 173, 178
Taylor-Guthrie, Danielle .. 157, 159, 168
Test Act 9
theocentrization 6
theocracy 6
theocratization 6
Thomas Auld 60
Tiddeman, Edmund 27
Tlali, Miriam 110
Toleration Act 9
Tolstoy, Leo 25, 26, 29, 33
Tonton Macoutes 140, 149
Traansvaal 115
Transformation 121

trauma ... 38, 73, 76, 109, 130, 131, 134, 141
travails 12, 19, 21, 25, 27, 30, 31, 32, 96
tribulations 3, 12, 19, 21, 25, 30, 31, 32, 93
Triennial Act 9
Troy 78, 79, 80, 82, 84
Truth and Reconciliation Commission 109
Tual, Jacques 21, 35, 92

V

Vagrancy Act 9
Valiant Sixty 106
Venus Hottentot 174, 175
Vidal-Naquet 133
Voltaire 29, 33, 35

W

wa Thiong'o, Ngugi 136
Walker, Alice 119
Walker, Margaret 153, 164
Wannsee 134
Washington 73, 135
Wastberg 111
Weekly Standard, The 84
West, Cornell 112, 172
Wheatley, Phyllis 135
Whitman, Walt 29
Wiesel, Elie 109, 134, 142, 143, 149
Wilberforce 114

Wilcox, Catherine M. 35
Williams, Hank 80
Wilson, August 37, 39, 40, 42, 43, 47, 48, 49, 50, 73, 74, 78, 79, 80, 82, 83, 128
Wilson, Matt 41
Wizard of Oz, The 171, 172, 173
Wolfe, Andrea Powell 66
Wolfe, Thomas 37, 38, 39, 40, 41, 42, 44, 45, 47, 50
Woods, Tim 111, 112, 127, 134, 139, 147
Woodstock 80
Wordsworth, William 171, 181
World War II 78, 142

X

Xhosa 113

Y

Yankah, Kwesi 114
Yellin, Jean Fagan 64, 71

Z

Zandile 111, 113
zero degree, the 13
Zulu 113
Zulu/Xhosa 113